𝕰𝖑𝖒𝖜𝖔𝖔𝖉 𝕰𝖉𝖎𝖙𝖎𝖔𝖓

THE COMPLETE WRITINGS OF
JAMES RUSSELL LOWELL

WITH PORTRAITS, ILLUSTRATIONS, AND FACSIMILES

IN SIXTEEN VOLUMES

VOLUME XVI

Mr. Lowell in 1884

LETTERS

OF

JAMES RUSSELL LOWELL

EDITED BY CHARLES ELIOT NORTON

IN THREE VOLUMES

VOLUME III

BOSTON AND NEW YORK

HOUGHTON, MIFFLIN AND COMPANY

The Riverside Press, Cambridge

CONTENTS

VIII

1877–1880

IX

1880–1885

X

1885–1889

XI

1889–1891

RETURN TO ELMWOOD. — DECLINING HEALTH. — VISIT FROM LESLIE STEPHEN. — THE END.

LIST OF ILLUSTRATIONS

LETTERS OF
JAMES RUSSELL LOWELL

LETTERS OF
JAMES RUSSELL LOWELL

VIII

1877–1880

To Mrs. S. B. Herrick

ELMWOOD, *January* 14, 1877.

DEAR Mrs. Herrick, — This morning
I poured some ink for the first time into
your pretty inkstand, and, as in duty
bound, hansel it by writing to you. It has been
standing on the shelf of my secretary, its mouth
wide open with astonishment at my ingrati-
tude in not writing to thank you, ever since
it came. It need n't have been so jealous

though, for I have written to nobody else meanwhile, and it should remember that I can at any
moment shut it up tight, deny it ink, pen, and
paper, and thus cut it off from all its friends.
" Monster ! " I seem to hear it say, " you would
not surely deny me the sad consolation of sending my love to Mrs. Herrick and telling her
how homesick I am ? There are all kinds of
fine things in me, as good as were ever in any
inkstand that ever lived, if you had but the wit
to fish them out. If I had stayed with my dear
mistress I should ere this have found a vent for
my genius in a score of pleasant ways, but with
you I fear lest I go to my grave an *encrier in-
compris !* " " Well, well, so long as you don't
make me uneasy with your reproaches, I shall
be sure to treat you kindly for the sake of your
old mistress, . . . who is always contriving pleasant ways of making her friends grateful." . . .

I hope you maintain your tranquillity in this
ferment of politics. I do, for, as I made up my
mind deliberately, so I do not change it to please
the first man I meet. As I consider the question
of good government and prosperity in the Southern States the most pressing one, I voted for Mr.
Hayes on the strength of his letter. I think it
would be better for North and South if he were
President. He would carry with him the better
elements of the Republican party, and whatever
its shortcomings (of which none is more bitterly

conscious than I), the moral force of the North and West is with them and not with the Democrats. Above all, if Mr. Hayes should show a wise sympathy with the real wants and rights of the Southern whites (as I believe he would), it would be felt at the South to be a proof that the whole country was inclined to do them justice. From Mr. Tilden and the Democrats it would be received as a matter of course. You see what I mean? Of course I am not one of those who would have Mr. Hayes " counted in."

I shall have the pleasure of seeing you now in a few weeks. We have decided that, on the whole, it is best that Mrs. Lowell should not come with me. We both regret it, but it is wise. Wisdom always has a savor of regret in it ever since Eve's time. We have been having a noble winter. The old fellow has been showing a little feebleness for a year or two, and we thought he had abdicated. But now he has grasped his icicle again and governs as well as reigns. The world looks like a lamb in its white fleece, but some of us know better.

Mrs. Lowell sends her love, and I wish you and yours many happy returns of the New Year. Unhappily it is generally the Old Year that comes back again. However, we all *play* it is the New, and that is something.

Good-by.   Affectionately yours,

J. R. LOWELL.

To James B. Thayer
ELMWOOD, *January* 14, 1877.

Dear Sir, — I am heartily thankful to you for your very encouraging note. I write verses now with as much inward delight as ever, but print them with less confidence. For poetry should be a continuous and controlling mood, the mind should be steeped in poetical associations, and the diction nourished on the purest store of the Attic bee, and from all these my necessary professional studies are alien. I think the " Old Elm " the best of the three,[1] mainly because it was composed after my college duties were over, though even in that I was distracted by the intervention of the Commencement dinner.

But what I wished to say a word to you about (since you are so generous in your judgment) is the measures I have chosen in these as well as the " Commemoration Ode." I am induced to this by reading in an article on Cowley copied into the " Living Age " from the " Cornhill " (and a very good article too, in the main) the following passage, "As lately as·

---

[1] *Three Memorial Poems:* " Ode read at the One Hundredth Anniversary of the Fight at Concord Bridge, April 19, 1775 ; " " Under the Old Elm," poem read at Cambridge on the hundredth anniversary of Washington's taking command of the American army, July 3, 1775 ; an " Ode for the Fourth of July, 1876."

our own day " (*my* ear would require " *So* lately
as," by the way) " Mr. Lowell's ' Commemoration Ode ' is a specimen of the formless poem
of unequal lines and broken stanzas supposed
to be in the manner of Pindar, but truly the descendant of our royalist poet's ' majestick numbers.' " Now, whatever my other shortcomings
(and they are plenty, as none knows better than
I), want of reflection is not one of them. The
poems were all intended for public recitation.
That was the first thing to be considered. I
suppose my ear (from long and painful practice
on Φ. B. K. poems) has more technical experience
in this than almost any. The least tedious measure is the rhymed heroic, but this, too, palls
unless relieved by passages of wit or even mere
fun. A long series of uniform stanzas (I am
always speaking of public recitation) with regu-
larly recurring rhymes produces somnolence
among the men and a desperate resort to their
fans on the part of the women. No method
has yet been invented by which the train of
thought or feeling can be shunted off from the
epical to the lyrical track. My ears have been
jolted often enough over the sleepers on such
occasions to know that. I know *something* (of
course an American can't know much) about
Pindar. But *his* odes had the advantage of
being chanted. Now, my problem was to contrive a measure which should not be tedious

by uniformity, which should vary with varying moods, in which the transitions (including those of the voice) should be managed without jar. I at first thought of mixed rhymed and blank verses of unequal measures, like those in the choruses of "Samson Agonistes," which are in the main masterly. Of course, Milton *deliberately* departed from that stricter form of the Greek Chorus to which it was bound quite as much (I suspect) by the law of its musical accompaniment as by any sense of symmetry. I wrote some stanzas of the "Commemoration Ode" on this theory at first, leaving some verses without a rhyme to match. But my ear was better pleased when the rhyme, coming at a longer interval, as a far-off echo rather than instant reverberation, produced the same effect almost, and yet was grateful by unexpectedly recalling an association and faint reminiscence of consonance. I think I have succeeded pretty well, and if you try reading aloud I believe you would agree with me. The sentiment of the "Concord Ode" demanded a larger proportion of lyrical movements, of course, than the others. Harmony, without sacrifice of melody, was what I had mainly in view.

The "Cornhill" writer adds that "Keats, Shelley, and Swinburne, on the other hand, have restored to the ode its harmony and shapeliness." He and I have different notions of harmony. He evidently means uniformity of recurrence. It is n't true of Shelley, some of whose odes certainly were written on the Cowley model. All of Wordsworth's are, except the " Power of Sound " and the " Immortality," which is irregular, but whose cadences were learned of Gray. (Our critic, by the way, calls the latter, whose name he spells with an *e*, a " follower of Cowley." Gray's odes are regular.) Coleridge's are also Cowleian in form, I am pretty sure. But all these were written for the closet — and mine for recitation. I chose my measures with my ears open. So I did in writing the poem on Rob Shaw. That *is* regular because meant only to be read, and because also I thought it should have in the form of its stanza something of the formality of an epitaph.

Pardon me all this. But I could not help wishing to leave in friendly hands a protest against being thought a lazy rhymer who wrote in *numeris* that seem, but are not, *lege solutis*, because it was easier. It is n't easier, if it be done well, that is, if it attain to a real and not a merely visual harmony of verse. The mind should be rhymed to, as well as the ear and eye. *Mere* uniformity gives the columns and wings and things of Herbert and Quarles. If I had had more time to mull over my staves they would have been better.

Gratefully yours,   J. R. LOWELL.

To C. E. Norton

BALTIMORE,[1] *February* 18, 1877.

. . . It happened that Judge Brown spoke of a letter he had received recommending somebody for the Professorship of Philosophy here. This gave Child a chance to speak of —— (Judge Brown is one of the trustees of the Johns Hopkins), which he did as excellently well as he lectures on Chaucer and reads him, and that is saying a great deal. You lost, by the way, a very great pleasure in not hearing him read the Nonnes Prestes tale. I certainly never heard anything better. He wound into the meaning of it (as Dr. Johnson says of Burke) like a serpent, or perhaps I should come nearer to it if I said that he injected the veins of the poem with his own sympathetic humor till it seemed to live again. I could see his hearers take the fun before it came, their faces lighting with the reflection of his. I never saw anything better done. I wish I could inspire myself with his example, but I continue dejected and lumpish. . . .

Child goes on winning all ears and hearts. I am rejoiced to have this chance of seeing so much of him, for though I loved him before, I did not know *how* lovable he was till this intimacy. . . .

[1] This visit to Baltimore was for the purpose of giving a course of lectures on Poetry at Johns Hopkins University .

To Miss Norton
"Bahltimer," *February 22, 1877.*

. . . We have just come back from celebrating our Johns Hopkins Commemoration, and I came home bringing my sheaf with me in the shape of a lovely bouquet (I mean nosegay) sent me by a dear old Quaker lady who remembered that it was my birthday. We had first a very excellent address by *our* President Gilman, then one by Professor Gildersleeve on Classical Studies, and by Professor Silvester on the Study of Mathematics, both of them very good and just enough spiced with the personality of the speaker to be taking. Then I, by special request, read a part of my Cambridge Elm poem, and actually drew tears from the eyes of bitter secessionists — comparable with those iron ones that rattled down Pluto's cheek. I did n't quite like to read the invocation to Virginia here — I was willing enough three or four hundred miles north — but I think it did good. Teakle Wallace (Charles will tell you who he is), a prisoner of Fort Warren, came up to thank me with dry eyes (which he and others assured me had been flooded), and Judge Brown with the testifying drops still on his lids.

Silvester paid a charming compliment to Child, and so did Gildersleeve. The former said that he (C.) had invented a new pleasure for them in his reading of Chaucer, and G., that you almost saw the dimple of Chaucer's own smile as his reading felt out the humor of the verse. The house responded cordially. If I had much vanity I should be awfully cross, but I am happy to say that I have enjoyed dear Child's four weeks' triumph (of which he alone is unconscious) to the last laurel-leaf. He is *such* a delightful creature. I never saw so much of him before, and should be glad I came here if it were for [nothing but] my nearer knowledge and enjoyment of *him*.

We are overwhelmed with kindness here. I feel very much as an elderly oyster might who was suddenly whisked away into a polka by an electric eel. How I shall ever do for a consistent hermit again Heaven only knows. I eat five meals a day, as on board a Cunarder on the mid-ocean, and on the whole bear it pretty well, especially now that there are only four lectures left. I shall see you, I hope, in a week from to-morrow. Going away from home, I find, does not tend to make us *under*value those we left behind. . . .

Your affectionate old friend,

J. R. L.

To Mrs. E. Burnett

ELMWOOD, *June* 5, 1877.

. . . It must be kept close, but I have refused to go either to Vienna or Berlin. Indeed
I have no desire to go abroad at all. But I had
said that "I would have gone to Spain," sup-
posing that place to have been already filled.
But on Saturday I saw Mr. Evarts (by his request) at the Revere House, who told me that
the President was much disappointed by my
refusal. He (Mr. Evarts) thought it possible
that an exchange might be made, in which case
I shall have to go. It will be of some use to me
in my studies, and I shall not stay very long
at any rate. But it is hard to leave Elmwood
while it is looking so lovely. The cankerworms
have burned up all my elms and apple trees, to
be sure, but everything else is as fresh as Eden.
I tried troughs and kerosene round the two elms
near the house, and they are not wholly con-
sumed, but are bad enough. The crow blackbirds, after prospecting two years, have settled
in the pines and make the view from the
veranda all the livelier. It is a very birdy year
for some reason or other. I can't explain it,
but there is a great difference in the *volatility*
(as Dr. Hosmer would have said) of the
seasons. . . .

* *To Miss Grace Norton*
ELMWOOD, *July* 1, 1877.

. . . We have been having a very busy week,
as you know. The President's visit was really
most successful, so far as the impression made
by him went. He seemed to me simple and
earnest, and I can't think that a man who has
had five horses killed under him will be turned
back by a little political discomfort. He has a
better head than the photographs give him, and
the expression of the eyes is more tender. I
was on my guard against the influence which
great opportunities almost always bring to bear
on us in making us insensibly transfer to the
man a part of the greatness that belongs to the
place. . . . Mrs. Hayes also pleased me very
much. She has really beautiful eyes, full of
feeling and intelligence, and bore herself with
a simple good-humor that was perfectly well-
bred. A very good American kind of princess,
I thought. Don't fancy I am taken off my feet
by the enthusiasm of contagion. You know I am
only too fastidious, and am too apt to be put at
a disadvantage by the impartiality of my eyes.
No, I am sure that both the President and his
wife have in them that excellent new thing we
call Americanism, which I suppose is that
" dignity of human nature " which the philosophers of the last century were always seeking

and never finding, and which, after all, consists, perhaps, in not thinking yourself either better or worse than your neighbors by reason of any artificial distinction. As I sat behind them at the concert the other night, I was profoundly touched by the feeling of this kingship without mantle and crown from the property-room of the old world. Their dignity was in their very neighborliness, instead of in their distance, as in Europe. . . .

You must remember that I am " H. E." now myself, and can show a letter with that superscription. I have n't yet discovered in what my particular kind of excellency consists, but when I do I will let you know. It is rather amusing, by the way, to see a certain added respect in the demeanor of my fellow-townsmen towards me, as if I had drawn a prize in the lottery and was somebody at last. Indeed, I don't believe I could persuade any except my old friends of the reluctance with which I go. I dare say I shall enjoy it after I get there, but at present it is altogether a bore to be honorabled at every turn. The world is a droll affair. And yet, between ourselves, dear Grace, I should be pleased if my father could see me in capitals on the Triennial Catalogue.[1] You remember John-

---

[1] The triennial (now quinquennial) catalogue of the graduates of Harvard College ; now, since Harvard has grown to a University, deprived alike of the dignity of its traditional

son's pathetic letter to Chesterfield. How often I think of it as I grow older ! . . .

To Thomas Hughes

ELMWOOD, *July* 2, 1877.

. . . I should have written to you at once, when I finally made up my mind to go to Madrid, but that I heard of the death of Mrs. Senior. Just after this I lost one of my oldest and dearest friends in Jane Norton, and then went Edmund Quincy, an intimate of more than thirty years, at a moment's warning. I had always reckoned on their both surviving me (though Quincy was eleven years my elder), for they both came of long-lived races. Of Mrs. Senior I have a most delightful remembrance when we rowed together on the Thames, and she sang " Sally in our Alley " and " Wapping Old Stairs " in a voice that gave more than Italian sweetness to English words. I thought that her sympathy with the poor, and her habit of speaking with them, had helped to give this sweetness to her voice. If heaven were a place where it was all singing, as our Puritan forbears

Latin and of those capitals in which the sons of hers who had attained to public official distinction such as that of Member of Congress, or Governor of a State, or Judge of a U. S. Court, were elevated above their fellow-students. To have one's name in capitals in the catalogue was a reward worth achieving.

seem to have thought, the desire to hear that voice again would make one more eager to get there. I was in a very gloomy mood for a week or two, and did n't like to write. There is no consolation in such cases, for not only the heart refuses to be comforted, but the eyes also have a hunger which can never be stilled in this world. . . .

To Miss Grace Norton

Grosvenor Hotel, Park Street,
LONDON, *July 29*, 1877.

. . . I have just come in from Hyde Park, whither I go to smoke my cigar after break-fast. The day is as fine as they can make 'em in London: the sun shines and the air is meadowy. I sat and watched the sheep crawl through the filmy distance, unreal as in a pastoral of the last century, as if they might have walked out of a London eclogue of Gay. Fancy saw them watched by beribboned shepherdesses and swains. Now and then a scarlet coat would cross my eye like a stain of blood on the in-nocent green. The trees lifted their cumulous outlines like clouds, and all around was the ceaseless hum of wheels that never sleep. . . . This scene in the Park is one of which I never tire. I like it better than anything in London. If I look westward I am in the coun-try. If I turn about, there is the never-ebbing

III

stream of coaches and walkers, the latter with
more violent contrasts of costume and condition
than are to be seen anywhere else, and with
oddities of face and figure that make Dickens
seem no caricaturist. The landscape has the
quiet far-offness of Chaucer. The town is still
the town of Johnson's London. . . .

To the Same

Hôtel de Lorraine, 7 Rue de Beaune,
Paris, August 8, 1877.

. . . Here we are in the same little hotel in
which you left us five years ago, and I never
walk out but I meet with scenes and objects
associated with you. It is the same Paris, and
more than ever strikes me as the handsomest
city in the world. I find nothing comparable to
the view up and down the river, or to the liveli-
ness of its streets. At night the river with its
reflected lights, its tiny bateaux mouches with
their ferret eyes, creeping stealthily along as if in
search of prey, and the dimly outlined masses of
building that wall it in, gives me endless pleasure. I am as fond as ever of the perpetual torch-
light procession of the avenue of the Champs
Elysées in the evening, and the cafés chantants
are more like the Arabian Nights than ever. I
am pleased, too, as before with the amiable ways
and caressing tones of the French women —
the little girl who waits on us at breakfast treats

us exactly as if we were two babies of whom she had the charge—and with the universal courtesy of the men. I am struck with the fondness of the French for pets, and their kindness to them. Some Frenchman (I forget who) has remarked this, and contrasted it with their savage cruelty towards their own race. I think, nevertheless, that it indicates a real gentleness of disposition. The little woman at the kiosque where I buy my newspapers asked me at once (as does everybody else) after John Holmes. (She had a tame sparrow he used to bring cake to.) " Ah ! " exclaimed she, "*qu'il était bon ! Tout bon ! Ce n'est que les bons qui aiment les animaux ! Et ce monsieur, comme il les aimait !* ". . . .

To George Putnam

Hôtel de Paris, Madrid,
Thursday, August 16, 1877.

. . . We are obliged to go about somewhat in the heat of the day house-hunting. We can't go in a cab like ordinary mortals, but must have coachman and footman in livery, with their coats folded over the coach-box in a cascade of brass buttons. The first day it rather amused me, but yesterday the whole thing revealed itself to me as a tremendous bore — but essential to the situation. *Tu l'as voulu, Georges Dandin !* There are moments when I feel that I have sold my soul to the D—l. I am writing post-haste now because this leathern inconveniency will be at the door in half an hour, and I must find work for it or— . . .

To Mrs. Edward Burnett

Legacion de los Estados Unidos
    de America en España.   MADRID, *August* 24, 1877.

. . . We arrived here on Tuesday, the 14th, and on Friday, the 17th, I started with Mr. Adee (the late chargé-d'affaires here) for La Granja. This is a summer palace of the king, about fifty miles from Madrid, among the mountains. You go about half the distance (to Villalba) by rail, and there we found awaiting us the private travelling-carriage of the prime minister, which had been very courteously put at our disposal. Our journey was by night and over the mountains, the greatest height reached by the road being about that of Mt. Washington. Eight mules with red plumes and other gorgeous trappings formed our team. A *guardia civil*, with three-cornered hat, white cross-belts, and rifle, mounted the rumble, and with a cracking of whips quite as noisy as a skirmish of revolvers in Virginia City, and much shouting, away we pelted. After crossing the pass and beginning to go down-hill the road was very picturesque, through a great forest of heavy-needled pines whose boughs, lighted up by our lamps, were like heavy heaps of smoke in a still air. We reached La Granja at midnight, beating the *diligence* by more than an hour. Our rooms at the only inn had been engaged by telegraph, so we supped and to bed. The next morning the second Introducer of Ambassadors (the first was at the seashore) came to make arrangements for my official reception and Mr. Adee's (late chargé) audience of leave. The introducer was in a great stew (for he had never tried his hand before), and made us at least six visits, to repeat the same thing in the course of the forenoon. At ten minutes before two a couple of royal coaches arrived, the first for Mr. Adee and the second (more gorgeous) for me. Mounted guards, with three-cornered hats and jack-boots, looking like the pictures of Dumas *père's* mousquetaires, rode on each side in files. The introducer, blazing with gold and orders, sat on my right, and we started at a footpace for the palace, about a hundred yards away. The troops and band saluted as we passed, and, alighting, we were escorted through long suites of rooms to the royal presence. There I found the king, with as many of the court dignitaries as were at La Granja, in a long semicircle, his majesty in the middle. I made one bow at the door, a second midway, and a third on facing the king. I made my speech in English, he answered me in Spanish, then came forward and exchanged a few compliments with me in

French, and all was over. Then I was taken
to another wing of the palace to pay my respects to the Princess of the Asturias, the king's
sister. Next morning (Sunday, 19th) we break-
fasted *en famille* with Señor Silvela, Minister
of State. At two the Duke of Montpensier
(just arrived) held a reception in my honor.
All the diplomats at La Granja sat in a circle.
At the end of the room farthest from the door
sat the duke and duchess, with an empty chair
between them to which I was conducted. After
five minutes of infantile conversation the duke
rose and the thing was over. At five some of
the *grandes eaux* in the garden were played for
Uncle Sam. It was a pretty and picturesque
sight. The princesses and their ladies walked
in front abreast, followed by the king, his household, and foreign ministers. I was beckoned to
the king's side, and he talked with me all the
way — even quoting one of my own verses.
He had been crammed, of course, beforehand.
The waters were very pretty, and the garden,
set as it is in a ring of mountains, far finer than
Versailles. At eight o'clock dinner at the palace, where I sat on the left of the Princess of
Asturias, the Duke of Montpensier being on
her right, and the king opposite. The king,
by the way, is smallish (he is not nineteen),
but has a great deal of *presence*, is very intelligent and good-looking. So young a monarch

in so difficult a position interests me. The
same night, at two o'clock, we started for
Madrid. . . .

To H. W. Longfellow

MADRID, *November* 17, 1877.

Dear Longfellow, — I have just had a visit
from Sñr. D. Manuel Tamayo y Baus, secretario
perpetuo de la Real Academia Española, who
came to tell me that they had just elected you a
foreign member of their venerable body. When
your name was proposed, he says, there was a
contest as to who should second the nomination,
*porque tiene muchos apasionados aquí el Señor Long-
fellow*, and at last the privilege was conceded to
the Excmo. Sñr. D. Juan Valera, whose literary
eminence is no doubt known to you. You may
conceive how pleasant it was to hear all this, and
likewise your name pronounced perfectly well
by a Spaniard. Among all your laurels this leaf
will not make much of a show, but I am sure
you will value it for early association's sake, if
for nothing more. I told the Sñr. Secretary that
one of your latest poems had recorded your
delightful memories of Spain.

It made me feel nearer home to talk about
you, and I add that to the many debts of friendship I owe you. I wish I could walk along your
front walk and drop into your study for a minute. However, I shall find you there when I

come back, for you looked younger than ever when I bade you good-by. (I forgot to say that your *diploma* will be sent to me in a few days, and that I shall take care that you receive it in good time.)

I have had a good deal of *Heimweh* since I got here, and a fierce attack of gout, first in one foot and then in the other. I am all right again now, and the November weather here (out of doors) is beyond any I ever saw. It beats Italy. And such limpidity of sky! Within doors it is chilly enough, and one needs a fire on the shady side of the house.

I have made few save diplomatic and official acquaintances thus far — very pleasant — but I miss my old friendships. But I don't know how many times I have said to myself, "Tu l'as voulu, Georges Dandin, tu l'as voulu!"

Keep me freshly remembered in your household, to the whole of which I send my love. Eheu!

Good-by. God bless and keep you!

Your affectionate friend,

J. R. LOWELL.

To George Putnam

MADRID, *December* 23, 1877.

Dear Putnam, — . . . You talk jauntily of journeys to Granada and the like! You 've no notion how much there is to do here. My secretary, who was eight years in the State Department, says it is the hardest-worked legation of all. I am getting used to it, though I shall never like it, I think, for I am too old to find the ceremonial parts even amusing. They bore me. Then I had seven weeks of gout before I had learned to take my work easily, and I worried myself abominably over it. 'T is a vile thing to have a conscience! But fancy a shy man, without experience, suddenly plumped down among a lot of utter strangers, unable to speak their language (though knowing more of it than almost any of them), and with a secretary wholly ignorant both of Spanish and French. (An excellent fellow, by the way, whom I like very much, and whose knowledge of official routine has been a great help.) And I was to get an indemnity out of them! It was rather trying, and I feared seriously at one time, while I was shut up, it would affect my brain — for what with gout and anxiety I sometimes got no sleep for three days together. However, the gout let go its hold of my right foot just long enough for me to hobble with a cane and finish my indemnity job, and then went over into my left and pulled me down again.

From the first, however, I insisted on transacting all my business with the Secretary of State in Spanish, and now I get along very well, going to an interview with him quite at my ease.

The offices of the legation are a mile from my
house, and I have been there every day during
office hours except when I was jugged with the
gout. I hope to see Granada in the spring.

Next month we shall have prodigious doings
with the king's wedding — such as could not
be seen anywhere else, I fancy, in these days —
for they purposely keep up or restore old fashions here, and have still a touch of the East in
them so far as a liking for pomp goes. I like
the Spaniards very well so far as I know them,
and have an instinctive sympathy with their
want of aptitude for business. My duties bring
me into not the most agreeable relation with
them, for I am generally obliged to play the
dun, and sometimes for claims in whose justice
I have not the most entire confidence. Even
with the best will in the world, Spain finds it
very hard to raise money. Fancy how we should
have felt if a lot of South Carolinians during
our civil war could have got themselves naturalized in Spain, and then (not without suspi-
cion of having given aid and comfort to the
enemy) should have brought in claims for damage to their estates by the Union Army! I think
they would have had to wait awhile! . . .

To the Same

<small>MADRID, *January* 28, 1878.</small>

. . . We are just getting done with the fes-
tivals incident to the king's marriage, to the
great relief of everybody concerned. The dis-
play, in certain respects, has been such as could
be seen nowhere out of Spain, but the fatigue
and row have been almost unendurable. I had
just had two more of those dreadful attacks in
the stomach to which I have been liable for the
last few years, one on Tuesday, and a second
still worse on Saturday — so bad, indeed, that
I really thought something was going to happen that would drive the legation to black wax.
Ether was of no avail, but on Sunday my feet
began to swell and the stomach was relieved. I
was forced to keep my bed for ten days. I am
now all right again, except that I have to wear
cloth shoes and cannot do any walking. But I
took such care that I was able to show myself
at the more important ceremonies. I never saw
a crowd before, and one night, on my way to a
reception at the prime minister's, I was nearly
mobbed (that is, my carriage was), and so were
several other foreign ministers. We were obliged
to go round by a back street — the mob being
furious, and I don't blame them.

The most interesting part of the ceremonies,
on the whole, was the dances of peasants from

the different provinces of Spain before the king yesterday morning. It took place in the *plaza de armas* before the palace, and afterwards they were all brought up and ranged in a row for our inspection. The costumes were marvellous, and we could never have otherwise had such a chance to see so many and so good. In the evening the king dined the diplomatic body, and afterwards held a grand reception. The uniforms (there are six special embassies here with very long tails) and diamonds were very brilliant. But to me, I confess, it is all vanity and vexation of spirit. I like America better every day. . . .

To Miss Grace Norton
MADRID, *March* 7, 1878.

. . . I don't care where the notion of immortality came from. If it sprang out of a controlling necessity of our nature, some instinct of self-protection and preservation, like the color of some of Darwin's butterflies, at any rate it is there and as real as that, and I mean to hold it fast. Suppose we don't *know*, how much *do* we know after all? There are times when one doubts his own identity, even his own material entity, even the solidity of the very earth on which he walks. One night, the last time I was ill, I lost all consciousness of my flesh. I was dispersed through space in some inconceivable fashion, and mixed with the Milky Way. It

was with great labor that I gathered myself
again and brought myself within compatible
limits, or so it seemed; and yet the very fact
that I had a confused consciousness all the while
of the Milky Way as something to be mingled
with proved that *I* was there as much an indi-
vidual as ever. . . .

To John W. Field
MADRID, 7 Cuesta de Sto. Domingo,
March 14, 1878.

. . . Thanks, too, for the "République Fran-
çaise." The article amused me. Devotion to
money quotha! The next minute these Johnny
Crapauds will turn round and say, "Was there
ever anything like us? See how we paid the
German indemnity, and all out of our old
stockings — the savings of years." The don-
keys! You can raise more money for public
purposes by subscription in a Boston week than
in a French twelvemonth. *That's* not the weak
point of democracy, whatever else may be.
And in Gambetta's paper, too! What has been
the strength of his Jewish ancestors and what is
the strength of his Jewish cousins, I should like
to know! That they could always supply you
or me with an accommodation at heavy interest.
Where would a Jew be among a society of
primitive men without pockets, and therefore
a fortiori without a hole in them? . . .

To George Putnam

MADRID, *March* 16, 1878.

. . . What I meant by my not blaming the crowd that night was that the whole street from one end to t'other was so crammed with people that a carriage passing through really endangered life or limb. I intended no communistic sentiment, but, though I am one of those who go in chariots for the nonce, I confess that my sympathies are very much with those who don't. Communism seems to have migrated to your side of the water just now. But I confess I feel no great alarm ; for if history has taught us any other lesson than that nobody ever profits by its teachings, it is that property is always too much for communism in the long run. Even despite the Silver Bill, I continue to think pretty well of my country, God be praised ! . . .

To H. W. Longfellow

MADRID, *March* 16, 1878.

Dear Longfellow, — I meant to have sent the diploma by Field, but as it was locked up in our safe at the Legation (I don't live there), I forgot it. I sent it yesterday to Paris by Mr. Dabney, our consul at the Canaries, who will deliver it to Ernest, and he will soon find a safe hand by whom to send it home. I am charmed with your simple Old Cambridge notion of our despatch-bags. God knows we have despatches enough to write, but we have only one bag, which we use only when we have reason to send a special courier to London, and the last one we sent left it behind him, so that we are bag-less as Judas when he hanged himself (Old Play). I could n't send the diploma, according-ly, with our regular despatches without folding it, which would have disfigured it abom-inably ; and meanwhile you are as much an academician as if you had it, though I hope still young enough to wish to hold it in your own hand. By the way, the *Académicos del Número* are entitled to wear a gorgeous decoration round the neck. If it had been that, I should n't wonder at your feeling a little anxious, for if I had n't stolen it I should have wondered, like Clive, at my own moderation.

Thank you for the poem, which Mrs. Lowell and I enjoyed together, and is so characteristic " that every line doth almost read your name." I should have known it everywhere, and liked it very much — all the more that it convinced me you were as young as ever and with no abatement of natural force.

The forsythia is already in bloom here, and the almond trees were three weeks ago. The leaves are peeping. And yet to-day it is really cold again, and I suppose there was a fall of snow on the Guadarramas last night, for it was tumultu-

ous with wind. It is a queer climate — the love-
liest I ever saw — and yet it sticks you from
behind corners, as we used to think Spaniards
employed all their time in doing. After all,
Cambridge is best.

My love and best wishes on your latest birthday (I was going to write "last," and super-
stitiously refrained my pen). I won't read the
milestone, but I am sure it is on a road that
leads to something better. Two countrymen in-
terrupt me, and I end with love from your

Affectionate
J. R. LOWELL.

To F. J. Child

MADRID, *Palm Sunday, April* 14, 1878.

Dear Ciarli,[1] — I have noticed that Class and
Phi Beta poems almost always begin with an
" as " — at any rate, they used to in my time,
before a certain Boylston professor took 'em in
hand ; e. g., —

> As the last splendors of expiring day
> Round Stoughton's chimneys cast a lingering ray,
> So —

And sometimes there was a whole flight of
as-es leading up to the landing of a final *so*,
where one could take breath and reflect on what
he had gone through. Now you will be sure

[1] " Ciarli " was the attempt of an old Italian beggar at
Professor Child's name.

that I did n't mean to begin my letter thus, but
it was put into my head by the earthquake you
have been making in Baltimore, the wave from
which rolled all the way across the ocean and
splashed audibly on these distant shores; and as
all my associations are with dear Old Cambridge,
why naturally I found myself murmuring, —

> As, when the Earthquake stomps his angry foot,
> A thousand leagues the frightened billows scoot,
> So when my Ciarli, etc.

I was delighted to hear of it, though it was just
what I expected, for did n't my little bark at-
tendant sail more than a year ago? It gave me
a touch of homesickness too, for I look back on
that month as one of the pleasantest of my life,
and here I am not as who should say altogether
and precisely happy. Yet I hope to get something out of it that will tell by and by. The
ceremonial, of which there is plenty, of course
is naught, and I make acquaintance so slowly
that I hardly know anybody (except officially)
even yet, but I have at last got hold of an intelligent bookseller, and am beginning to get a
few books about me. . . . Gayangos has some
exquisite old books, by the way — a Góngora,
among others, that would have tempted me to
ruin had it been for sale. It is a manuscript on
vellum, made as a present to the Conde-duque
de Olivares when he was in the flush of his *pri-
vanza*. Each poem is dated on the margin, and

III

in the index the copyist marks certain ones as falsely attributed to Góngora, and says the poet told him so himself. It is exquisitely done, like that little Greek book in Mr. Sibley's showcase — Anacreon, is n't it?

I have just succeeded in getting a copy of the series printed for the *Bibliofilos Españoles*, which is very hard to come at, and cost me $105 in paper. It contains one or two things worth having, but I bought mainly with a view to the College Library one of these days. I have also bought the *photolithographie* of Cuesta's *editio princeps* of "Don Quixote" for the sake of Hartzenbusch's notes, which, by the way, show a singular dulness of perception, and *correct* Cervantes in a way that makes me swear. But they are worth having, as showing the emendations that have been made or proposed, the *when* and *by whom*. I have, too, the Burgos 1593 *Crónica* of the Cid, a very fair copy, and Damas-Hinard's edition of the *Poem*. . . .

I fear what you say of my being thrown away here may turn out true. There is a great deal to do, and of a kind for which I cannot get up a very sincere interest — claims and customs duties, and even, God save the mark! Brandreth's pills. I try to do my duty, but feel sorely the responsibility to people three thousand miles away, who know not Joseph and probably think him unpractical. . . .

. . . We have seen Seville, Cordova, Granada, and Toledo, each excellent in itself and Toledo queer, even after Italy and Sicily. But the *shrinkage* is frightful. Toledo especially is full of ruin, and, what is worse, of indifference to ruin. Yet there is something oriental in my own nature which sympathizes with this " let her slide " temper of the *hidalgos*. They go through all the forms of business as they do of religion, without any reference to the thing itself, just as they offer you their house (dating their notes to you *de su casa*) and everything in it. But they are very friendly, and willing to be helpful where they can. I love the jauds for a' that. They are unenterprising and unchangeable. The latest accounts of them are just like the earliest, and they have a firm faith in Dr. Mañana — he will cure everything, or, if he can't, it does n't signify. In short, there is a flavor of Old Cambridge about 'em, as O. C. used to be when I was young and the world worth having. . . .

Good-by, dear old fellow.

Your affectionate

J. R. L.

To C. E. Norton

7 Cuesta de Sto. Domingo, 2°, izqᵃ.
(second floor, left-hand door),
April 15, 1878.

. . . I write now because I am going away for two months and have n't time to write at all. Whither we shall go I hardly can tell. I have a furlough of sixty days, and am going first into southern France to see Toulouse and Carcassonne, which I never saw. Then I think we shall go to Genoa and Pisa, staying some little time, perhaps, in the *vituperio delle genti*. Then we may go on to Naples, take the steamer there, and be carried round to Athens. I am obliged to take my vacation now, to bring it within the year. My heart is as heavy as dough, so does the thought of travel always depress me. I don't know how I can come to grief — but am sure I shall always.

I believe I have performed my functions here tolerably well, except those of society, and even those I have not wholly neglected. I have been out a great deal — for *me*. The hours here are frightfully late. They go to a reception *after* the opera, so that half past 11 is early. At a dance they are more punctual, and I have even known them to begin at 10, but they keep it up till 2 or 3. They seem childishly fond of dancing. But there is no such thing as conver-

sation, nor any chance for it. As for scholarship, there is, I should say, very little of it, in
the accurate German sense. I don't think they
value it any more than they do time, of which
they always have more on their hands than they
know what to do with, and therefore vastly less
than they want.

My own time has been very much broken up
by my not being well. I think I told you that
I have had three fits of gout since I came, and
I *worry* over my duties. . . .

But I am learning something, I hope. I get
along very well in Spanish now, and when I
come back am going to fasten an *abbé* to my
skirts, so as to be forced into talking. I have
tried in vain to find out for you whether there
are any letters of Velasquez or not. What they
call their *archives* have never been sorted. They
don't know what they have. And then Siman-
cas is ever so far away, and Government won't
consent to have their documents brought to
Madrid — nor even to Valladolid. There are
local jealousies in the way — stronger even than
ours. But next winter, when I am more familiar
with things and men, I hope to do something.
There are no scientific booksellers — not one —
and I can't even procure what has been actually
printed about Cervantes. I bought the other
day the photolithographic copy of the first edition of " Don Quixote," for the sake, mainly,

of Hartzenbusch's notes. But they are mostly
worthless — of value mainly as collation. He
does n't understand his author in the least,
whose delightfully haphazard style is too much
for him. I shall, however, bring home some
books you will like to see. I buy mainly with
a view to the College Library, whither they will
go when I am in Mount Auburn, with so much
undone that I might have done. I hope my
grandsons will have some of the method I have
always lacked.

. . . My little world is getting smaller and
smaller, and I am *not* reconciled. Still, I long
for the Charles and the meadows, and walk
between Elmwood and Shady Hill constantly.
I feel much older in body and mind — I can't
quite say why or how, but I feel it. I cling to
what is left all the more closely. . . .

Always your loving

J. R. L.

To Mrs. E. Burnett

ARLES, *April* 27, 1878.

. . . Mamma has told you that we were to
go off on a leave of absence, and we have now
been on our travels eleven days. Thus far we
have enjoyed it very much. Our itinerary has
been : from Madrid to Tarbes, then Toulouse,
then Carcassonne, then Nismes, then Avignon,
and then hither. We have thus had a pretty

good glimpse of the south of France, and very lovely it is. At Toulouse and Carcassonne I had never been before, and Toulouse, I confcss, disappointed me, though thcrc was an interesting old church (St. Sernin) and an old house worth seeing. But Carcassonne is wonderful, a fortified place of the twelfth and thirteenth centuries, as perfect as if it had been kept in a museum. As you look across the river at it from the *new* town (six hundred years old) it seems like an illumination out of some old copy of Froissart. I positively thought I was dreaming after looking at it for long enough to forget the modernness about me. Its general aspect is of the dates I have given, but parts are Roman, parts Visigothic, and parts Saracenic. The past is ensconced there as in a virgin fortress, and will hold out forever.

From Nismes we drove out about twelve miles to the Pont du Gard. It rained all the way out ; but just as we got there it cleared, and all the thickets (in every one a nightingale) were rainbowed and diamonded by the sun. The *Pont* is a Roman aqueduct, which crosses the deep valley of a pretty river on three rows of arches, one above another. It is really noble, and these gigantic bones of Rome always touch and impress me more the farther away they are from the mother city. Then we had some bread and sausages and wine in a little arbor,

served by a merry old man, who, when I told
him I had been there twenty-six years before,
challenged me to come back as many hence;
" but," said he, touching his white whiskers,
and with a sly glance at mine, " *les blancs ne se
refont jamais bruns.*" Jacques (our servant) re-
sented this, as in duty bound, and insisted that
monsieur was n't in the least white yet, at which
the heartless old boy only laughed, and I joined
him in order to put a good face on the matter.
I complimented him on his daughter, who was
making a pretty nosegay for mamma. "*Ah,*"
said he, "*je lui lègue les bouteilles vides et les
bouchons, mais avec de la santé et la bonne
volonté on arrive.*" So we parted, agreeing to
meet in 1904! Before we were halfway home
(if I may call a hotel so) it began to rain again.
So you see what luck we had.

From Avignon we drove twenty miles to
Vaucluse (which I had not visited before), and
found it worthy of all Petrarca had said of it.
The *onde* are as *chiare* and *fresche* as ever, and
the fountain one of the most marvellous I ever
saw. You follow a ravine deeply hollowed in
the soft rock for about half a mile, and there,
at the foot of a huge precipice, is the basin,
which feeds a considerable stream. A clear,
calm pool. You see no bubbling of springs
from below, no fissure in the rock, and per-
ceive no motion in the water except where it

escapes towards the valley. It is lined with fac-
tories now, and French visitors have daubed
the rocks with their vulgar names in black paint
in every direction. You can't find a fragment
to sit on without feeling discomforted by a
guilty sense of complicity in hiding half a
dozen of these profanations from the angry
glare of the sun. We might have lunched at
any one of three cafés — one of which invites
you with the advertisement painted on its front
that here Petrarch wrote his 129th sonnet! It
is the Café de Pétrarque et Laure. "Great
Cæsar dead and turned to clay," etc. . . .

I don't care to say how soft my heart gets
when I think of you all at home. I fancy I am
growing old. . . .

To the Same

ATHENS, *May* 17, 1878.

. . . Here we are in Athens, and just come
in from a visit to the Acropolis, which has
served to balance our first impressions, which
were rather depressing. For to drive from the
Piræus through a dreary country, in a cloud of
dust, drawn by two wretched beasts that ought
to have been in their graves long ago, and unable to stop the driver from lashing because we
could speak no tongue he could understand,
and then to enter a shabby little modern town,
was by no means inspiriting. I was for turning

about and going straight back again, but am
getting wonted by degrees, and I dare say shall
come to like it after a while. I was stupid
enough to be amused last night at hearing the
boys crying the newspapers in Greek — as if
they could do it in anything else — and fancied
I caught some cadences of the tragic chorus in
the bray of a donkey, the only " Attic warbler "
that I have heard " pour his throat."

. . . Our first sight of Greece was the shores
of the Morea, and anything more sterile and
dreary I never saw. I thought some parts of
our New England coast dreary enough, but this
is even grimmer. We had for fellow-passenger
a pretty little land-bird, which found the land
inviting in spite of all, and flew away when he
thought we were near enough. I could n't help
thinking how much better off he would be than
we, having a command of the language where-
ever he lighted. The first natives we saw were
two gulls (an imperishable race), probably much
less degenerate from their ancestors than the
men who now inhabit the country.

The position of the Parthenon, by the way,
is incomparable, and, as mamma said, the general sadness of the landscape was in harmony
with its ruin. It is the very abomination of desolation, and yet there is nothing that is not
noble in its decay. The view seaward is magnificent. I suppose the bird of Pallas haunts the

temple still by nights, and hoots sadly for her lost mistress. There was a strange sensation in looking at the blocks which Pericles had probably watched as they were swung into their places, and in walking over the marble floor his sandals had touched. . . .

To C. E. Norton

ATHENS, *May* 21, 1878.

. . . On the day of my arrival I was profoundly depressed, everything looked so mean — the unpaved and unsidewalked streets, the Western coat and trousers, and what costumes there were so filthy. And yet I was in luck, for the town is full of Thessalian insurgents, so that I see more that is characteristic than I had a right to expect. They are dreadful ruffians to all appearance, and reminded me of Macaulay's Highlanders. In consequence of them I refused to go out to Marathon with Jebb, who is here, and who, after all, went and came safely. But for my official character I should have gone. I could not afford the time to be sequestered (as we call it in Spain), and the Minister of State thought it risky. The returning patriots are of a class who are quite indifferent whether they learn the time of day from a Moslem or Christian timepiece, and to whom money from whatever pocket is orthodox.

In the afternoon of the day of my arrival I

walked up to the Acropolis, and tuned my nerves and mind to a manlier key. It is noble in position and sublime even in ruin. The impression was all I could wish — profound beyond expectation and without artificial stimulus. You know I prefer Gothic to Grecian architecture, and yet (I cannot explain it) the Parthenon was more effective in its place than a shattered cathedral would have been. But imagination plays such tricks with us —

MADRID, *August* 2, 1878.

I was in the middle of a reflection, my dear Charles, when in came Santiago to tell me that the steamer for Constantinople would leave the Piræus in three hours. It was my only chance, and I decided for going — Athens only half seen. But then, you know, I have a theory that peaches have only one good bite in 'em, and that a second spoils *that*. I am glad we went. The view of Constantinople as you draw nigh is incomparable, and one sees at once what an imperial eye Constantine had. Planted firmly in Europe, it holds Asia subject with its eye. The climate is admirable — Eastern sun and Western rains. The harbor ample for all the navies of the world — the Bear, if he planted himself here, would get wings and turn aquiline. We went as far as the Black Sea in the track of the Argo and saw the Symplegades, very harm-

less-looking rocks, like certain women when
their claws are sheathed. The captain of the
French steamer we came back to Marseilles in,
who had been in all seas, told me that in winter
the Black Sea was the worst of all. Our four
days at Constantinople were nothing more nor
less than so many Arabian Nights. I could n't
have believed that so much was left. Santa
Sofia is very noble, *really* noble, and one sees
in it the germ, if not the pattern, of all Oriental
architecture — Cordova, Granada, Seville, nay,
Venice and St. Mark's. This struck me very
much.

The Turks are the most dignified-looking
race I have ever seen — a noble bearing even
in defeat and even in rags. Their exceeding
sobriety of life no doubt helps this — for all
their faces look pure — and perhaps their fatal-
ism. Do you remember I prophesied (against
Godkin) that they would make a better fight
than was expected ? I think they did, and that
with competent leaders they would have beaten
the Muscovite, who, after all, to my thinking,
is a giant very weak in the knees.

I saw Layard, by the way, just as he was
concluding the Cyprus business, as I found out
afterwards. I thought he seemed in tempestu-
ous spirits, and no wonder ! I am inclined to
like the Asia Minor arrangement (because I
wish digging to be done there !), and I think

England strong enough for the job. I think if Beaconsfield were n't a Jew, people would think him rather fine. But they can't get over an hereditary itch to pull some of his grinders.

My Eastern peep has been of service in enabling me to see how oriental Spain still is in many ways. Without the comparison, I could n't be sure of it. . . . I am beginning to feel competent to make some observations on the Spaniards, but shall keep them till they are riper. These things have to stand in solution a long while till the introduction of some new element, we scarce know when or how, precipitates out of mere vagueness into distinct and hard crystals which can be scientifically studied and assigned. I fancy it is otherwise with history, which is not so much " philosophy teaching by example " as clarified experience. It only has to stand on the lees long enough. One apothegm I have already engraved in brass : " The Spaniard offers you his house, but never a meal in it." I like them and find much that is only too congenial in their genius for to-morrow. I am working now at Spanish as I used to work at Old French — that is, all the time and with all my might. I mean to know it better than they do themselves — which is n't saying much. . . .

To Mrs. Edward Burnett

MADRID, *July* 26, 1878.

. . . I was very far from well and in miserable spirits before my journey. I have come back a new man, and have flung my *blue* spectacles into the paler Mediterranean. I really begin to find life at last tolerable here, nay, to enjoy it after a fashion. . . .

I am turned schoolboy again, and have a master over me once more — a most agreeable man — Don Herminegildo Giner de los Rios, who comes to me every morning at nine o'clock for an hour. We talk Spanish together (he does n't understand a word of English), and I work hard at translation and the like. I am now translating a story of Octave Feuillet into choice Castilian, and mean to know Spanish as well as I do English before I have done with it. This morning I wrote a note to one of the papers here, in which my teacher found only a single word to change. Was n't that pretty well for a boy of my standing? It was about Miss Dana's recollections (or records rather) of the convent days of our poor little Queen Mercedes. Anything more tragic than the circumstances of her death it would be hard to imagine. She was actually receiving extreme unction while the guns were firing in honor of her eighteenth birthday, and four days later we saw her dragged

to her dreary tomb at the Escorial, followed by
the coach and its eight white horses in which
she had driven in triumph from the church to
the palace on the day of her wedding. The
poor brutes tossed their snowy plumes as
haughtily now as then. Her death is really a
great public loss. She was amiable, intelligent,
and simple — not beautiful, but *good*-looking —
and was already becoming popular. Her malady was not thought serious at first, and, I fear,
was all along mistakenly treated. . . .

To Miss Grace Norton
7 Cuesta de Sto. Domingo, *August* 11, 1878.

. . . Madrid is the noisiest city I ever dwelt
in. The street cries are endless, and given with
a will and with such distortions of face as must
be seen to be believed. None are musical. One
always stirs my fancy by its association with
Aladdin — the *lamparero*. Shall I try my luck?
I think not, for in his cry I have the material
for rows of palaces, whereas if I bought a lamp
I might rub in vain. The first sound in the
morning is the tinkle of bells on the necks of
the she-asses that come in to be milked at the
customer's door for surety. I know not who
the customers are, but there must be many if
there be any truth in the vulgar belief that children take after their nurses. Then there is a
succession of blind players on the guitar, on the

pipe and tabor, and on what I suppose to be the
gaita. They sometimes also sing, but commonly have with them a boy or girl who shrieks
a *romance*. All the tunes are the same so far as
I can make out — just as in a school of poetry.
Then the town is full of parrots and caged
quails. I don't suppose we are exceptional, but
there are five parrots in this house and the next
together, all birds of remarkable talents. One
hangs in the courtyard of our house and sings,
shouts, calls names, and swears all day long. In
this same *patio*, by the way, I have heard songs
issuing from the servants' quarters in every
floor and from the grooms in the courtyard at
the same time. The voices are seldom agreeable and the tunes always monotonous. Indeed,
they seem to have but one. I can't catch much
of the words, but the other day I heard, " *Yo
soy el capitán de la tropa*," and presently, " *Yo
soy el duque de Osuna*," from which I surmised a
Lord of Burleigh who was gradually revealing
himself. I was wrong in saying that all the
street cries are harsh. There is a girl who passes
every day crying radishes, who really makes a
bit of melody with her *Rábanos!* It is seldom
that one does not hear (night or day) a thrum-
ming or a snatch of nasal song, and I am pretty
well persuaded that it was the Spanish dominion
which planted the seeds of the Neapolitan
street-music.

III

At this season they sleep in the day a good
deal, and at night are as lively as certain skipping insects, with which many of them are only
too familiar. Far from being a grave people,
they seem to me a particularly cheerful one; and
yet I am struck with the number of deeply
furrowed faces one meets, the mark of hereditary toil. I turn half communist when I see
them. The porters especially stir an angry
sympathy in me, sometimes old men (nay,
often) tottering under incredible burthens, which
they carry on their backs steadied by a cord
passed round the forehead. Every day I recall
that passage in Dante where he stoops from
sympathy, like an ox in the yoke. The traditional figures of the *genre* painters one sees rarely
now, and yet there is no lack of costume. One
meets constantly men in the very costume of
Velasquez's "Lanzas," which sometimes has a
very odd effect on my fancy. The reality makes
a very different impression from the attempted
illusion of the stage, and has made me understand better why I don't care for such pictures
as many of Meissonier's and the like, clever as
they are. But here is theme for a dissertation.
I suppose that in some remote way the notion
of *sincerity* has something to do with it, and
here, I suspect, is to be found the distinction
between the *reality* of Dante and modern real-
ism. A great deal of what is called pre-Raphaelite

on canvas and in verse gives me the same uncomfortable feeling of *costume*. You will guess
what I mean if I am not very clear. To come
back to statistics.

I never saw anything like the fruit in Madrid
for abundance and variety. The oranges, plums,
melons, apricots, and nectarines are the best
I ever saw. I have sometimes eaten finer
melons of my own growing — but my average
was never so high. Then we have grapes,
pomegranates, pears (not nearly so fine as ours),
apples (ordinary), prickly pears, peaches (tolerable), medlars. What surprises me is how long
the season is. We are never without something. Grapes begin in June and last till
December.

The city of Madrid at first disappointed me
greatly by its modern look. I had expected
to find the *mise en scène* of Calderon. But I
gradually became reconciled, and now like it.
Moreover, I begin to suspect that I had n't
understood Calderon, and that his scenery is
applicable to the present city — at least, in a
measure. The Prado with its continuations is
fine, and the Buen Retiro as agreeable a drive as
I know — more agreeable, I add on reflection,
than anything of the kind I know of in any
other city. But then I am bewitched with the
Campiña. To me it is grander than the Campagna; of course I do not count the associations.

I mean as a thing to look at and fall in love
with. The Guadarramas are quite as good as or
better than the Alban mountains, and their color
is sometimes so ethereal that they seem visionary rather than real. The Campiña, I admit, is
sombre — but its variety and shift of color, its
vague undulations! At night, especially, it is
like the sea, and even in the day sometimes.
We are, you know, twenty-five hundred feet
above the sea, but beside that, Madrid stands
on hills more considerable than those of Rome
and commanding wider horizons. The climate
thus far has been incomparable. In our year
here we have had, I believe, only three days
when it rained. All blue, night and day, and
such a blue! Nothing so limpid have I ever
conceived. I should hate such a climate were I
living in the country. I should sympathize too
keenly with my trees, should be always feeling
the drouth of their roots, and being wretched.
But here it makes no odds. The trees are
watered daily, and there are really beautiful
gardens.

This is the course of my day: get up at 8,
from 9 sometimes till 11 my Spanish professor,
at 11 breakfast, at 12 to the Legation, at 3
home again and a cup of chocolate, then read
the paper and write Spanish till a quarter to 7,
at 7 dinner, and at 8 drive in an open carriage
in the Prado till 10, to bed at 12 to 1. In

The Palace, Madrid

cooler weather we drive in the afternoon. I am very well — cheerful and no gout. . . .

Your affectionate

J. R. L.

To Mrs. Edward Burnett

MADRID, August 25, 1878.

. . . Things go on here much as usual. The death of Queen Cristina (the king's grandmother) I feel mainly because it gives us two months more of full mourning, and I am already tired of my sables. It will, besides, cost mamma a new dress. Such are the painful responsibilities of diplomacy! Our flag is floating at half-mast and wreathed in crape, from the balcony; and what a handsome flag it is, by the way! . . .

I see that some good people at home are in a very desperate mood over tramps and defalcations and socialism and what not. For my part, I have been assured so often in the course of my life that the bottom of the world had at last dropt out for good and all, and yet have survived to see it hold water very tolerably nevertheless, that I am not much scared. I, who saw the Irish mobbed in Boston ten years before you were born, for the very same reason that the Chinese are now hounded by the Irish in California, think it a good sign that Kearney can address his countrymen in Faneuil Hall and talk as much nonsense to 'em as he likes. It proves the good sense of our people (in that respect at least) and the solidity of our social framework. I expect to find you all safe and well when I come home next summer — for I mean to come on a visit, if not to stay. I begin to feel as if I should like to remain here longer, now that I have served my apprenticeship and feel at home in my business. But I have resolved nothing as yet, and what I say you must keep to yourself.

I am having a slight touch of gout since the last few days — not enough to keep me in the house, but only to remind me that I have joints in my feet. I have had to put on my cloth shoes again, but am in other respects in excellent health and spirits — very unlike what I was last year. Then I had not the spirit to be interested in anything, and wished myself at home every five minutes. Now I begin to be amused with what I see in the streets — for example, with the boys playing bullfight under my window. One boy (the bull) covers his head with a long basket with which he plunges at the rest, who irritate him with colored handkerchiefs and rags. When this has gone on for some time one of them goes to the sidewalk for two sticks sharpened at one end, which represent the *banderillas*. If he succeed in sticking them both through the interstices of

the basket so that they stand up firmly, the
bull drops and is despatched, and a fresh boy
dons the basket and the bullship. They make
me think of Jem and Joe, and are *somebody's*
grandsons, I suppose, at any rate. . . .

To Mrs. W. E. Darwin
September 1, 1878.

. . . I have just been doing something that
reminds me of you all the time. I should be
willing to give you a thousand guesses and you
would n't divine what. . . . However, I will
answer my own conundrum for you. I am
turned Spanish author! "Why should that remind you of *me*, pray? Is there anything Spanish about *me?*" No, I 'm sure there 's not,
but my authorship is of a very humble kind,
indeed. "Worse and worse! Is there anything
so *very* humble about me, sir?" No, I did n't
mean that, but — in short, I have been translating into Spanish a sketch of Mr. Darwin's
life — no, not *your* Mr. Darwin, certainly, you
foolish little person, but his father. Not that
I like science any better than I ever did. I
hate it as a savage does writing, because he
fears it will hurt him somehow; but I have
a great respect for Mr. Darwin, as almost the
only perfectly disinterested lover of truth I
ever encountered. I mean, of course, in his
books, for I never had the pleasure of seeing

him. So I volunteered my services as drago-
man, and when the opuscule is printed (which
will not be for some time yet), I shall ask
permission to lay a copy at your feet, as we
say here. . . .

To George Putnam

MADRID, *September* 9, 1878.

. . . Your tobacco came safely (except that
the Spanish customs officer stole one package
and filled the gap with brown paper. I mention it because their system of appointment is
just like ours) and is a great blessing. I wish
you would send me a hundred more packages
by the same route. Don't suppose I am con-
suming all this enormous quantity of smoke like
a new-fashioned furnace. I want it for quasi-
diplomatic service. I found that my friend the
Minister of State (for foreign affairs), who has
been everything I could wish in amiability towards me, smokes a pipe in the secrecy of his
despacho at home, and as I was sure he must be
blistering his tongue with Spanish mundungus,
I sent him a package of mine. He writes to
say that " *es el mejor que he fumado en mi vida;
no tenia idea de cosa tan buena!* " So I sent
him yesterday ten more, and have promised to
keep his pipe full for so long as I am here. By
the way, he is going to have me elected a cor-
responding member of the Spanish Academy

(this is between ourselves), which will be very agreeable, as I shall be able to attend the weekly meetings and discuss the new edition of the Dictionary. I am to be proposed by the Prime Minister Cánovas del Castillo, the Minister of State; and Excmo. Sñr. Nocedal, leader of the Ultramontanes — an odd combination for me. . . .

To Miss Grace Norton
MADRID, *October 2, 1878.*

. . . Yesterday (I mean night before last) we went to the Teatro Español, and saw a very clever comedy of Alarcon. Of course, it had been *adapted*, as all the old comedies have to be ; but they are not capable of being Rowed and Cibbered as Shakespeare is, for they have not the complexity of coherence (if I may venture the Johnsonism) that characterizes him. It was the *Semejante á si mismo.* The hero, with that whimsical jealousy of an accepted lover of which Spanish playwrights are so fond, resolves to test his mistress. His cousin Don Diego has just arrived from Peru, a perfect stranger, and has not yet presented himself to his relatives. Don Juan persuades him to give *him* his letters of credence, pretends a voyage to Peru, takes solemn leave, and presently returns as Don Diego. He contrives to have news arrive of his other self's loss at sea, and makes love to

Doña Ana. She very readily accepts and even returns his advances. He is thus in the comical position of being jealous of himself. In his anger he tells her who he is. She excuses herself by saying that it was not with the name of Juan or Diego that she was in love, but with the qualities she found in the bearer of both. At last, after a very pretty complication, in which everybody refuses to believe that he is Don Juan, all ends happily. I was very much interested — it was so pleasant to *see* what I had so often had to imagine in reading Spanish plays. The acting was good — especially that of the *gracioso*. The heroine was perfectly a portrait by Vandyke in the Museo, so that by an odd trick of imagination she seemed real, a person I had already known. . . .

To C. E. Norton

MADRID, *November* 10, 1878.

. . . We have had General Grant [here], and I gave him a dinner and reception. As he speaks nothing but English, he was as incommunicable as an iceberg, and, I think, is rather bored by peregrination. What he likes best is to escape and wander about the streets with his Achates Young. After being here two days, I think he knew Madrid better than I. He seemed to me very simple-minded, honest, and sensible — very easy to be led by anybody he likes. He

is perfectly unconscious and natural, naïvely
puzzled, I fancied, to find himself a personage,
and going through the ceremonies to which he
is condemned with a dogged imperturbability
that annotated for me his career as General.
He seemed anxious to explain to me his quarrel
with Sumner — or Sumner's with him. " Sumner is the only man I was ever anything but
my real self to ; the only man I ever tried to
conciliate by artificial means " — those are his
very words. . . . Grant has an excellent memory and narrates remarkably well. . . .

To Thomas Hughes
MADRID, *November* 17, 1878.

My dear Friend, — Now and then there is
an advantage in being a dilatory correspondent ;
as, for example, if a friend had written to me
offering the splendid opportunity of enrolling
myself among the shareholders of the Emma
Mine, I should have been as safe as are the
pyramids from cholera. More punctual men
would have been bitten, but I should have
found so many reasons for not writing to-day
nor to-morrow nor next day, that by the time
I dipt my pen in the ink I should have been
as likely to subscribe for shares in that rail-
way to the moon chartered by the legislature
of New Hampshire as in the enterprise of
Messrs. Schenck & Park. Again, if I were one

of those admirable persons who always reply by
return of post, I should now find myself entangled in a web of contradictory opinions and
prophecies about the Eastern Question, and
should long ago have had to deliver an opinion
or die, on the vext question whether the Pleni-
pos at Berlin had applied a plaster or a blister
to their unhappy patient. As it is, I have only
been called on to shake my head and leave my
interlocutors to guess what new shape I had
thus given to my ideas. Between ourselves, by
the way, I am satisfied that Dizzy's policy has
done a good deal to restore the prestige of
England among the " rest of mankind " ;
and as I back the English race against the field,
I am not sorry for it. I hope you won't have
a war, but at all events a war between England and Russia would be a war between
civilization and barbarism. Moreover, I like
the Turks for about as good a reason as the
man had for not liking Dr. Fell, but still I
like them. And then I think a good deal of
the prejudice against Beaconsfield is mediæval,
of a piece with the enlightened public opinion
which dictated the legend of Hugh of Lincoln.
There are plenty of other modern versions of
the story of Joseph — only people know not
Joseph, that is, his pedigree.

Yes, I am beginning to feel handier in my
new trade, but I had a hard row to hoe at first.

All alone, without a human being I had ever seen before in my life, and with unaccustomed duties, feeling as if I were beset with snares on every hand, obliged to carry on the greater part of my business in a strange tongue — it was rather trying for a man with so sympathetic and sensitive a temperament as mine, and I don't much wonder the gout came upon me like an armed man. Three attacks in five months! But now I begin to take things more easily.

Still, I don't like the business much, and feel that I am wasting my time. Nearly all I have to do neither enlists my sympathies much nor makes any call on my better faculties. I feel, however, as if I were learning something, and I dare say shall find I have when I get back to my own chimney-corner again. I like the Spaniards, with whom I find many natural sympathies in my own nature, and who have had a vast deal of injustice done them by this commercial generation. They are still Orientals to a degree one has to live among them to believe. But I think they are getting on. The difficulty is that they don't care about many things that we are fools enough to care about, and the balance in the ledger is not so entirely satisfactory to them as a standard of morality as to some more advanced nations. They employ inferior races (as the Romans did) to do their intellectual drudgery for them, their political economy, scholarship, history, and the like. But they are advancing even on these lines, and one of these days — but I won't prophesy. Suffice it that they have plenty of brains, if ever they should condescend so far from their *hidalguia* as to turn them to advantage. At present they prefer the brook to the mill-pond. They get a good deal out of life at a cheap rate, and are not far from wisdom, if the old Greek philosophers who used to be held up to us as an example knew anything about the matter. . . .

To Miss Grace Norton
MADRID, *January* 15, 1879.

Dear Grace, — I wrote some verses thirty odd years ago called "Without and Within," and they originally ended with the author's looking up at the stars through six feet of earth and feeling dreadfully bored, while a passer-by deciphers the headstone and envies the supposed sleeper beneath. I was persuaded to leave out this ending as too grim — but I often think of it. They have a fine name for this kind of feeling nowadays, and would fain make out pessimism to be a monstrous birth of our century. I suspect it has always been common enough, especially with naughty children who get tired of their playthings as soon as I do — the absurdity being that then we are not content with smashing

the toy which turns out to be finite — but everything else into the bargain. . . .

I wonder if somebody else, if I myself when
I was younger, could n't find enough that was
interesting to say about this New World, that
has become new by dint of staying pretty much
where it was when Columbus left it to find another — because this, I suppose, had grown tiresome. I shall have a good deal to tell by the
chimney-corner if ever I get back to it, I have
no doubt, but it takes a great while for things
to settle and separate themselves in my memory.
Shall I tell you of a reception at the palace? It
is so comically like what one sees on the stage,
and really *is* so much a mere piece of acting
here, that it seems hardly worth while. Or shall
I write of the weather? That, after all, in spite
of the fun that has been made of it as a topic
of conversation, is the only one of universal and
permanent interest, and you will be glad to know
that we have had a rainy winter, on the whole,
but roses have been in bloom all the while, and
the daisies were opening their eyes in the grass
more than a week ago. There are great patches
of green on the brown gaberdine of the Campiña, and there is a sound of spring in the voice
of the sparrows. But the Guadarramas (the
tallest of them) are dreamy with snow, and don
ever and anon (don anon!) a kind of luminous
mantilla of cloud that is wonderfully fine. I ex-

plain this nebular radiance by the vapors being comparatively low, so that the sunshine is reflected through them from the snow behind. I think I have told you that I like the Campiña better than the Campagna. It is serious, it is more than that — it is even sad, but it is the sadness and incommunicativeness of nature and not the melancholy of ruin. It is vast and grows vaster the more you see it, and one conceives the rotundity of the earth, as at sea. It always looks to me like a land not yet taken possession of by man, rather than one that he has worn out. . . .

To George Putnam

MADRID, *March* 3, 1879.

. . . I have pretty much made up my mind to stay on here for at least another year — perhaps for two, if they don't Motleyize me. I have now learned my business, and after two years of a discomfort that has sometimes been almost intolerable I should like to get a little pleasure and profit out of my exile. . . .

To Miss Grace Norton

MADRID, *March* 4, 1879.

. . . Since I have been here I have been reading a good many travels in Spain, beginning with a Bohemian knight of the fifteenth century and ending with Théophile Gautier. It is very

curious in how many particulars the earliest and
latest agree, proving, I suspect, that the condition of the country is not due to the expulsion
of Moors and Jews, or to the House of Austria,
or the Bourbons, so much as to something in
the character of the people.

Generally the balls I have to attend are a
bore, but I was interested in one the other night
at the Duke of Osuna's, who lives in a real
palace with family portraits and relics. The duke
represents ten grandeeships of the first class —
which ought to give him the right to wear ten
hats in the presence of the king. He sums up
in himself Bejar, Olivares, Lerma, and other
names we all know. He is ruined, but comfort-
ably so, for he is allowed a hundred thousand
dollars a year by his creditors. But he cannot
live on it. He has ruined himself magnificently.
While ambassador at St. Petersburg he sent all
his clothes home to be washed in the Manza-
nares, and had a table of fourteen covers set
every day in his palace here. He seems to have
inherited his magnificent wastefulness, for Lord
Auckland speaks of a ball given by his grandfather (I suppose) in 1788 that cost £8000. It
is a wonder he inherited anything else.

Field is still with us, and we propose, as he
no doubt has told you, a little excursion together
to the Balearic Islands, but as the ministry re-
signed yesterday I suppose I shall have to stick

in Madrid for the present. Politics here are in one respect interesting and worth study. They are so personal and so much moved by springs of intrigue that they help one to a more vivid understanding of those of the last century. I can make no guess as to what is to take place. . . .

To W. D. Howells

MADRID, *May* 2, 1879.

Dear Howells, — When Aldrich passed through here he brought me some excuse or other from you for not having answered a letter of mine. Was it an abominable sarcasm sent all the way over the ocean with its subtile barb dipt in sweetened poison — the worst kind of all ? If not, the sensation is so novel that I ought not to endanger it by any clumsy interferences of mine. I am as sure as I well can be of anything that no man ever before accomplished the feat of owing me a letter. Believe me, my dear boy, it is your most exquisite literary achievement. My own debts of this kind commonly gather and gather till bankruptcy is the only possible outlet — and without a dividend. Never a court in Christendom would whitewash me. Now I am going to astonish you by paying you a penny in the pound.

And yet I can't say that you had wholly neglected me. I always fancy that an author's works are more intimately addressed to his

friends, have passages in them written in sympathetic ink invisible to the vulgar, but revealing themselves to the penetrating warmth of
friendship. And your " Lady of the Aroos-
took " was to me a delightful instance of this
cryptography. I read it as it came out in the
" Atlantic," and was always as impatient for
more as the French ladies used to be for more
Arabian Nights. It is delightful, and there was
never a slyer bit of satire than your Englishman who loves the real American flavor, while
his wife is abolishing herself as hard as she can
in a second-hand Anglicism. I am quite in love
with your heroine, and am grateful to you accordingly. . . .

I am painfully struck, by the way, with the
amount of discussion going on just now, which
somehow implies a certain consciousness of in-
feriority on our part as compared with our English cousins. (I confess, let me say in passing,
that I am tired to death of———'s laborious
demonstration that we have a right to our
mother-tongue ! If he would devote himself to
hunting down American vulgarisms and cor-
ruptions — I observe that even the " Atlantic,"
in some sort the child of my entrails, confuses
will and *shall* — more power to his elbow !) I
think we were less conscious when I was a
youngster. Nowadays Europe, and especially
England, seems a glass of which everybody is

uncomfortably aware, an horizon which, instead
of suggesting something beyond itself, cuts us
all off with reflections of (perhaps I should say
on) our unhappy selves. We are all the time
wondering what is thought of us over there,
instead of going quietly about our business.

However, my opinion is of no earthly consequence, for I feel every day more sensibly
that I belong to a former age. A new generation has grown up that knows not Joseph, and
I have nothing left to do but to rake together
what embers are left of my fire and get what
warmth out of them I may. I still take an
interest, however, in what some of the young
ones are doing, as a gambler who has emptied
his pockets still watches the game, and especially in you who always do conscientious work.
So I venture to tell you that I think your new
book especially *wholesome* and admirable.

You can't imagine how far I am away from
the world here— I mean the modern world.
Spain is as primitive in some ways as the books
of Moses and as oriental. Spaniards have, I
believe, every possible fault— and yet I love
the jades for a' that! They find themselves in
the midst of a commercial age, poor devils!
with as little knowledge of book-keeping as the
Grand Turk. But there is something fine in
this impenetrability of theirs, and the grand
way they wrap themselves in their ragged *capa*

of a past and find warmth in their pride. Their indifference to legitimate profit is a continual comfort, and they have no more enterprise than an Old Cambridge man.

Good-by. Write another story at once, and don't forget

Your affectionate old friend,

J. R. L.

To C. E. Norton

MADRID, *May* 4, 1879.

. . . One thing I have remarked here, not without serious foreboding. I mean the analogy between the Spanish civil service with its inevitable results, and our own. Politics here is a scramble for office. Leaders, therefore, represent not a principle, but simply a chance. A government once in power cooks the elections to its fancy, and there is absolutely no way to a change except through a *pronunciamiento*. Are we not moving more or less rapidly in the same direction? As we have no standing army, we choose the more cowardly way of fraud rather than the bolder of brute force. But the root of the matter seems the same — the hopelessness of getting power and place against the patronage and myriad means of influence of the cabal in possession. I have great faith in the good sense of our people, but deterioration of national character is always so gradual and imperceptible, and we are receiving so strong a dose of alien and more impatient blood, that there is certainly room for doubt. It all depends on our force of digestion, but with the utter decay of the principle of authority the world has a new problem before it. Perhaps Judge Lynch is not so bad a fellow after all from some points of view. . . .

To Leslie Stephen
MADRID, *June* 8, 1879.

My dear Stephen, — . . . What you say of politics and the D—l reminds me of the Universalist who announced his conversion to Calvinism during our civil war, because " he was satisfied that Hell was a military necessity." But to me over here in Spain, which is pretty much what it was when Gil Blas saw it, *any* kind of administration looks ideal. " War-horses" and " Favorite Sons" are plentier here than in the best country in the world.

Over there, by the way, I see they are in a great taking over the new California Constitution. I am rather pleased with it myself, for it is going to show how really healthy our body politic is. It is the great advantage of our system that one State can try quack medicines while the others look on and await the result. No Dennis Kearney was ever yet contrived who could make himself master of the helm. . . .

To Miss Grace Norton
MADRID, *Corpus Christi, June* 12, 1879.

. . . I am still reading old travels in Spain, and with profit as well as interest. And this, with Harry James's and Howells's stories, has made me very vividly conscious of a sad change. The old travellers tell what they see, and talk of men as impartially — of men and their ways I mean — as they would of animals of any other species. They are interested, and seem rather glad than otherwise to come across strange habits as a relief from the general monotony of existence. They record facts, and neither draw conclusions nor make comparisons. Nations seem to have had an individuality that satisfied themselves and other people. Now they have become self-conscious. There is a standard somewhere or other to which they all strive more or less eagerly to prove themselves conformable, and which every traveller seems to carry in his pocket. No nation seems to be free from this weakness, or to have that high style of manners that comes of perfect self-possession or from interest in loftier matters than whether they eat with their knives — we Americans least of all. I know, of course, that there is a standard of good manners, and that the comfort of life and the security of civilization are in some measure dependent on its maintenance. But this is not precisely what I mean. (Here I was interrupted by a visitor, and can't knit together again the broken ends of my thread of thought.) But one thing seems clear to me, and that is that the Americans I remember fifty years ago had a consciousness of standing firmer on their own feet and in their own shoes than those of the newer generation. We are vulgar now precisely because we are afraid of being so. The English press is provincializing us again. I don't object to English criticism, but I do to English influence, for England seems to me the incarnation of the Kingdom of this World. . . .

To the Same

Madrid, *August* 16, 1879.

. . . Life does seem sometimes a hard thing to bear, and all that makes it bearable is to occupy the mind with the nobler moods of contemplation — not shutting our eyes to what is mean and ugly, but striving to interpret it rightly. However we explain it, whether as implanted by God or the result of long and laborious evolution, there is something in the flesh that is superior to the flesh, something that can in finer moments abolish matter and pain, and it is to this we must cleave. I do not see how even the loss of mind tells against a belief in this superior thing — for is the mind really dying in the same way as the body dies? or is it only

that the tools it works with are worn out or bent
or broken? . . :

To the Same
MADRID, *September* 12, 1879.

. . . They talk a good deal about *fetiches*
nowadays, but I confess that I have sometimes
lately been in a state of mind when I could have
vowed a gigantic candle to a saint. And why
not, if I was baby enough to be quieted a moment by a toy? I think the evolutionists will
have to make a fetich of their protoplasm before
long. Such a mush seems to me a poor substitute for the Rock of Ages — by which I understand a certain set of higher instincts which
mankind have found solid under their feet in
all weathers. At any rate, I find a useful moral
in the story of Bluebeard. We have the key
put into our hands, but there is always one
door it is wisest not to unlock. I suppose there
are times when the happiest of us ask ourselves
whether life is worth living, but did you ever
happen to hear of a pessimist sincere enough to
cut his own throat? . . .

To F. J. Child
MADRID, *December* 30, 1879.

. . . I will try, when I can pull myself together again, to see if I can get you any inedited
folk-songs. But I greatly doubt. The Spaniards

are singularly indifferent to such things, if not contemptuous of them. There is almost no scholarship here in our sense of the word, and most of the criticism is in the good old *isime* style. So entire a self-satisfaction I never saw in any people.

. . . The *penitus divisos ab orbe Britannos* were nothing to them in point of seclusion from the rest of mankind. But I love the jades for a' that — perhaps on account of a' that. I shout with laughter over their newspapers sometimes. For example, the " Imparcial " (a very clever paper by the way) had an article not long ago on " Longevity in Europe," based on one by Max Waldstein in a Viennese review. Here is a bit of it : " Salimos los Españoles los menos aventajados en eso de vivir mucho tiempo ; pero *como es necesario dudar siempre de la veracidad de los extrangeros en todo cuanto atañe á nuestro pais,*" etc., etc. Isn't that delicious ? Commonly they bluntly attribute this malice of facts to envy. They fancy themselves always in the age of Charles V., and the perfect gravity with which they always assume the airs of a Great Power is not without a kind of pathetic dignity. We all wink at the little shifts of a decayed gentleman, especially when he is Don Quixote, as this one certainly is. . . .

To Mrs. Edward Burnett

MADRID, *January 22,* 1880.

. . . Day before yesterday I was startled with a cipher telegram. My first thought was, " Row in Cuba — I shall have no end of bother." It turned out to be this: " President has nominated you to England. He regards it as essential to the public service that you should accept and make your personal arrangements to repair to London as early as may be. Your friends whom I have conferred with concur in this view." You see that is in very agreeable terms, and at least shows that Government is satisfied with my conduct here. I was afraid of its effects on mamma [1] at first; but she was pleased, and began at once to contrive how I could accept, which she wished me to do. I answered: " Feel highly honored by the President's confidence. Could accept if allowed two months' delay. Impossible to move or leave my wife sooner."

The papers already announce the appointment of my successor here, but say nothing about me. The doctor says I could safely leave mamma now for a few weeks, in which case I could go to London and present my letters of credence and come back here. The rent of my house is paid to March 1st, and I should feel easier now the Fields are here. It is certainly

[1] Mrs. Lowell was recovering from a long, desperate illness.

an honor to be promoted to the chief post in our diplomatic service, and I should like to serve (if only for a year) for the sake of my grandchildren if nothing else. By this time you probably know more about it than I. . . .

To Mrs. W. E. Darwin

MADRID, *January* 26, 1880.

. . . You look at only one side of the matter (and it is one great merit of your sex that they always do), and don't consider, first, whether I can afford it — though that is the least, for I have no profound faith in fuss and feathers, and it is they that cost most; but, second, you don't consider how I hate snobs and bores, and how many of our richer countrymen have to be thus labelled by the scientific inquirer. Madrid is a kind of Patmos in comparison with London, and yet even here I have been hunted down by Monsieur Jourdains, whose great object in life seemed to be to inform everybody that they travelled with *two* servants or with a courier, or that somehow or other they were not Americans exactly.

And the worst of it is that the Eastern States provide most of these vermin. Your Westerner, thank God! if he has n't the manners of Vere de Vere, has at least that first quality of a gentleman, that he stands squarely on his own feet and is as unconscious as a prairie. You can fancy how many of our countrymen are speedily convinced that I am wholly unfit to represent the great republic — and all of 'em pass through London ! But, after all, the Senate has n't confirmed me yet. . . .

To R. W. Gilder
MADRID, *January* 26, 1880.

Thank you for your congratulations. I know not whether I deserve them or no. At any rate, I had no choice, for I was nominated without consultation. Otherwise I hardly should have accepted. As I had consented to come hither for my own pleasure, I felt bound to obey orders.

I shall probably go to London to present my credentials, and then come back hither to remove Mrs. Lowell, who is better, but not yet able to leave her bed.

However, the Senate have not acted on me yet, so I may not come after all. . . .

IX

1880–1885

In London. — Vacation tour in Germany and Italy. — Death of Mrs. Lowell. — Departure from England. Letters to C. E. Norton, H. W. Longfellow, Mrs. W. E. Darwin, R. W. Gilder, Mrs. Lowell, John W. Field, T. B. Aldrich, W. D. Howells, F. J. Child, J. B. Thayer, George Putnam, Mrs. W. K. Clifford, Thomas Hughes, O. W. Holmes, Miss Grace Norton.

To C. E. Norton
37 LOWNDES STREET, S. W., *August 17, 1880.*

. . . I find that you have been very lenient in your judgment on my poems and have used a far finer [*sic*] sieve than I should have chosen if I had done the sifting. They always make me sad, thinking how much better I might have done if in the early years I *had* improvised less, and if in the later other avocations and studies had not made my hand more clumsy through want of use than it might have been had I kept more closely to verse and to the mood which that implies. But it is something that three such friends as you and George Curtis and Child should still retain a certain amount of interest in what I have written. I not only approve, but shall perhaps go further if I once begin. The question was simply one of leaving out *any*thing — for the terrible *manet litera scripta* was staring me in the face, and positively made me unwilling to reprint at all. By the way, I spent Sunday with Mr. Leveson Gower (Lord Granville's brother and a charming host), and coming in from out of doors came upon John Bright reading aloud from the " Commemoration Ode." It sounded better than I feared — but when I am asked to read I never can find anything that seems to me good enough. . . .

To H. W. Longfellow
37 LOWNDES STREET, S. W., *October* 3, 1880.

My dear Longfellow, — I have just been reading, with a feeling I will not mar by trying to express it, your " Ultima Thule." You will understand the pang of pleasurable homesickness it gave me. I cannot praise it better than by saying that it is like you from the first line to the last. Never was your hand firmer. If Gil Blas had been *your* secretary he never need have lost his place. I have n't a Dante by me, and my memory is in a very dilapidated state, but you will remember the passage I am thinking of, where the old poet in Purgatory says to him, *Or sei tu colui,* and so on. *Io mi son uno che quando Amor mi spira* is a part of it. If I could only drop into your study as I used, I should call you "old fellow," as we do boys, without any reckoning of years in it, and tell you that you had misreckoned the height of the sun, and were not up with *Ultima Thule* by a good many degrees yet. Do such fruits grow there?

But you have made me more homesick than ever, and I feel like the Irishman whose friend was carrying him for a wager up to the roof on a ladder — "Begorra, whin you were at the thurrud story I had hopes!" So I begin to think it would n't be so bad if Hancock were elected, for he would recall me. I like my present life as Touchstone did his in the forest. However, I dare say Garfield will have somebody he would like to send in my place.

I hope the Club still persists. I have never found such good society and don't expect it. I forwarded to you yesterday a box containing a drawing of the Minnehaha Fall by Lord Dufferin. It goes to the care of the State Department, which I thought would save trouble. I hope it will arrive safely. Good-by, hoist sail again without delay, and correct your geography. You are sure of a welcome in every port.

Affectionately yours,

J. R. L.

To Mrs. W. E. Darwin

LONDON, *October* 10, 1880.

. . . As you intervened unofficially (or *benevolently*, as we diplomatists say) in the affair of the Workingmen's College, I have the honor to report that I have fulfilled your instructions by talking to the unfortunate youth who compose the Body — as the teachers do the Soul — of that excellent institution. That part of Dogberry's charge to the watch in which he inculcates the duty of "*comprehending* all vagrom men," seems to me a very fair expression of the painful position in which a quasi-compulsory audience is placed by itinerant lecturers. But some pity is also due to the unfortunate creature who is obliged to inflict his particular form of aphasia (is n't that the word ?) upon them. As for me, who value my own wisdom less the older I grow, and who found it absolutely impossible to prepare anything, I shall not attempt to pathologize for you the pangs I underwent. When I saw directly under me a row of eight reporters, I was abashed by the feeling that I was decanting my emptiness into a huge ear-trumpet which communicated with the four winds of heaven, whose duty it would be to bear every idle word I uttered to the uttermost parts of the earth. If you had been there, you would have swallowed it all without a wry face, and

III

would have told me afterwards that it was a
" splendid success," with that sweet partiality
which characterizes all your sex . . . and which
is one of the few things that make life endur-
able to its victims. I did not quite break down
— but I heard several ominous cracks under
me as I hurried over the slender and shaky
bridge which led from my exordium to my
peroration. . . .

To R. W. Gilder

Legation of the United States,
LONDON, *September* 4, 1881.

Dear Mr. Gilder, — Your telegram scared
me, for, coming at an unusual hour, I thought
it brought ill news from Washington.[1] My relief on finding it innocent has perhaps made
me too good-natured towards the verses I send
you, but I have waited sixty-two years for them,
and am willing to wait as many more (not here)
before they are printed. Do what you like with
them. They mean only my hearty good-will
towards you and my hope for your success in
your new undertaking. . . .

Faithfully yours,

J. R. LOWELL.

If I could see the proofs, very likely I could
better it — they sober one and bring one to his
bearings. Perhaps the metaphysical (or what-

[1] Of President Garfield's condition.

ever they are) stanzas — what I mean is *moralizing* — were better away. Perhaps too many compound epithets — but I had to give up " visionary " in order to save " legendary," which was essential. Perhaps a note, saying that so long as the author can remember a pair of these birds (give ornithological name — *muscicapa ?*) have built on a jutting brick in an archway leading to the house at Elmwood — or does everybody know what a *phœbe* is ? I am so old that I am accustomed to people's being ignorant of whatever you please.

PHŒBE

Ere pales in heaven the morning star,
    A bird, the loneliest of its kind,
Hears Dawn's faint footfall from afar
    While all its mates are dumb and blind.

It is a wee sad-colored thing,
    As shy and secret as a maid,
That, ere in choir the robins ring,
    Pipes its own name like one afraid.

It seems pain prompted to repeat
    The story of some ancient ill,
But *Phœbe! Phœbe!* sadly sweet
    Is all it says and then is still.

It calls and listens. Earth and sky,
    Hushed by the pathos of its fate,
Listen, breath held, but no reply
    Comes from its doom-divided mate.

Phœbe ! it calls and calls again,
    And Ovid, could he but have heard,
Had hung a legendary pain
    About the memory of the bird;

A pain articulate so long
    In penance of some mouldered crime
Whose ghost still flies the Furies' thong
    Down the waste solitudes of Time ;

Or waif from young Earth's wonder-hour
    When gods found mortal maidens fair,
And will malign was joined with power
    Love's kindly laws to overbear.

Phœbe ! is all it has to say
    In plaintive cadence o'er and o'er,
Like children that have lost their way
    And know their names, but nothing more.

Is it a type, since nature's lyre
    Vibrates to every note in man,
Of that insatiable desire,
    Meant to be so, since life began ?

Or a fledged satire, sent to rasp
    Their jaded sense, who, tired so soon
With shifting life's doll-dresses, grasp,
    Gray-bearded babies, at the moon ?

I, in strange lands at gray of dawn
    Wakeful, have heard that fruitless plaint
Through Memory's chambers deep withdrawn
    Renew its iterations faint.

So nigh ! yet from remotest years
   It seems to draw its magic, rife
With longings unappeased and tears
   Drawn from the very source of life.

To the Same

Legation of the United States,
LONDON, *September* 5, 1881.

Dear Mr. Gilder, — I sent off the verses yesterday, and now write in great haste to say that
in my judgment the stanza beginning " Or waif
from young Earth's," etc., were better away.
Also for " doom-divided " print " doom-dissev-
ered." I have not had time to mull over the
poem as I should like.

Faithfully yours,

J. R. LOWELL.

P. S. I may write in a day or two suppress-
ing more, after I have had time to think.

To the Same

Legation of the United States,
LONDON, *September* 6, 1881.

Dear Mr. Gilder, — I bother you like a boy
with his first essay in verse. I wrote yesterday
to ask the omission of a stanza ; but last night,
being sleepless, as old fellows like me are too
often apt to be, I contrived to make a stanza
which had been tongue-tied say what I wished.

Let it go thus, —
> Waif of the young World's wonder-hour
>
> .　.　.　.　.　.　.　.
>
> .　.　.　.　.　.　.　.
>
> .　.　.　.　to overbear, (comma).

Then go on —
> Like Progne, did it feel the stress
> And coil of the prevailing words
> Close round its being and compress
> Man's ampler nature to a bird's?

This manages the transition, which was wanting. Perhaps this might follow : —
> One only memory left of all
> The motley crowd of vanished scenes,
> Hers — and vain impulse to recall
> By repetition what it means.

Faithfully yours,

J. R. LOWELL.

To the Same

Legation of the United States,
LONDON, *September* 8, 1881.

Dear Mr. Gilder, — This is positively the last! I wish to omit the stanza beginning " Or a winged satire," etc. I have been convinced by a friend whom I have consulted that it was a cuckoo's egg in my nest. *Item*. The verse that had bothered me most of all was this : —

> Listen, breath held, but no reply, etc.

I wished to have a distinct pause after " listen,"

in accordance with the sense. Somehow I could
not get the right, and " breath held " was clearly
the wrong one, awkward, and with the same
vowel sound in both halves. Print —

> Listen : no whisper of reply
> Is heard of doom-dissevered mate.

No ; that won't do either, with its assonance
of " heard " and " disse*vered* " — so, though I
prefer " dissevered " for sense, I will go back
to the original word " divided," which I suppose was instinctive.

This is positively my last dying speech and
confession. You need fear nothing more from
me. I fancy you ducking your head for fear of
another rap every time the postman comes.

I hope you will like my little poem, and tell
me so if you don't.

Kindest regards to Mrs. Gilder.

Faithfully yours,

J. R. LOWELL.

To the Same

Legation of the United States,
LONDON, *September* 12, 1881.

Dear Mr. Gilder, — With (I am sorry to
say) not unheard-of selfishness I forgot, in writing about my own little affairs, a much more
important one of Aubrey de Vere. He is going to send you a poem (founded on an Irish
legend) which is sure to be good — though

whether good enough I cannot say, for I like him so much and have liked him so long that I can't tell for the life of me why and how he falls short. I told him I feared the poem would be too long for you, etc., etc., but the dear old boy has a self-possession of hope which would be creditable at ten years. He is naturally anxious about his manuscript, and I beg you to be careful of it and return it to Mr. Norton at Cambridge if you should n't want it.

As I am writing, I add that if you think (as I am half inclined)

> no whisper of reply
> Comes from its doom-dissevered mate

better than the other reading, print it so.

Faithfully yours,

J. R. Lowell.

We are sadly anxious to-day about the President.

To Mrs. Lowell

Victoria Hotel, Dresden, *October* 16, 1881.

. . . It is just twenty-five years since I was in Dresden, and there is something sad in coming back an old man to a place familiar to you when much younger. But I must take up my diary again. When I wrote yesterday [from Weimar] I was uncertain whether I should see Goethe's house (I mean the inside of it) or not.

At any rate, I would see the garden-house he built when he first came to Weimar. So I took the drollest little bow-legged *valet-de-place*, who touched his hat and called me *Excellenz* whenever he could catch my eye. I had taken him with the express stipulation that he should n't open his mouth, and this was the compromise he made. Our walk led through the Park and along the Ilm. The Park, except the paths, is left pretty much to nature. It is very charming. The garden-house turned out to be about twenty minutes' walk. . . . It was a very simple affair of stone, about twenty feet square, roughly built, but beautifully set on the edge of a meadow sloping to the river. It was odd to find that my associations with Weimar, which are so vivid that I seem to have seen the persons and can hardly persuade myself I did not know Frau von Stein, should be more than a century old. Goethe was building this house just as our Revolution began. When I got back I found a card from Baron v. Brincken, informing me that Herr v. Goethe would be glad to see me at half past one. So I saw what I went to Weimar for after all. There was a small collection of antique gems, of drawings and engravings, and of very good majolica. There were also some bronzes, none of them remarkable. The *Studienzimmer* was what interested me most — the plain little table and

desk, with the chair waiting its master. Out
of it opened the sleeping-room with the bed in
which he died — about as large as a Spanish
alcoba, and showing how little good air has to
do with long life. Everything was very dingy,
and the study especially ill-lighted. I have an
engraving of it somewhere, so that I have been
wondering ever since if I had not seen it before.

I am going out presently to see the Sistine
Madonna and a few other old friends again.
They will not have changed or grown older. . . .

To R. W. Gilder

Hôtel Danieli,
VENICE, *October* 24, 1881.

Dear Mr. Gilder, — If you put up a warning
hand to point at your new address — then, *a
fortiori*, *I* may, who am in Venice. It is raining : never mind, I am in Venice ! Sirocco is
doing his worst : I defy him, I am in Venice ! I
am horribly done at my hotel : but what could
I expect ? I am in Venice ! But it is base in
me to crow in this way over a young poet who
perhaps would be more in keeping here than
my gray hairs can hope to be. I find on looking back that I have crowed once oftener than
the cock crowed at St. Peter ; and as he (I mean
the bird) was divinely inspired, he probably
went to the precise limit that human nature

could bear. Forgive me. I change my figure.
I have seen a grave horse of thirty years, and a
parson's, too, gallop and fling up his heels and
roll and do all kinds of indecorous things on
being turned into the pasture. I am that animal
— or even lengthen my ears if you will and I
am *that* animal; I am an escaped prisoner of
the Bastile; I am a fugitive slave; more than
all, I am an American public nigger out for a
holiday! And I am come here to find a
bateau mouche plying up and down the Grand
Canal!

Thank you for the printed copy. Of course
I am disgusted with it. Print somehow is like
a staring plaster-cast compared with the soft and
flowing outlines, the modest nudity of the manuscript clay. But it is a real pleasure to me that
you like it.

"Robins *ring*" is right, and whenever you
spend a June night at Elmwood (as I hope you
will so soon as I am safe there once more) you
will recognize its truth. There are hundreds
of 'em going at once, like the bells here last
night (Sunday), with a perfect indecency of dis-
regard for rhythm or each other. Mr. Bur-
roughs, I hear, has been criticising my knowledge of outdoors. God bless his soul! I had
been living in the country thirty years (I fancy
it must be) before he was born, and if anybody
ever lived in the open air it was I. So be at

peace. By the way, I took Progne merely because she was changed into a *little* bird. I should
have preferred a male, and was thinking of a
fellow (transformed, I think, by Medea), but
can't remember his name. While I am about
it, I question *wee*. Is it English? I had no
dictionary at hand. But there is one atrocity —
" *mold*ered." Why do you give in to these ab-
surdities? Why abscond into this petty creek
from the great English main of orthography?
'T is not quite so bad as " I don't know *as* "
for " I don't know *that*," but grazes it and is
of a piece with putting one's knife in one's
mouth.

As for your "remuneration" — it was most
generous, and I had a kind of qualm as I im-
peticosed your gratillity. I fear for authorship
with these luxurious rates.

Thank you for your good opinion of my
ministerial performances. I suppose I may be
recalled, just as I have learned to be easy in my
seat. Such is the lot of an American Minister
— he fleeth away as a shadow and hath no abid-
ing *place*. Give my kindest regards to Mrs.
Gilder and the Boy. As for writing a sonnet —
in Venice?! Ask me to saw wood.

Faithfully yours,
J. R. LOWELL.

P. S. My flock of s on the other side
remind me of my doves. I have just fed them

at my balcony. They came in scores, their wings whistling like shafts of Phoibos and so beautiful! *Now* I have touched the quick; I see you wince with your "Union Square," marry come up!

To Mrs. Lowell

Hôtel Bristol, ROME, *November* 11, 1881.

. . . I came hither yesterday from Florence through beautiful weather . . . and a country which is to me always the most pathetic in the world. I don't know why, but the desolation of Greece touches me less nearly. I saw Cortona in the distance sunning its long wall on the slope of the hill, and close by the station were some roofs all gilt with lichen, on one of which a pair of white doves were philandering. Then Orvieto on its crag . . . and queer, nameless little burghs that sought the hills for safety, and are now, consequently, *too* safe from the iron highway. Then there came slopes smoky with olives, which somehow are quite another thing in Italy than in Spain, and the groves of oak I remembered so well and through which I loitered in a vettura so many years ago.

I am sitting in the shadow of the Barberini as I write, and am growing into a furious socialist at the sight of these upstart palaces that shut out the sun from Diogenes. . .

To the Same

Hôtel Bristol, ROME, *November* 13, 1881.

. . . My windows here look out on one side towards the Barberini, and on the other towards the old Triton. . . . The weather is as fine as fine can be, and I do nothing with commendable assiduity — thawing myself out in the sun like a winter fly. William and John [1] and I idle about, telling over old stories and reviving old associations. . . .

I told you of the *vaporetto* on the Grand Canal (between ourselves, it was only sentimentally disagreeable, and, in point of fact, a great blessing to the poorer class), but I hesitate to tell you what I have seen here. The only costumes left now are on the brazen-faced models, and one sees below — what? Those hateful boots with a high heel in the midst of the sole, on which they tottle about as on peg-tops. When I was first here every peasant woman one met wore sandals. I have always hated those eternal repetitions of women with a dirty towel on their heads which express the highest aspiration and conviction of modern art — but this is like the cloven hoof. . . .

Wordsworth speaks of a motion this way or that which is fateful — and I often think of it as I look at pictures and statues, and try to

[1] Mr. William W. Story and Mr. John W. Field.

Frances Dunlap Lowell

make out *what* it is that makes some eternally fascinating and leaves us cold before the rest. It is so little and it is everything — and the earth is full of the same beauty the Greeks and Venetians saw. Why should they be the only ones that ever saw it? . . .

To R. W. Gilder

10 Lowndes Square, S. W.,
January 9, 1882.

Dear Mr. Gilder, — I forgot all about the photograph — my misfortunes in the way of engraved portraiture (the only set-off to which is security against identification by the police) having made me callous, if not indifferent. I don't know which you have got from Mrs. Carter, for your description of it as " sitting in a chair " does n't help me much. Pray, what should the poor thing be sitting in? Go on and do your worst — or rather (vanity would say) your prettiest. The Storys showed me an old photograph of myself in Rome the other day, which I should not have believed taken from me but for their assurance. How young it looked! and what a wealth of curls! It must have been about thirty years old — I mean the photograph. Was *I* ever thirty? It seems impossible, though folks tell me I am no more than that now. *Posthume! Posthume!*

I don't think much of any international copyright bill which is drawn by publishers — always in the interest of the manufacturers and not the makers of books. The clause you mention was no doubt meant for a sop to our protectionists. The British Government has already expressed its indifference thereanent. But I don't see how it can do you much harm.

I have just heard of the death of my old schoolmate Dana [1] — a friend of more than fifty years. I am so glad that I saw him in Florence and Rome lately — for we never expect these things. He was a very able and high-minded man, who (if Captain Ill had not so much influence in politics) should have been one of the Senators from Massachusetts. But he would never condescend to the means of such advancement, and I dare say is the happier for it now.

With kindest regards to Mrs. Gilder and young Prince Aureole,

Yours always,

J. R. Lowell.

To John W. Field

[London], *January* 17, 1882.

. . . I was greatly startled by the death of Dana, of which we got news by telegraph before hearing that he was ill. It is the first time Death has so distinctly nudged me with his elbow, for, though four of my own classmates have died

[1] Mr. Richard Henry Dana.

this year, he, if a year or two older than I, belonged more immediately to my own set, and I had known him lifelong. I am very glad now that I saw as much of him as I did in Florence and Rome. He is a very great loss in every way — a loss to the world no less than to his country and friends — and he died prematurely, before building the monument for which he had gathered the material. He never had the public career he should have had, both for his own sake and ours, and it was from a quality of character pushed to excess. He was, as you say, a " high-minded man," but he was more than that. He was a *lofty*-minded man, and could not meet his fellows on such terms (nowise degrading) as is needful for success in a democracy. He ought to have been Senator from Massachusetts, Minister to England — indeed, he might have been almost anything but for this weakness. I do not know that he would have been happier for it, but at least the syllogism of expectation would have been more complete.

What you tell me Mrs. Dana said after the burial was very touching. Take care of yourself, my dear John. The lesson for us is to *close up*, and I think we *are* drawn nearer by these things — though Death seems less solemn than he used, now that we have seen him so often look at the number on our own door, as he was on his way to knock at a neighbor's. " Who

III

knows?" and "Do I *really* wish it may be?"
are all that the nineteenth century has left us of
the simple faith we began life with. . . .

To T. B. Aldrich

Legation of the United States,
LONDON, *May* 8, 1882.

Dear Aldrich, — If I could, how gladly I
would![1] But I am piecemealed here with so
many things to do that I cannot get a moment
to brood over anything as it must be brooded
over if it is to have wings. It is as if a sitting
hen should have to mind the door-bell. I speak
as of the days of Æsop, which I mention lest
some critic should charge me with not knowing
what a mixed metaphor was — or rather an
incongruous conception.

Now, you who are young and clever will at
once divine what I mean you to divine from
that last sentence — namely, that a man with his
mind in so self-conscious a state as that can't write
*any*thing to advantage, and I should wish to do
my best for a man so intimately associated with
what is dearest to me. No, you must wait till I
come home to be boycotted in my birthplace by
my Irish fellow-citizens (who are kind enough
to teach me how to be American), who fought
all our battles and got up all our draft riots.

[1] Mr. Aldrich, then editor of the *Atlantic Monthly*, had
asked Lowell to write a paper upon Mr. Dana.

Then, in the intervals of firing through my loop-holes of retreat, I may be able to do something for the " Atlantic."

I am now in the midst of the highly important and engrossing business of arranging for the presentation at Court of some of our fair *citoyennes*. Whatever else you are, never be a Minister!

With kind regards to Mrs. Aldrich,

                    Faithfully yours,

                              J. R. LOWELL.

To W. D. Howells

Ashridge, BERKHAMPSTEAD,
December 21, 1882.

Dear Howells, — I was very glad to get your letter, though it put me under bonds to be wiser than I have ever had the skill to be. If I remember rightly, Panurge's doubts were increased by consulting the Oracle, but how did the Oracle feel? Did it ever occur to you that a certain share of our sympathy should go in that direction?

My best judgment is this, and like all good judgment it is to a considerable degree on both sides of the question. If you are able now, without overworking mind or body, to keep the wolf from the door and to lay by something for a rainy day — and I mean, of course, without being driven to work with your left hand because the better one is tired out — I should refuse the offer,[1] or should hesitate to accept it. If you are a systematic worker, independent of moods, and sure of your genius whenever you want it, there might be no risk in accepting. You would have the advantage of a fixed income to fall back on. Is this a greater advantage than the want of it would be as a spur to industry? Was not the occasion of Shakespeare's plays (I don't say the motive of 'em) that he *had* to write? And are any of us likely to be better inspired than he? Does not inspiration, in some limited sense at least, come with the exercise thereof, as the appetite with eating? Is not your hand better for keeping it in, as they say? A professorship takes a great deal of time, and, if you teach in any more direct way than by lectures, uses up an immense stock of nerves. Your inevitable temptation (in some sort your duty) will be to make yourself *learned* — which you have n't the least need to be as an author (if you only have me at your elbow to correct your English now and then, naughty boy!). If you can make your professorship a thing apart — but can you and be honest? I believe the present generation does n't think I was made for a poet, but I think I could have gone nearer convincing 'em if I had not estranged the muse by donning a professor's gown. I speak of myself because you wanted my experience. I am naturally indolent, and be-

[1] Of a Professorship of Literature.

ing worked pretty hard in the College, was willing to be content with the amount of work that was squeezed out of me by my position, and let what my nature might otherwise have forced me into go. As I said before, if you can reckon on your own temperament, accept. If you have a doubt, *don't*. I think you will divine what I am driving at.

I find everybody here reading your books, and you know very well how much pleasure that gives me. They wish to see you, and I hope when you come back you will stay and let 'em do it. I wish you could know my hostess, for instance — noble in all senses of the word. I am staying here for a few days with a large party in a house as big as a small town, and a beautiful country of hill and dale and gray birch woods. Enough to say that there was once a convent here. The monks always had an eye for country.

You will have to be very fine when you show yourself in England, to look like the portrait I have painted of you — but I am willing to take the venture.

Inexorable lunch has sounded, and I must say good-by. I should say, on the whole — it is safe to ask my advice, but not to follow it. But then people never do. . . . Love to all.

Affectionately yours,

J. R. L.

To F. J. Child

10 LOWNDES SQUARE, S. W.,
February 2, 1883.

Dear Ciarli, — Thank you over and over again for your beautiful book,[1] the only fault I can find with which is the "Esq." you have added to my name, and which seems to hold me at arm's length from you, as it were. But I won't be held there, do what you will!

I have been reading it with delight and wonder. The former you will understand better than anybody; the latter, called forth by the enormous labor you have spent on it, you will be modestly incredulous about. You have really built an imperishable monument, and I rejoice as heartily as the love I bear you gives me the right in having lived to see its completion. I did not know you were to begin printing so soon, and I wish my name to appear on the list of subscribers, as it ought. I hope it is not too late. I am particularly gratified with the dedication, which will delight Furnivall, and which he in all ways so truly deserves.

I am getting old, and my beard has now more white than brown in it, but I on the whole enjoy my life here, and feel that in some ways I have been and am useful. London I like

[1] The first part of *The English and Scottish Popular Ballads.*

beyond measure. The wonderful movement of life here acts as a constant stimulus — and I am beginning to need one. The climate also suits me better than any I ever lived in. I have only to walk a hundred yards from my door to see green grass and hear the thrushes sing all winter long. These are a constant delight, and I sometimes shudder to think of the poor dead weeds and grasses I have seen shivering in the cast-iron earth at home. But I shall come back to them to comfort them out of my own store of warmth with as hearty a sympathy as ever.

I need not tell you how glad I was of the revulsion in our politics. I think we shall keep all the ground we have won, and before long bring the country forward — or back — to better ways. If not, I see no hope. Spain shows us to what a civil service precisely like our own will bring a country that ought to be powerful and prosperous. It was n't the Inquisition, nor the Expulsion of Jews or Moriscos, but simply the Boss System, that has landed Spain where she is.

Give my love to all who care for it, and be sure that I am always, as I have always been,

Most affectionately yours,

J. R. L.

To C. E. Norton

10 Lowndes Square, S. W.,
April 22, 1883.

. . . If one wait for the right time to come
before writing, the right time never comes. I
have been sitting like Horace's *rusticus* waiting
for the stream of daily occupations to run dry,
to be convinced only of the *labitur et labetur.*
So I will prorogue no longer, but write a line
to send you my love and to thank you for the
" Carlyle-Emerson Correspondence," which I
have read with pathetic interest. You can well
imagine how many fading frescos it brightened
in the chambers of my memory. It pleased,
but not surprised me in what an ampler ether
and diviner air the mind and thought of Emerson dwelt, than those that were habitual to his
correspondent. . . . I suppose you have read
by this time Mrs. Carlyle's " Correspondence."
A very painful book in more ways than one.
There are disclosures there that never should
have been made, as if they had been caught up
from the babblings of discharged housemaids.
One blushes in reading, and feels like a person
caught listening at the keyhole. . . .

I linger on here, partly from *vis inertiæ* and
partly because I have been, and may again be, of
some use. A year ago it would have been easy
for the wrong man to have made trouble between

the two countries. The Irish howl against me at home, by the way, received its signal from here.

I like London, and have learned to see as I never saw before the advantage of a great capital. It establishes one set of weights and measures, moral and intellectual, for the whole country. It is, I think, a great drawback for us that we have as many as we have States. The flow of life in the streets, too — sublimer, it seems to me often, than the tides of the sea — gives me a kind of stimulus that I find agreeable even if it prompt to nothing. For I am growing old, dear Charles, and have n't the go in me I once had. Then I have only to walk a hundred yards from my door to be in Hyde Park, where, and in Kensington Gardens, I can tread on green turf and hear the thrushes sing all winter. I often think of what you said to me about the birds here. There *are* a great many more and they sing more perennially than ours. As for the climate, it suits me better than any I ever lived in, and for the inward weather, I have never seen civilization at so high a level in some respects as here. In plain living and high thinking I fancy we have, or used to have, the advantage, and I have never seen society, on the whole, so good as I used to meet at our Saturday Club.

Always affectionately yours,

J. R. LOWELL.

To the Same

LONDON, *December* 4, 1883.

. . . On Saturday I went down to Cambridge to see " The Birds." It was really delightful, and more instructive than a tragedy, because its wild fancy is harder to conceive in visible types. The birds seemed to have been left inadvertently behind by a dream — such an unreal reality had they to the waking sense, and such a feeling had one that one had seen them somewhere before in some Zoo of Dreamland. I was glad to find that I knew more Greek than I expected, though that was hardly more than Swift bids us in his supplement to the " Beatitudes." They are now thinking of giving the " Œdipus Rex."

I can see that the Democrats have come to the conclusion that it would be wise to have some principles about them in case of a sudden call, and this I think increases the probability of my being your neighbor again eighteen months hence. A worse thing might befall me.

I am not yet rector of St. Andrew's. There is a question of eligibility. You will know what I mean when I say that I am utterly indifferent except on the score of the Quinquennial College Catalogue. By the way, please say *à qui de droit* to note me as Member of Spanish Academy and of Philosophical Society at Philadelphia. I wish to justify Parson Wilbur's augury, now nearly forty years old. . . .

To James B. Thayer
LONDON, *December 24, 1883.*

Dear Mr. Thayer, — Many thanks for your *Rettung*, as Lessing would have called it, which is excellently done, and just both to Emerson and his critic. From what I have heard it was much needed, for though, of course, the personal *equation* is to be allowed for in all criticism, there seems to be a tendency in America (fatal to sound judgment) to treat it as if it were the same as personal *bias.*

As for Emerson's verse (though he has written some as exquisite as any in the language) I suppose we must give it up. That he had a sense of the higher harmonies of language no one that ever heard him lecture can doubt. The structure of his prose, as one listened to it, was as nobly metrical as the King James version of the Old Testament, and this made it all the more puzzling that he should have been absolutely insensitive to the harmony of verse. For it was there he failed — single verses are musical enough. I never shall forget the good-humoredly puzzled smile with which he once confessed to me his inability to apprehend the value of accent in verse.

I liked particularly what you say about his mastery of English. No man in my judgment ever had a greater, and I greatly doubt whether

Matthew Arnold is quite capable (in the habit of addressing a jury as he always is) of estimating the style of one who conversed with none but the masters of his mother-tongue. Emerson's instinct for the best word was infallible. Wherever he found one he *froze* to it, as we say in our admirable vernacular. I have sometimes found that he had added to his cabinet the *one* good word in a book he had read. Sir T. Browne is the only man I know of worthy to be named with [him] in the imaginative felicities and audacities — the *O altitudos*, as he himself would have called them — of speech. I think that Matthew Arnold, like Renan (who has had an evil influence over him), is apt to think the *super*fine as good as the fine, or better even than that.

Look at the list of prophetic honors with which Parson Wilbur has decorated himself in the preface to the "Biglow Papers," and you will condole with me in being excluded by my official position from the rectorship of St. Andrew's. As a lawyer, you will be amused to know that it is my extra-territoriality (an awful word and fit to conjure with!) that makes me ineligible. If I picked his saintship's pocket — fancy stealing from a Scottish saint! — I could snap my fingers at the local tribunals. So I shall never be able to read Univ. Sanct. Andr. Scot. Dom. Rect.[1] Could n't they count me

---

[1] In the *Quinquennial Catalogue of Harvard University*.

as they do Louis XVII., though I never
reigned?

Faithfully yours,

J. R. LOWELL.

Alas for the Holmes House,[1] so dear and
sacred in my memory!

To C. E. Norton

LONDON, 31 Lowndes Square,
January 11, 1884.

. . . We have been having a very mild winter, with thrushes and robins in full song. I
often think of what you said to me years ago
about English singing-birds. I remember I
went to the Waverley Oaks and made a list of
those I heard there, which pretty well matched
the catalogue in the " Squier of Low Degre."
But you were right. In early summer every
bush here is musical. It is partly older civilization (there are few song-birds in the woods) and
partly climate. The thrushes twitch out earth-
worms here all winter long, and constantly remind me of their cousins our robins. . . .

To John W. Field

[LONDON], January 19, 1884.

. . . I wonder, by the way, when we shall
see an American politician able to appreciate

[1] One of the fine Old Cambridge houses, then about to be
pulled down.

and shrewd enough to act on Curran's saying about his countrymen, that "An Irishman is the worst fellow in the world to run away from." . . .

To F. J. Child

31 LOWNDES SQUARE, 1884.

Dear Ciarli, — . . . When I got up this morning it was snowing, and I had been lying for some time watching the flakes fluttering up and down, like the ghosts of moths seeking vainly the flowers they used to pillage, and thinking of home, as I always do when it snows. Almost my earliest recollection is of a snow-storm and putting crumbs on the window-sill for the redbreasts that never came. Yesterday there was one singing cheerily in Kensington Gardens. A thrush, too, was piping now and then, and the grass was as green as May. I think the climate more than anything else keeps me here. It is the best I have ever seen — at any rate the best for me, and the vapory atmosphere is divine in its way — always luminous, and always giving the distance that makes things tolerable. But I have pangs sometimes. . . .

I have no news except that my official extra-territoriality will, perhaps, prevent my being rector at St. Andrews, because it puts me beyond the reach of the Scottish courts in case of malversation in office. How to rob a Scottish

university suggests a serious problem. I was
pleased with the election and the pleasant way
it was spoken of here, though I did not want
the place. Had I known what I know now, I
should not have allowed myself to be put up.
But I was in Paris, and had forgotten among
the bookstalls that I was an Excellency. . . .

To George Putnam
LONDON, *April* 8, 1884.

. . . On Monday we go to Edinburgh, where
they are to have a most emphatic tercentenary,
and make doctors enough for the three centuries to come. This will be my fourth gown, so
that I beat Dogberry by two. I shall be able
to keep myself warm without Harvard.[1] . . .

To C. E. Norton
31 LOWNDES SQUARE, S.W.,
Easter Sunday, April 13, 1884.

Dear Charles, — How strange a vision rose
before me in the two letters you enclosed! I
thought of that little picture of Rossetti's that
you have, where the two lovers, walking in the
selva oscura, meet the ghosts of their old selves.
And what a foreign yet familiar thing the ghost
of one's old self is. It is memory with its sharp
edges renewed, memory without any softening

[1] Harvard conferred upon him the honorary degree of
LL. D. at her commencement in June of this year.

perspective. But one must learn to face these *revenants* from the past. How vividly my old study under the roof (where you first knew me) comes back, and the dreary year I dragged through there thirty years ago in solitary confinement, finding a strange consolation in repeating the service for the dead which I had learned by heart. I see the old scribblings on the wall which I had traced there as prisoners are wont. . . . I remember the ugly fancy I had sometimes that I was another person, and used to hesitate at the door when I came back from my late night walks, lest I should find the real owner of the room sitting in my chair before the fire. A well-nigh hermit life I had led till then, and my fate often seems to me a strange one — to be snatched away and set down in the midst of Babylon the great city, obliged to interest myself in what to me are the mirages of life, and, above all, to make speeches (which I loathe), and to be praised for them, which makes it more bitter. But for my sense of humor, I could n't stand it. I feel that my life has been mainly wasted — that I have thrown away more than most men ever had; but I have never been able to shake off the indolence (I know not whether to call it intellectual or physical) that I inherited from my father. . . .

To Mrs. W. K. Clifford

31 LOWNDES SQUARE, S. W.,
October 9, 1884.

Dear Mrs. Clifford, — . . . How delightful it is to have woman friends — they are such impartial critics. No, I am not a genius, and very far from thinking myself one. I was half meant for one, but only half. A genius has the gift of falling in love with the side-face of truth, going mad for it, sacrificing all for it. But I must see the full face, and then the two sides have such different expressions that I begin to doubt which is the sincere and cannot surrender myself.

I was very sorry that I could not tea with you yesterday, but I got home too late and fearfully tired. I shall try to find you this afternoon.

Yes, your note was a *little* extravagant, but I could not help liking it all the same. My address would have been far better if I had been plain J. R. L. and not His Excellency.

Faithfully yours,

J. R. LOWELL.

To C. E. Norton

31 LOWNDES SQUARE, S. W.,
October 17, 1884.

. . . I send you a copy of my address at Birmingham.[1] It has made a kind of (mildish)

[1] On Democracy. Mr. Lowell was the guest, during his

sensation, greatly to my surprise. I could n't
conceive, as I told Du Maurier, that I had
made so great a splash with so small a pebble.
I hear that even the G. O. M. has read it with
interest. It *was n't* revised (as they say it was)
by me. I did but insert some passages I spoke,
but which were not in the notes given to the
press.

The most interesting part of my visit to
Birmingham was a call I made by appointment
on Cardinal Newman. He was benignly cour-
teous, and we excellencied and eminenced each
other by turns. A more gracious senescence I
never saw. There was no "monumental pomp,"
but a serene decay, like that of some ruined
abbey in a woodland dell, consolingly forlorn.
I was surprised to find his head and features
smaller than I expected — modelled on lines of
great vigor, but reduced and softened by a cer-

---

stay at Birmingham, of Mr. Wilson King. "Professor
Mahaffy, of Dublin, was also my guest at the time," writes
Mr. King, "and the two 'took to' each other at once, and
I never heard so much good talk in four days before or since.
Mahaffy went off in the morning, and when, somewhat
later, I was driving Mr. Lowell to the station, he put his
hand on my knee and said, 'I think, on the whole, that is
the most delightful fellow I ever met, and I wish you 'd
tell him I said so.' Of course it was pleasant for me to have
such testimony to the success of my party. When I told
Mahaffy, his characteristic reply was, 'Poor Lowell, never
to have met an Irishman before.' "

tain weakness, as if a powerfully masculine face had been painted in miniature by Malbone. He was very kindly and sympathetic — his benignity as well as his lineaments reminding me of the old age of Emerson. He has not been able to preach, he told me, for two years. . . .

To Thomas Hughes
31 LOWNDES SQUARE, S. W.,
October 20, 1884.

Dear Friend, — I send back your boy's letter, which gave the old man real pleasure. It even encouraged him to read one of the " Biglow Papers " aloud to his naval attaché yesterday, who seemed interested by the unwonted performance of his chief. He (the old man) was rather surprised with a certain pithiness in the poem, and with the quantity of meaning he used to have in himself. As his habitual feeling is that he has never done anything, it is not disagreeable now and then to find somebody who thinks that he has.

I am in the midst of Froude — two new volumes of Carlyle. Very interesting I find them, and him more problematic than ever, but fine on the whole. A kind of sentimental *Ajax furens.* I don't think that sincerity towards his hero justifies Froude in printing Carlyle's diatribes (result of dyspepsia mainly) — about Gladstone, for example. In a world where there is so much unavoidable pain, why add to the avoidable? Gladstone won't mind, but his wife and daughters?

With love to your wife,

> Affectionately yours,
>
> J. R. LOWELL.

To Mrs. W. K. Clifford

31 LOWNDES SQUARE, S. W.,
November 9, 1884.

. . . I enjoyed my visit to the country. I was among friendly people who all bewailed the chance of my being recalled, and one charming person told me that "all the women of England would rise as one man, if I were." I had no notion how charming I was — had you?

As for whether I shall be or not — I mean recalled, not charming — you, as one of the women of England, must be anxious to know what the chances are. All I can say to comfort you is, that you know as much about it as I do. I fear the chances are against me. Well, I shall have enjoyed my five years in England, where everybody has been kind to me, and shall find people to be kind to me at home also. It has been my luck to find them everywhere.

I wish I had some news of the Great World to send you, but there never has been any since I can remember, except that it was going to be wise one of these fine days. But no day has yet been fine enough for its purpose, and fine days are so rare in London! Yes, I have one bit of secret intelligence. His Excellency and Mrs. Lowell are going to see the Lord Mayor's Show to-morrow for the first time! Don't you envy us? Real camels and real elephants, with men atop of them, and Queen Bess in all her glory! I mean to be ten years old for the nonce. Generally I am younger. . . .

To the Same
HURSTBOURNE, *November* 16, 1884.

. . . Everybody has gone to church, and I have just come in from walking up and down the avenues of meditation, by which orientalism I mean an avenue of autumnal trees, in one of which (an elm that has changed all its leaves into fairy gold) a thrush has been singing to me, like Overbury's fair and happy milkmaid, as if he never could be old. I have been thinking that the decay of nature is far more beautiful than that of man, that autumn is rather pensive than melancholy, that the fall of the leaf does not work such dilapidation on the forest as on us the fall of the hair, but gives its victims a new beauty. I have been thinking— to about as much purpose as the deer who were browsing or dozing all about me, and now I have come in to answer your letter.

I am quite willing you should prefer disagreeable men (there are enough of them!), provided you will tolerate me. For my part, I prefer agreeable women. I must keep copies of my letters if I would understand the answers to them. Could I have been such an ass as to ask if I was charming? It is out of the question. Even if I thought I was, I should be too clever to inquire too nicely about it, for I hold with my favorite Donne that

"Who knows his virtue's name and place hath none."

And yet I should infer from your letter that I had been stupid enough to ask something of the kind. Nothing in my life has ever puzzled me so much as my popularity here in England — which I have done nothing and been nothing to deserve. I was telling my wife a day or two ago that I could n't understand it. It must be my luck, and ought to terrify me like the ring of Polycrates.

No, the Lord Mayor's Show was pure circus and poor circus at that. It was cheap, and the other adjective that begins with n. 'T was an attempt to make poetry out of commonplace by contract. 'T was antiquity as conceived by Mr. Sanger. Why, I saw the bottoms of a Norman knight's trousers where they had been hitched up into a tell-tale welt round the ankle by his chain armor! There was no pretence at illusion; nay, every elephant, every camel, every chariot was laden with disillusion. It was worth seeing for once, to learn how dreary prose can contrive to be when it has full swing.

It is cold here. Twelve degrees of frost this morning. My fingers are numb and my thoughts crawl slowly as winter flies. Are you making notes as I bade you? I have no news about myself yet, though I have heard the name of somebody who expects to be my successor. A very agreeable man, by the way, so you won't like him. That's some comfort.

Faithfully yours,
J. R. LOWELL.

To the Same

31 LOWNDES SQUARE, S. W.,
November 26, 1884.

. . . I should have answered your letter before if I had not had somebody staying with me who took up all my spare time. "If he couldn't *find* time he should have *made* it!" I hear you exclaim, and if I had been at St. Ives I would, but here there is nothing to make it with. I am not sure that I could have done it anywhere, for the material of the manufacture is *method,* and I have too often turned all my pockets inside out and never found that I had any about me. I am stealing the time I need for this note — I hope nobody else will miss it.

'T is a strong argument against communism that time is one of the few things we hold in common, and there is none that we worse misuse. . . .

To C. E. Norton

LONDON, *December*, 1884.

. . . Politics are rather interesting here just now. You will like to hear this : the other day I said to Gladstone that I was very glad he had included Ireland in the Franchise Bill — or rather had not excluded her. " I had rather the heart were torn out of my breast than that clause out of the bill," said he. A day or two ago I met Morley at dinner, who regretted that I had not heard Gladstone a few nights ago, when he turned on Sir Stafford Northcote (his whilom private secretary) and rent him. I said that from what I had heard of it, I thought it must have been a fine exhibition — something lion-like in the leap of it — but that mockers said that the passion was simulated. Morley laughed and said that in the lobby afterwards he had said to (I forget the name), " What an old lion it is !' " What an old fox ! " smiled the other. I think Gladstone's late illness (and I have pretty good intelligence) partly moral and partly diplomatic, by the way. Egypt is beyond even his powers of explanation, and Pharaoh seems to harden his heart and won't let Gladstone's people go. What

puzzles and sometimes bores me in Gladstone
is that he takes as much interest in one thing as
in another, and is as diffusively emphatic about
it—in "John Inglesant" (which I could n't read)
as in Gordon. Gordon, by the way, sent me his
regards from Khartoum — which pleased me like
a friendly message from Judas Maccabeus. . .

To the Same
31 LOWNDES SQUARE, S. W.,
December 8, 1884.

. . . I post with this a corrected copy of my
Address. Of course you must read between the
lines. I could n't speak my mind freely whether
for this latitude or that. I see our blots only
too plainly, and have not forborne my com-
mentary on them in time past. I fear you see
them *large* — and perhaps I see them *small*, as
some artists do the heads they paint. We have
enormous and exceptional difficulties in our
foreign and half-digested population. I do not
find the tone much higher here — for example,
in the private talk about the Corrupt Practices
in Elections Act — though I admit that this is
a less dangerous symptom here where the traditions are all aristocratic.

As for the small majority for Cleveland, I am
more than satisfied with *any*, considering the
obstacles. That we are saved from Blaine is
enough for the nonce. There are four more

years to work in before the next election. The
great vice is in the system of conventions, as I
learned at Cincinnati in '76. . . .

To John W. Field

LONDON, *December* 11, 1884.

. . . As for coming to live in Washington,
my dear boy, that is all very well for people
that have "struck ile." But I have n't, and
never shall. Besides, I have but one home in
America, and that is the house where I was
born and where, if it shall please God, I hope
to die. I should n't be happy anywhere else,
and might as well stay here where we are nearer
the world's navel. . . .

To Mrs. W. K. Clifford

31 LOWNDES SQUARE, S. W.,
December 14, 1884.

. . . You have now all the prose I have collected into volumes. I am really glad that you
find something in them to like, for I have a
worse opinion of myself than of most authors,
knowing only too well how much I have wasted
such gift as I had.

I do not know whether I was happier when
I wrote the second volume of "Among my
Books,"as you suppose. I am never very happy
when I am writing about books that I like. I had
much rather like them and say nothing about

it — for one should be secret about one's loves
and not betray the confidence they have put in
one. But I *had* to write because I had foolishly
allowed myself to be made a professor, and you
will understand better the defects of some of my
essays when I tell you that they were patched
together from my lectures, leaving out a great
part of the illustrative matter, and compressing
rather than dilating as one should do for a mis-
cellaneous audience.

As for happiness, a man with a sense of humor (as I in some measure have) has always a
clot of black blood in his veins, always circulat-
ing, always lodging in the most unforeseen and
discomforting places, and if it once get into the
heart or brain, always fatal to all that illusion
which is the substance of content. And then
I have inherited a Puritan conscience that will
not let me alone. Every now and then my
good spirits carry me away and people find me
amusing, but reaction always sets in the moment I am left to myself.

But enough of Me! I am not very interesting to myself, except as a puzzle sometimes,
and I do not wish to propose myself to you as
a conundrum.

I have been reading Taine's new volume. It
is interesting as a collection of *pièces justifica-
tives*, but not judicial, as it seems to me. 'T is
argument of counsel, and not the charge of a

judge weighing both sides. The way in which authors, especially French, who have found the *moyen de parvenir*, look backward and downward on the class they have risen from is bitterly amusing. There are no such aristocrats. They kick down the ladder behind them, quite unconscious that the height they have climbed to is the pillory. The agreeable aristocrats are those who are born to it and therefore unconscious — and women, who all have it in their blood. . . .

To the Same

31 Lowndes Square, S. W.,
December 15, 1884.

. . . What you say about correctness of style both pleases and amuses me. The great fault I am always taxing myself with is impatience of revision. I am too prone to extemporize. A note on p. 76 of the " Essay on Dryden " will show that we are of one mind on this point. You will be glad to hear that a man once devoted an entire volume to the exposure of my *solecisms*, or whatever he chose to call them. I never read it — lest it should spoil my style by making it conscious. A *Scotsman*, too, gave me a dressing, I am told — but I don't mind their theories about English (which is always a foreign tongue to them), and, besides, he liked me all the same. By the way, a Scots-

man had the ill-manners one day to compliment
me on my English. " Why, I should n't know
you were n't an Englishman. Where did you
get it ? " I could n't resist, and answered with
a couple of verses from a Scottish ballad —

> " I got it in my mither's wame,
>   Whaur ye 'll get never the like ! "

He will never compliment me again, I fear. . . .

To the Same

31 LOWNDES SQUARE, S. W.,
Christmas Day, 1884.

. . . I dare say you will have seen by the
papers (for you seem to read them) what I have
been about. But they won't have told you that
I made a very stupid speech at Peterhouse
Monday night. I could n't help it. I was
dazed by the consciousness that there were to
be eighteen speeches, and that everybody but I
had his speech neatly written out in his pocket.
I really had something pretty to say — I mean
I might have had — but after hearing six or
seven my mind was a blur. They droned away
over their flowers of rhetoric as bees do over
a tuft of lime-blossoms when they know that
they have the whole day before 'em, and that
the longest of the year. Why, we did n't rise
from table till half past one ! Sir Frederick
Bramwell made the best speech. He was called
on to answer for Applied Science. " At this

time of night," said he, " the only illustration
of the toast I can think of would be the application of the domestic safety match to the bedroom candle." Whereupon I wrote on my *menu*
and handed over to him,

> Oh, brief Sir Frederick, might the others catch
> Your happy science and supply your match !

I give it you as the best evidence of the coma-
tose state to which I was reduced. But I enjoyed my visit at Peterhouse Lodge, where I
was the guest of the master, Dr. Porter, an old
friend of Leslie Stephen. . . .

To O. W. Holmes

31 LOWNDES SQUARE, S. W.,
December 28, 1884.

Dear Wendell, — I was about to write thank-
ing you for your " Emerson," when your letter
was brought to me. I found the Emerson very
interesting. You, more than anybody else, have
the literary traditions of New England in your
blood and brain. It was this special flavor that
pleased my palate as I read. I felt as when I
walk along one of our country lanes in early
autumn — stone walls on either hand, a somewhat thrifty landscape, and yet fringed all along
with hardhack and golden-rod. I recognize our
surly limitations, but feel also the edging of
poetry — northern, not tropical, but sincere
and good of its kind. Nay, with you I may

trust a homelier image. You know that odor
of sweet herbs in the New England garret
and its pungency of association, and will know
what I mean when I say that I found much of
it in your book. You have never written better than in some of the genially critical parts.
There are admirable things in the chapter about
Emerson's poetry, many that made me slap my
thigh with emphatic enjoyment. You say the
book tired you, but I see no sign of it, and your
wind is firm to the end. I thank you for helping me to a conclusion (or a distinction) I was
fumbling for. If Emerson show no sensuous
passion in his verse, at least there is spiritual
and intellectual passion enough and to spare —
a paler flame, but quite as intense in its way. I
go back, you see, to my hardhack and golden-
rod again. I talked with him once about his
versification, by the way, and he humorously
confessed that he couldn't see the difference
between a good verse and a bad one — so in
that line you cite from his "Adirondacks."

The first number of your new portfolio whets
my appetite. Let me make one historical correction. When I accepted the editorship of the
"Atlantic," I made it a condition precedent that
you were the first contributor to be engaged.
Said I not well? Underwood will remember this.

It was very good of you to take all that
trouble about me and my poor affairs with

Mr. Cleveland and Boyle O'Reilly. As for the former, I shall be satisfied with whatever he thinks fit to do in my case, for I have a high respect for his character, and should certainly have voted for him had I been at home. As Minister I have always refused to have any politics, considering myself to represent the country and no special party in it. As for Mr. O'Reilly, it is *he* that misunderstands the rights of naturalized citizens, not I; and he would n't have misunderstood them had they been those of naturalized Germans, nor would Bismarck have been as patient as Granville. I made no distinction between naturalized and native, and should have treated you as I did the " suspects " — had there been as good ground. There is a manifest distinction, however, between a native American who goes abroad and a naturalized citizen who goes back to the country of his birth, and we acknowledge it in our treaties — notably with Germany — making two years' residence in the native country a forfeiture of the acquired citizenship. Some of my Irishmen had been living in their old homes seventeen years, engaged in trade or editing nationalist papers or members of the poor-law guardians (like MacSweeney), and neither paying taxes in America nor doing any other duty as Americans. I was guided by two things — the recognized principles of international law, and the conduct of Lord Lyons

when Seward was arresting and imprisoning British subjects. We kept one man in jail seven
months without trial or legal process of any
kind, and, but for the considerateness and moderation of Lyons, might have had war with
England. I think I saved a misunderstanding
here. . . . When I had at last procured the
conditional (really unconditional) release of all
the suspects, they refused to be liberated.
When I spoke of this to Justin McCarthy (then
the head of the Irish Parliamentary party, Parnell being in Kilmainham), he answered cheer-
fully, " Certainly : *they are there to make trouble.*"

But enough of these personal matters. I shall
come home with the satisfaction of having done
my duty and of having been useful to the true
interests of both countries — of the three if
you count Ireland. The fun of the thing is that
here I was considered a radical in my opinions
about Ireland. I have always advised them to
make Davitt or Parnell Irish Secretary.

Good-by and a happy New Year !

Affectionately yours,

J. R. LOWELL.

To Miss Grace Norton

31 LOWNDES SQUARE, S. W.,
January 15, 1885.

. . . Do you remember that in a month I
shall be sixty-six? Luckily I am not reminded of

III

it often, our decays are so full of *prévenances* and come to us shod in felt. Don't you know how we sometimes become instinctively aware that we have lost or forgotten something, we don't know what? So it is with the thefts of old age. We grow conscious of them only after all is over. . . .

A German band is noisy before my window as I write, and it is a rainy day and there is a blue tinge in the atmosphere that mezzotints the bare trees of the square, seeming to wrap their nerves against the east wind. . . .

To George Putnam

Legation of the United States,
LONDON, *March* 2, 1885.

. . . I am more than ever at a loss what to do with myself. We had always taken it for granted together that she would outlive me, and that would have been best. But I cannot live alone in the old home. It would be too dreary. Whatever I decide, I shall come home for a visit. . . .

To Mrs. W. K. Clifford

10 LOWNDES SQUARE, S. W.,
March 19, 1885.

Dear Mrs. Clifford, — In trying to piece together the broken threads of my life again, the brightest naturally catch the eye first. I write only to say that I do not forget. . . .

I am getting on as one does — gradually getting my wits together. . . .

I have at last found something I can read — Calderon. He has stood me in stead before.

By and by I will write again.

Faithfully yours,

J. R. LOWELL.

To C. E. Norton

31 LOWNDES SQUARE, S. W.,
April 16, 1885.

. . . I sail for home on the 10th June (earlier if I can), and will tell you all I have to say. My future is misty to me. What you write falls in with my own inward presentiment. . . . I should be happy nowhere but at Elmwood. There I cannot live now. . . .

To W. D. Howells

31 LOWNDES SQUARE, S. W.,
April 17, 1885.

Dear Howells, — I return your grasp of the hand with another as sincere, but in silence. What is there to be said?

If all go well I shall see you again in June — one of the greatest favors I have to thank President Cleveland for.

With kindest regards to Mrs. Howells,

Affectionately yours,

J. R. LOWELL.

To R. W. Gilder
Deerfoot Farm, SOUTHBOROUGH,[1] MASS.,
June 14, 1885.

. . . I was to have gone to Washington last week (carrying my head, as Bertran de Born did, like a lantern) to take a look at my decapitators, but the illness of Mr. Bayard prevented me.

I am now waiting fresh orders here, where I ramble over the hills, hearing familiar birds and plucking familiar flowers. I find that my life hooks together across the eight years' gap as if nothing had happened so far as the outward world is concerned. Inwardly there is a breach, as you can imagine.

I should like to run down for a day to Marion, and will if I can. . . .

[1] The home of his daughter, Mrs. Edward Burnett.

X

1885–1889

To W. D. Howells

SOUTHBOROUGH, MASS., *July* 1, 1885.

DEAR Howells,— Many thanks for your welcome home — if home I may call it now. I had been counting on seeing yours among other dear faces, and you are as inaccessible as if I were still where the epigraph on my paper puts me.[1]

I have been reading your "Silas Lapham" with great interest and admiration. I have generally found romance more interesting and often

[1] The paper bears his old London address.

more true than reality — but I am as weak as Falstaff and can't help liking whatever you do, whatever it may be. This is more your fault than mine, however, for it is sure to be good. . . .

To Sybella Lady Lyttelton [1]

SOUTHBOROUGH, *July* 2, 1885.

Your delightful letter reached me the day before yesterday; 't was my first letter from my old world. The political news was especially welcome, for I left London before the catastrophe, and see no English papers here.

So you have been dining with Chamberlain. As for his Irish notions, you know that I have always insisted that Ireland should be "governed through the Nationalists." Let 'em try and 't will make Conservatives of every mother's son of them. Gladstone of course will be in the thick of the fight again. The *gaudia certaminis* are essential to his vigor (if not to his health) of body and mind. He is like the soapboiler who sold out his business with the stipulation that he should always have the right to come back on melting-days.

I am here making the acquaintance of my grandchildren and gradually acquiring *l'art d'être grand père*. There are five of them, as you know. . . .

---

[1] The late Dowager Lady Lyttelton had been one of the most intimate and kindest of friends of both Mr. and Mrs. Lowell during their residence in England.

I have a large room at the top of the house, and look out on a superb sea of rye from one window and on a pretty gleam of water from another, where the cloud-shadows are pillowed by day, and where the flash of the fireflies repeats itself by night as they go zigzagging over it. A bullfrog with a bass like Lablache practises his deeper notes there when the rest of the world is asleep. Pretty hills bound my prospect on both sides. 'T is a narrow world after London, you will say, and so it is. But all worlds are only as broad as we have the wit to make them, and my bullfrog does n't say the same thing over again *much* oftener than I heard folks do in larger places. . . .

I hear that Mr. Phelps is as popular already at the start as I at the end of my race. I don't like to think of you at 31 Lowndes Square and I not there. But *ainsi va le monde!* It happens as often in life as in death that the place that knew us knows us no more, and perhaps we find it harder to bear before we are fairly tucked up in the only bed where sleep is sure.

To C. E. Norton
Deerfoot Farm, SOUTHBOROUGH,
July 22, 1885.

. . . I am already in love with Southborough, which is a charmingly unadulterated New England village, and with as lovely landscapes as I

ever saw. I entrench myself in a flannel shirt,
and wander over the hills and in the lonely
pastures, rejoicing in the immitigable sunshine.
'T is an odd shift in the peep-hole of my pano-
rama from London to this Chartreuse. For the
present I like it, and find it wholesome. I fancy
myself happy sometimes — I am not sure —
but then I never was for long.

I shall appear in Ashfield in time for your
rustic feast — though the notion of a speech
embitters my future. . . .

To the Same

DEERFOOT FARM, *August* 13, 1885.

. . . I got back yesterday morning from
Washington, where I spent four days very
pleasantly with Bayard, whom I liked before,
but now like thoroughly. He is a gentleman
all through, and as courageous as a tender heart
will let him be. I mean that he has the sensitiveness as well as the high spirit of a refined
organization, and that it would be better for
him, perhaps for the country, if he could be
brutal on occasion. His commerce has much
of the same charm that Dufferin has beyond
any man I ever knew, whose very teeth are
engaging, though in Dufferin one sometimes
fancies that one sees the ear-tip of highly per-
fected art. Cleveland I liked, but saw only for
half an hour. I told him that I came to him

like St. Denis, with the head he had cut off
under my arm, at which piece of humor he
laughed heartily — and I think, on the whole,
was not sorry that he should be represented in
England by somebody else.

I took my grandson James with [me], and
we went to Mount Vernon together, whither I
was taken by my father fifty-nine years ago. I
remembered everything as if from yesterday,
and went straight to the key of the Bastile and
to the honey-locusts in the garden. Washington must have found it hard to die and give up
the view from his veranda. It combines gran-
deur and placidity, as he did himself. I was
struck in travelling with Jem to find how much
less the boys of this generation know about
American history than I did when I was seven
years his junior. . . .

To the Same

DEERFOOT FARM, *September* 11, 1885.

. . . I got home safely, bearing constantly
in mind our modern version of the Spartan
mother's parting words to her son — "with
your portmanteau, or on it" — for as I had a
special check and a very complicated ticket, I
felt myself walking in a series of pitfalls and
ambushes, where every baggage-smasher was a
secret foe. I waited three hours at Fitchburg,
and wiled away my time by eating a very dur-

able substitute for what is elsewhere called a beefsteak and in visiting the principal objects of interest, including the Cathedral and picture galleries. I saw also several signboards which promised well for the future of Fitchburgian art.

My hills here in Southborough I found lower than I left them, but they are growing daily, and will be as tall as ever in a few days. I find I was right in falling so deeply in love with the " June grass." We have it here, as I thought, but it has n't the same fine effects of color. I can't account for it, but the fact is so. Nature has these partialities, and makes no scruple of showing them. But we do very well, all the same. I climbed one of my hills yesterday afternoon, and took a sip of Wachusett, who was well content that Monadnock was out of the way. How lucky our mountains (many of them) are in their names, though they must find it hard to live up to them sometimes! The Anglo-Saxon sponsor would Nicodemus 'em to nothing in no time.

I found a bushel of cold letters awaiting me here, and I have spent most of my time with my hands across, gazing in despair at the outside of them. I am thinking seriously of getting a good forger from the State's-Prison to do my autographs, but I suppose the unconvicted followers of the same calling would raise the cry

of Convict Labor. Ashfield would be perfect
but that it has a post office. That fly would
corrupt a pot of ointment as large as the cup of
her horizon. . . .

To Lady Lyttelton

DEERFOOT FARM, *September* 14, 1885.

My life is so utterly uneventful that I have
nothing to write about except myself — an un-
edifying topic at best, and with ever-narrowing
limitations; for I begin to discover that our inward visual horizon, like our outer, grows less
and less wide with years. My only history is
that I have been making visits (and speeches,
of course) for the better part of a month. I
have been at the seashore with one of my nieces
and lately among the hills of western Massachusetts with my old friend Norton. All day I
climbed the hills and read Dante with Norton,
and in the evening the daughter of another
old friend, George Curtis, came in to accom-
pany Sally Norton's violin with the piano.
We had Bach and Beethoven and Handel and
Corelli and Schubert to our hearts' content.
I made them play *Ungeduld* and *Wenn die
Schwalben* over and over again. They made
me very happy. It was a pretty spectacle, and
the two girls, in the first flush of youth and
beauty, put their whole being into the music,
and made me feel that there are some chords in

us that the fingers of time never deaden. . . .
As for your forty-ninth birthday (or whatever
it was) I mock at it. Ask the first brook you
meet how long it has been running! It will
tell you it remembers the glaciers and is n't a
day older for it.

I have agreed to take a class in Dante and
one in Don Quixote at Harvard during the
first term, which ends in January. Then I shall
be free again till October, and mean to cross
the water again. . . .

Always your affectionate

J. R. L.

To the Same

Deerfoot Farm, *October* 30, 1885.

I am sitting in my room without fire and by
an open window, though the day is sullen and
sunless and as ready to cry on the smallest provocation as ever a woman was. . . . My room looks
south, and the landscape is changing wholly as
the trees shorten sail in preparation for winter.
I see the houses of neighbors invisible all
summer long, and my life is so eventless that
even this interests me as a change of Ministry
would you. The earth, too, seems to have
grown leaner and the bones show through as
never before. Our landscape is bonier than
yours, which has been petted and made comfortable so long. Luckily we can't wholly do-

mesticate Nature. She will become familiar and
purr when we stroke her, like a cat, but, like a
cat also, she keeps a bit of savage instinct hid
away somewhere that can fly out on occasion.
I am often struck with this in my lonely walks,
when, though she and I are so fond of each
other, an uncanny feeling comes over me that
I am in an enemy's country, after all. But I was
going to tell you how my room looked, that you
might fancy me more clearly. In the middle is
a great black table sent home from Spain and
already confusedly heaped with books (for I have
brought up a few from Elmwood), as I need not
tell you. My most impressive (and forbidding)
chairs are also huge Spanish ones of stamped
leather with brass studs as big as pygmy shields.
In one corner is an old Portuguese cabinet in-
laid with queer monsters showing the whites of
their eyes. On this are silhouettes of my father
and mother in their youth, which make me
wonder I am not better looking, and an engraved
great-uncle who was one of the signers of that
Declaration of Independence which was the
remote cause of my being Minister to England. Of other furniture there are a few shelves
of books, two portrait-landscapes of a lake in
the Adirondack wilderness and a group of oaks
(old friends of mine), Mrs. Cameron's photograph of Mabel, and one after a picture by
Velasquez.

I have an anecdote for you of which I am reminded by the shouts of the children just home from school and all so eager to see their mother as if she were a travelling circus. Frank came home the other day and said, " Mamma, M. N. used bad language, and I told him that my mamma didn't choose that I should hear bad language, and I knocked him down." . . .

To R. W. Gilder

SOUTHBOROUGH, *November* 9, 1885.

. . . As for writing, if *peut* and *veut* were the same thing (and how easily they might be — only they won't — when *p* so often changes to *b* and that to *v*) I would swamp all the magazines, and forty *Centuries* should behold my exploits as they beheld the soldiers of the only sublime charlatan on record. But — to take another illustration from Egypt — Horus didn't have to pick up his own *disjecta membra*, and I am trying to piece myself together again with no help save my own. When I am not answering letters, I strive for a little peace with my pipe and the small flock of books I have driven up hither from Elmwood — a flock which has the advantage of pasturing me instead of my doing it for them. It isn't Arcady exactly, but nobody knows how to find that nowadays except your friend Mr. Bunner, whose volume,[1]

[1] *Airs from Arcady.*

by the way, I read with so much pleasure. It
has some real stuff in it — and woven, too, with
no creak of machinery. But if it is n't Arcady
(" to resume," as the " Compleat Letter-writer "
would say), it pleases me for its analogy with
my favorite hero Don Quixote. Like him I
began with my tilt at windmills, and like him I
seek repose from discomfiture in another phase
of my monomania. Are n't the enchanters as
active as ever? Have n't they resuscitated
Sambo in a shape as *descomunal* as ever, after we
had dismounted him once and for all?

And then there is the " Atlantic." They
(O. W. H. and the rest) all say that I owe a duty
(and the first) to my own child, or, rather, the
adopted foundling I taught to go alone. And I
meanwhile have a sneaking disgust at the whole
of it, as knowing that my value is due less to
myself than to the abominable notoriety I have
unhappily achieved in these latter years. . . . .

To John W. Field

BOSTON, *December* 13, 1885.

. . . Where did you get that extract from a
letter of mine? [1] and to whom was it written?
It antedates my abolitionism by two years. I
thought it began in 1840. But when I read the
passage you quote, I remembered having writ-

[1] An extract from a letter to Dr. Loring, dated November
15, 1838; see vol. i. p. 41.

ten on my Class poem (in which I made fun of
the Abolitionists, 1838),

> Behold the baby arrows of that wit
>   Wherewith I dared assail the woundless Truth !
> Love hath refilled the quiver, and with it
>   The man shall win atonement for the youth. . . .

To R. S. Chilton
68 Beacon Street, Boston, *December* 17, 1885.

. . . No, I am not living at Elmwood, alas !
and never look forward to living there again.
I have let it, it being for me uninhabitable. I
hope to die there, however.

I received your volume, and ought to have
thanked you for it long ago. It revived so many
pleasant old associations ! I was naturally very
much pleased with the poem with which you
have honored me, but thought the entire tone
and manner of the book an honor to you. . . . .

To Miss Grace Norton
Deerfoot, *Christmas Day*, 1885.

. . . The " Scepsis," too, completes my Glan-
vill, for the " Sadducismus " has stood on my
shelves this many a year, and will feel warmer
with his brother beside him. I shall read the
" Scepsis " as soon as I have time, and I am
sure it will interest me as the other did, for I,
too, am a sceptic, with a superstitious imagination. . . .

To Lady Lyttelton
Deerfoot Farm, SOUTHBOROUGH, MASS.,
January 2, 1886.

. . . As for Ireland, it is hopeless, for the inexhaustible and unappeasable hate that is gnawing at the root of your supremacy there, and hitherto that has been the strongest passion in our nature except love, — and love is so long in coming! Moreover, the tenant farmers have tasted earth, which is worse than tasting blood, for the appetite it rouses. I should sympathize with them, as you know, were it not for you and one or two others. But no settlement can be arrived at which does not provide for the indemnification of you and such as you, — that is, unless England has ceased to be England, which I don't and won't believe. I think your politicians are too much afraid of what the Irish in this country can do. . . .

What have I been reading? Beaumont and Fletcher over again, for one thing, with mixed feelings of delight and disgust. How infinitely finer, as well as greater, is Shakespeare! And I have been reading a book you would like, — the " Life of Fawcett," by my friend Leslie Stephen. A really great life led by a man who was far from great. 'T is both a rebuke and a stimulus for those of us who are apt to waste themselves as some of us are. . . .

III

To the Misses Lawrence

Deerfoot Farm, Southborough, Mass.,

January 4, 1886.

. . . I am living quietly here with my son-in-law, my daughter, and five very creditable grandchildren, in a pretty country village, all hill and dale, and every hill a heap of boulders piled up by glaciers Heaven knows how long ago. I like my grandchildren, and this is in their favor, for I have none of that natural fondness for children which some people have, who also, I have observed, like puppies in the same indiscriminate way. I like my solitude, too, when I am allowed to have it all to myself, for a solitude *à deux* is possible only with a woman.

You must have had a pleasant continental trip, but I can't understand your not liking Weimar. I liked it immensely — a kind of puppet-theatre of the world, with its little Schloss and little Park and little Army and little Playhouse and little Court and little men and women. And as for the little stream that runs through the Park or along its edge, I fell in love with it, and so would you had you seen the horse-chestnuts lying in its bed, and more brilliant than balas rubies. And then there was the grand duke — a man of genius (on perpetual furlough), and one can get on very well where one has a man of genius to friend. And Frau v. Stein —

one can get on very well where there is one
charming woman. But I am glad you said what
you did, because it confirms me in something I
was going to say about Hawthorne — that men
of genius can manage anywhere, because they
make the best part of their own material. . . .

But you have Ireland still, and worse than
ever. 'T is the clot of blood in England's veins,
always discomforting, and liable always to lodge
in the brain. But then we all have our difficulties — that 's what we are put here for, and they
put here with us to test our doughtiness. I
often recall Hamlet's groan about the out-of-
joint world and the cruel spite — nevertheless.
But one can be philosophical three thousand
miles away !

What you say of Weimar convinces me of
how London has thrown its dust in your eyes.
But I like it too, and am glad even of a bit of
gossip thence now and then. . . .

You will divine, by what I say about gossip,
that I am growing old. I used to be as stern
about it as Wordsworth. You remember his " I
am not one," etc. ? 'T is senescence or London, I know not which — perhaps a mixture of
both. . . .

To R. W. Gilder

Deerfoot Farm, SOUTHBOROUGH,
January 16, 1886.

Dear Mr. Gilder, — I return the portfolio
with the verses[1] you ask for therein. It was an
effort of honesty on my part to send you back
the former, for I felt like " proud Dacres " when

> " he came aboard
> To deliver up his sword,
> He was loath to give it up — it looked so neat
> and handy, oh ! "

(Pronounce the sw in " sword " as in " swore,"
and " loath " " lawth," or you lose the local
tone of the period.) I have always thought this
passage delightful — a wonderful bit of sympathetic divination by the thrifty Yankee poet.
Ah me, how the times change and we with
them ! I have often seen rustics, buoyant with
Medford rum, dance the double shuffle on
the piazza of a country inn to the tune of
" Hull's Victory," and I saw that hero himself when his sword-belt would have lapt over
round a young elephant. As I looked down
on him, seated just under my perch in the gallery of Funnle Hall (they call it *fan-you-well*
now), he looked like a huge terrestrial globe
flanked with epaulets. I think it was when

[1] Autograph from *Commemoration Ode*, for reproduction,
to precede the *Life of Lincoln*.

General Jackson had a reception there. But I am getting garrulous.

The passage about Lincoln was not in the ode as originally recited, but added immediately after. More than eighteen months before, however, I had written about Lincoln in the " North American Review "— an article which pleased him. I *did* divine him earlier than most men of the Brahmin caste. The ode itself was an improvisation. Two days before the Commemoration I had told my friend Child that it was impossible — that I was dull as a door-mat. But the next day something gave me a jog and the whole thing came out of me with a rush. I sat up all night writing it out clear, and took it on the morning of the day to Child. " I have something, but don't yet know what it is, or whether it will do. Look at it and tell me." He went a little way apart with it under an elm tree in the College yard. He read a passage here and there, brought it back to me, and said, " Do? I should think so! Don't you be scared." And I was n't, but virtue enough had gone out of me to make me weak for a fortnight after. I was amazed at the praises I got. Trevelyan told me afterwards that he never could have carried through the abolition of purchase in the British Army but for the reinforcement he got from that poem. " I advise you to listen to this," Sumner used to say when he was talking about himself (as he commonly was); "*this* is historical!" So, having snubbed myself, I go on to say that I send the portfolio by express. . . .

To W. D. Howells

68 Beacon Street, Boston,
February 2, 1886.

Dear Howells, — I told you that I liked the plan of the new story when you gave me a sketch of it.[1] I like the story itself so thoroughly that I must please myself by telling you so. So far, 'tis the best yet. It made me forget eighteen hours in a sleeping-car and the loss of my only wearable-in-Boston hat.

But I won't let you say (when you reprint) as you do on page 5, 1st column, " bring us *in* closer relations," for that is n't what you mean. You don't mean "bring-in to us," but "bring us *into*"! That's what you mean. I am going to get up a society for the Prevention of Cruelty to Prepositions — I am getting so cross. Animals have certain natural means of defence. They can bite and prepositions can't. The skunk — but I forbear — you know what he can do in the newspapers. So beware, my dear boy! The society will be immitigable. It will spare neither age nor sex, and will be happiest when dancing a war-dance on the broken ties of friendship.

[1] *The Minister's Charge.*

On second thought, however (the hat having meanwhile come back), I still remain as always

Affectionately yours,

J. R. L.

Barring this bit of fruitless brutality, the story is simply delightful.

To the Same

My dear Valentine, — Come to 68 Beacon Street, Tuesday afternoon or late on Wednesday, for I don't wish to miss you.

I ought to have said, but forgot it, that you will find plenty of authority for *in* as you used it in our older writers. I remember it in Latimer (he was burned alive for that among other heresies, however) and elsewhere. But that sprang from a false analogy with the Latin, where the same preposition served both ends according to the case it governed. I believe some grammars still give no *cases*, but we have at best only one distinctive case-ending that I can think of — the genitive.   Affectionately yours,

J. R. LOWELL.

To Mrs. Leslie Stephen

. . . It is really too bad that I have been silent so long. But if you only knew how hard they work me with letters and speeches and things; and they have invented a new mode of torture — readings from one's poems, by Dr. Holmes and me, for the benefit of charities of one kind or another. We bow our necks to the yoke like patient oxen, and leaning away from each other as oxen will, strive to retrace our ancient furrows, which somehow will not gleam along the edge as when the turf was first broken. Admire, prithee, the aptness of my image, after first turning up in your Dixery the etymology of *verse*.

I am in Boston, and it is a rainy, dull day, such as we Americans, when we are in London, swear we never have at home. But we brought this wet with us also from the Old Home, and have improved upon it of course.

It rained all day yesterday, too, and when it rains here 't is after the reckless fashion of our people, as if we would spend all at once. None of your effete-monarchy drizzles such as you have in London, penurious as the last drops from a washerwoman's wringing. . . .

To C. E. Norton
DEERFOOT FARM, *March* 30, 1886.

. . . I send back the Dante, which you must have feared as irretrievably lost as Petrarch's copy of the " De Gloria.". . .

What I have for my book[1] makes only one

[1] *Democracy, and Other Addresses.*

hundred and forty pages, and they say it must be bigger. I had forgotten the Wordsworth address. Did I send you one? If so, send it to 68 Beacon Street, and let me use it to print from. I have another in London which I will give you.

I hate all the Addresses, now they are cold as Saul on Mount Gilboa. *Mi raccapricciono* — they give me the goose-flesh. As usual, I have n't left myself time to correct my proofs. What a pleasant life I shall have of it when I have all Eternity on deposit! Then the printers will say, "If you can with convenience return proofs before end of next century, you would oblige; but there is no hurry." 'T is an invincible argument for immortality that we never have time enough here — except for doing *other things*. . . .

To John W. Field
DEERFOOT FARM, *March* 30, 1886.

. . . I may be back before you leave Ashfield next summer, and if so, shall next see you there — as good a place as I know of this side heaven. Were I as good as you are, I should hope to meet you there also. If not, pitch me down a square of turf to stand upon when my birthday comes round. . . .

To Mrs. Edward Burnett
40 CLARGES STREET, PICCADILLY, W.,
May 3, 1886.

. . . I find myself very warmly welcomed
back, and shall soon be trotting round in the
old vicious circle of dinners and receptions. I
have had to make one speech at the dinner of
the Royal Academy, and have refused to make
five others. The editor of the " Contemporary
Review" has just gone out, having vainly en-
deavored (at the instigation of John Morley) to
persuade me that I should be doing a public
service by giving my views on Mr. Gladstone's
Home Rule project in that periodical. But I
prefer to keep clear of hot potatoes — and Irish
ones are apt to be particularly hot. Pretty nearly
Everybody who is Anybody here is furious —
there is no other word for it — and denounces
the G. O. M. as a kind of baser Judas Iscariot,
all the more contemptible because he will be
cheated of his thirty pieces. The Irish themselves are beginning to feel the responsibility of
governing Ireland, and Mr. —— has said that
they should " want an alien act to enable them
to deal with those d—d Irish-American scoun-
drels." (This is confidential.) The "situation"
is a very grave one, and everybody who is n't
excited is depressed.

I have been to see Irving's " Faust " (a won-

derful spectacle, but a very disagreeable play)
and Madame Sara Bernhardt, who has gone off
a little, but is still diabolically effective in certain rather unpleasant ways. I used to forget
who and what Rachel was, but can't divorce
Sara from her . . . self. Whom the Devil hath
joined together can't be put asunder. I am to
see her again, nevertheless, to-morrow night.
Both times I have gone by invitation of people
who had places to spare. So you see I am
emulating John Gilpin.

It has been very cold ever since I have been
here — but generally bright, which makes a great
difference, and oh, how goldenly green the grass
in the Parks is! The horse-chestnuts are getting ready their blossoms, and the thrushes need
strait-waistcoats every one of them.

I don't know whether I am glad I came or
not. My lodgings are good, but I have n't got
wonted yet and can't do anything. Yes, I can
preside at a dinner of the Dilettanti Society, as
I did last night. But all dinners are alike, except one I have just lost with Froude to meet
Matt Arnold and Morley. Unfortunately I
had promised myself for the Sunday at Hurstbourne. . . .

To R. W. Gilder

Care of Baring Brothers, LONDON

[*May?* 1886].

. . . I wish to do an act of charity to a dear old friend of mine here, and experience has taught me that it is more frugal to be vicariously beneficent. This won't give me a very high place in heaven perhaps, but I am modest, and with the pious Hebrew should be content with a por- tership in the House of the Lord — not only because it would keep me nearer earth, but be- cause in that office I could slam the door in the faces of bores, critics, and booksellers. I have chosen you for my vicar.

The case is this. Miss Mary Boyle is a de- lightful old lady. How old she is may be in- ferred, without breach of the *bienséances*, from the fact that Silvio Pellico wrote verses to her nearly sixty years ago. It is no fault of hers that they are not very good, still less that she should think them so. She is not only herself old, but comes of an old family, so that she has a double share of the infirmities of age. She is a descendant of that Earl of Orrery who antici- pated the dreary results of modern science by substituting balls of cork on the ends of wires for the lamps of heaven. (He was made Earl of Cork afterwards in recognition of this ser- vice.) She is also, I believe, a descendant of that

Honorable Robert Boyle whom Bentley roasted in his own bull of Phalaris. Let not these facts prejudice you against her. She has the blood of one martyr at least in her veins.

She has fifteen notes and letters of Landor (to her), and is willing to part with copies for publication. Here is no case of *dux femina facti*, for I suggested it. Some of the letters are very interesting, and all are characteristic. They have never been printed. Would they be worth £50 to you? or £40? I put the more generous sum first in deference to my own hopes and your character. If, when you get them, you think you have been cheated, I will make good the odds between my estimate and yours. When I get home (I come in September) I will write a short preface to them for nothing if you wish. They are not *important* letters, but they are Landor's. She is poor and nearly blind — as good as gold, but without the broker's art of changing herself into it. What say you?[1]

With all kindest regards to Mrs. Gilder,

Faithfully yours,   J. R. LOWELL.

> If my wild demand bewilders,
>   Think, 't is only fifty pound !
> Had I said as many Gilders,
>   Where could such a sum be found ?

[1] The letters were printed in the *Century*, with a pleasant introduction by Lowell, consisting mainly of his reminiscences of a visit to Landor. This may now be found in the volume of his *Latest Prose Essays*.

To Mrs. Edward Burnett
40 CLARGES STREET, PICCADILLY, W.,
June 7, 1886.

. . . My life here amuses without satisfying
me, and sometimes I am half sorry that I came.
The political situation, however, continues to
be interesting, and opinion about the fate of
Mr. Gladstone's bill varies from hour to hour.
I for a good while thought the second reading
would be carried by a small majority, but believe now that it will be defeated. I hear that
Mr. Gladstone said to the Duke of Argyll, " I
hoped in my old age to save my country, but this
is a bitter, humiliating disappointment." The
fate of the second reading depends somewhat
on the fear of a dissolution of Parliament, but
the general opinion now is that Government, if
defeated, will dissolve. I asked Mr. Chamberlain day before yesterday if he thought the
G. O. M. was angry enough to dissolve, and he
said *yes*. I met Gladstone a few days ago, and
he looked gay as a boy on his way from school.
From what I hear I am inclined to think that
what is called Irish public opinion in favor of
Home Rule is nearly as factitious as that of our
American meetings and resolutions. . . .

To the Same

40 Clarges Street, Piccadilly, W.,
June 19, 1886.

. . . From Osterley I went to Holmbury (Leveson-Gower's), where I spent a couple of days very pleasantly with Mr. and Mrs. Gladstone and other guests. Mr. Gladstone was in boyish spirits. He told me, among other things, that " in the whole course of his political experience he had never seen anything like the general enthusiasm of the country for Home Rule in Ireland." I asked slyly " if it was not possible that a part, at least, of this enthusiasm might be for the Prime Minister?" " Oh no, no, not a bit of it!" he answered with eager emphasis. And I am inclined to think he persuaded himself for the moment. This is one secret of his power as a speaker — that he is capable of improvising convictions. He left us to go down to Scotland, and I could n't help remembering that I first met him at a dinner at Lord Ripon's, in March, '80, when he was on the eve of starting for Midlothian on his first Scottish campaign. He was very confident, and the result justified him. Perhaps it will again, though the general opinion (as one hears it) is the other way. But I still think the people strongly with him.

. . . On the 29th I go down to the Vice-

Chancellor's at Baliol to wear my gown at Commemoration and help Dr. Holmes on with his.
He is enjoying himself immensely, and takes as
keen an interest in everything as he would have
done at twenty. I almost envy him this fresh-
ness of genius. Everybody is charmed with
him, as it is natural they should be. . . .

To the Same
40 CLARGES STREET, PICCADILLY, W.,
July 7, 1886.

. . . The elections are raging still, and I find
myself quoted on both sides. I made an epigram (extempore) one day on the G. O. M.,
and repeated it to Lord Acton : —

> His greatness not so much in genius lies
> As in adroitness, when occasions rise,
> Lifelong convictions to extemporize.

This morning I find the last lines quoted by
Auberon Herbert in a letter to the "Times," but
luckily without my name. It is a warning. Mr.
Gladstone has n't been as lucky with the con-
stituencies as I expected. Mr. Goschen, however, has been defeated at Edinburgh (for which
I am sorry), and this seems to console the
ministerialists for many other losses. I still remain convinced that Home Rule in some shape
will carry it one of these days. . . .

To C. E. Norton
40 CLARGES STREET, PICCADILLY, W.,
July 25, 1886.

. . . What you say of Carlyle is sympathetic (as it should be) and not dyspathetic. Of course every man that has any dimensions at all must have more than one side to him, and if he have dyspepsia one of those sides will have corners, and sharp ones, that find a sort of ease in the ribs of other folks. But, after all, Carlyle was a man of genius, and it is sheer waste of time to be looking one's gift-horse in the mouth and examining his hoofs, if he have wings and can lift us away from this lower region of turmoil at will. The rest is rubbish. Biographies (except Plutarch's) seldom do a man any good, and the less in proportion to the cleverness of the biographer, for your very clever one is sure to mix a good deal of auto- with his biography. The beauty and truth of impressions depend on the substance in which they are made. The main ingredient a biographer should contribute is sympathy (which includes insight). Truth is not enough, for in biography, as in law, the greater the truth sometimes the greater the libel. Happy those authors who are nothing more than airy tongues that syllable our names when they have a message for us ! Most Lives are more properly Deaths, or at least might

III

have for their title, like Chapman's D'Ambois, "The Life *and* Death of So-and-so."

I am living a futile life here, but am as fond of London as Charles Lamb. The rattle of a hansom shakes new life into my old bones, and I ruin myself in them. I love such evanescent and unimportunate glimpses of the world as I catch from my flying perch. I envy the birds no longer, and learn better to converse with them. Our views of life are the same.

As for politics — I saw Gladstone the other day, and he was as buoyant (*boy*ant) as when I stayed with him at Holmbury, just before he started for Scotland. I think the Fates are with him, and that the Tories will have to take up Home Rule where he left it. The great difficulty is in making up an able Cabinet. I suppose that ineptitudes will be neutralized with coronets (or signalized by them, as we mark shoals with buoys), and room made for younger and abler men. Lord Randolph Churchill is taken seriously now, and will have a front seat. He ought to build a temple to the goddess Push.

I spent two days in the country lately (at the George Lewises) with Burne-Jones, and found him delightful. As Mrs. Lewis says, "If he were not a great artist, there would be enough left of him to make a great man of." His series of Perseus (did you see any of them?) is to my

Charles Eliot Norton

thinking the greatest achievement in art of our time or of any time. It has mannerisms which I don't like, but it is noble in conception and execution. Above all, it has the crowning gift of making an old story as new as if nobody had ever told it before. I feel as if I had heard the waves rustle under the bows of the Argo.

I suppose you are at Ashfield, and that the hills are as dear as ever, and Monadnock as like a purpose unfulfilled. Is the June grass golden on the upper slopes? Do the cloud-shadows still linger and hate to leave their soft beds in the woods and grass? Above all, are you and yours well and remember me? And G. W. C.? Sometimes I hear faintly the notes of S——'s violin singing " Scheiden, ach, scheiden!" and think of many things. . . .

To Mrs. Edward Burnett

40 CLARGES STREET, PICCADILLY, W.,
August 6, 1886.

. . . There is n't a corner of England that has not its special charm, and the freaks of the atmosphere interest me more than any novel I ever read.

My last visit to the country was three days with the Darwins at Basset, which has more pleasant than sad associations for me. It was there that mamma began first to mend. I thought of you constantly. My bedroom window looked out towards the New Forest where the pony came from. We drove to the ruins of an old castle (*temp*. Henry II.), standing (or falling) in a park whose turf was like soft moss. If trees would only grow with us as they do here, where their leaves are washed and their roots drink every day ! . . .

To C. E. Norton
Deerfoot Farm, SOUTHBOROUGH, MASS.,
October 21, 1886.

. . . I am in despair about my address.[1] I have written a page only and made some notes. The bayonets must prick me more sharply from behind to set me going. Why did the Lord make us with ten fingers and toes that we might count up to fifties and hundreds and so make ourselves capable of this superstition of anniversaries ? Had he curtailed our left foot, for instance, of one toe, we should never have missed it except as a gout-trap, and could never have divided any multiple of nine so as to suit our stupid love of symmetry. The Japanese might have done it, but nobody else. There would have been no Cornelius, and Napoleon would have lost his pyramidal allusion, but I see no other harm it would have done.

I have no books up here, and have to trust

[1] For the two hundred and fiftieth anniversary of the foundation of Harvard University, delivered November 8, 1886.

to my memory, which I could leave, with Lord Bacon, to after-generations without impoverishing my heirs.

The only thing that has made me feel as if I had any life in [me] of late was the music I heard at Shady Hill. . . .

To the Same

Deerfoot Farm, SOUTHBOROUGH, MASS.,
October 26, 1886.

. . . The address drags like an ox-sled caught away from home by a January thaw. It *will* not take hold of me, do what I may. I have written a fair share of it, but I can't conquer our mutual alienation. My pitcher has gone once too often to the well. If I could scoop up a few drops with a shard of it, I were happy. But the well itself is dry !

What a scurvy trick —— has played me ! If he had reported what I really said, instead of his version of it, I should not feel so bitterly. Well, this also shall pass away, and so shall we, thank God, one of these days. . . .

. . . Happy Mirabeau, to whom Dumont supplied the substance of his speeches, leaving to him only the *fioriture* ! . . .

To W. D. Howells

Deerfoot Farm, Southborough, Mass.,
November 11, 1886.

. . . I was very sorry not to be able to
be with you to-day. I would have come if
I could, but I had most imperative proof-sheets
which I could correct only here, so I postponed
pleasure to duty. " Be virtuous and you will
be happy," says Whistler, "only you won't
have a good time."

I am happy in your well-earned fame, my
dear boy, and have just been reading your last
chapters with the feeling Gray had about Cré-
billon *fils*. Good-night.

To-morrow to fresh proofs and bothers new !

Affectionately yours,

J. R. Lowell.

To C. E. Norton

Deerfoot Farm, Southborough, Mass.,
November 22, 1886.

. . . I have been reading the book [1] with the
greatest interest. It not only makes Carlyle
more agreeable to me, but confirms an opinion
I formed several years ago in reading many of
these early letters (lent to me by Mr. Ireland),
that I know no man of letters so thoroughly *of
a piece* as Carlyle. The man who died sixty-four

[1] Carlyle's *Early Letters*.

years later is all there in the earliest of his writing that we have (potentially there, in character wholly there). And it is a fine character to my thinking, essentially manly and helpful to the core. . . .

To G. H. Palmer
Deerfoot Farm, SOUTHBOROUGH, MASS.,
November 30, 1886.

. . . I was n't thinking so much of the studies as of the method of teaching (by recitation and in divisions) when I wrote what gravels you.[1] I dare say also, as you suggest, that I was thinking more of what the College was than of what it is. There is a certain imprudence in letting one's self live to be sixty-eight for which one always has to pay. Had I been in Cambridge instead of Southborough, I dare say I should have written differently. I am sure I should had I heard that excellent essay of yours, of which I afterwards listened to a part with sincere admiration and profit.

You will observe that I have inserted a qualifying sentence, in which the influence of that essay may be traced.

Nothing could have been further from my thought than to give aid and comfort to the

---

[1] A sentence in the Harvard Address in which justice was hardly done to the advance lately made in the University in the methods of instruction, of discipline, and of investigation.

enemies of what I heartily approve in the main. *Nescit vox missa reverti*, but I shall be in Cambridge this week, and will talk over the matter with Norton. If I *can* frame such a note as you wish, I gladly will. . . .

To R. W. Gilder
Deerfoot Farm, SOUTHBOROUGH, MASS.,
December 2, 1886.

. . . I am one of those men who depend greatly on the kind offices of the *genius loci*, and am a good while in winning the confidence of a new one. I am just getting on speaking terms with the shy little fellow who has charge of the hills and pastures and woodpaths here, but am not yet in a position to ask him for a letter of introduction to his cousin in Boston, whom I don't know. I don't believe I can write anything there. But we shall see. At any rate, I have been mulling over Landor, and shall be able to do a page or two of personal reminiscence and (pemmican) criticism wound up [by] an epigram of my own. The letters are less trivial than I feared, and one (about his dog Pomero) really touching. . . .

To T. B. Aldrich
December 17, 1886.

. . . I have copied it all and I am tired, and it seems uninspired or ill-inspired, I hardly

know which. But I send another that you may
not be comfortless. It is shorter, and I advise
you to take, as I should, the smaller pill of the
two. I fear the long one (" Credidimus Jovem
Regnare ") will overrun your six pages, perhaps
I hope it. Cut out what you please. There
are two or three bright spots. If these be left,
all will be well. Don't be tempted by a paginal
vacuum to wrong your editorial conscience. Be
frank ; I am old and can stand it. My advice
is — cage the cuckoo ! 'T is of the last century
rather, but no harm in that. . . . If I had n't
lost a couplet I made last night while lying
awake, there would have been one good verse
in the longer poem. Always keep pencil and
paper, as bird-lime, at the head of your bed.
'T is worth more than " a twenty Bookes clothed
in black and red " — unless, indeed, they are
your own books. What shall I call it ? Will
" A Grumble " do ? [1] . . .

To C. E. Norton

Deerfoot Farm, SOUTHBOROUGH, MASS.,
December 24, 1886.

. . . I *can't* do what they wish me to do in
New York. The consciousness that I had it to
do would be so constantly foraging on my equa-
nimity and therefore laying waste my time, that

---

[1] The little poem was finally named " Fact or Fancy ? "
Both poems appeared in the *Atlantic Monthly*.

not a vine or a wheat-stalk would be left me.
If I could only so far conquer my shyness as
to be able to stand up and let myself run, I
would go with pleasure. How I envied the
rector of St. Olave's when the Pepys Memorial
was unveiled ! He simply flowed in the *labitur
et labetur* fashion as freely as if he had been a
Roman conduit. I knew my Pepys. I went
without notes but with my head full of delightful things to say about him, and when I got up
there was a kind of *er-r-r-oo* in my brain — the
noise of all my fine things flying away from me
like a flock of blackbirds when one comes suddenly on them over noiseless ploughed land.
I forgot even to say (though the only one there
who knew) that St. Olaf was the first viking ever
honored with that promotion — unless St. Mag-
nus was — and that therefore he would be sure
to take good care of the soul of a naval secretary which stood sadly in need of such official
intervention. I wonder at my own audacity
when I remember how I used to get up as
President of the Phi Beta or the Alumni and
trust to the spur of the moment. Yet I am
alive to tell you so ! No ; I must be left in
such peace as I can contrive for myself. Why,
my dear boy, I am going on to seventy. Nobody suspects it, least of all I.

I have got my Landor letters off my hands
at last — my " brief preface " resulting in twelve

quarto pages of manuscript as close-written as this ! I can't tell what it is till I see it in print. . . .

Now I shall buckle myself to my introduction to the " Progress of the World." It rather attracts me through my sense of humor. It will be pure creation made out of nothing, not even nebula or star-dust. . . .

To Miss Lawrence
Deerfoot Farm, Southborough, Mass.,
Christmas Day, 1886.

. . . Clever people are apt to be lucky, and when they are clever and nice too, as they sometimes are, they are sure to hit right. So I was n't a bit surprised that your kind letter, with its Christmas greetings, should arrive this very morning, as if it had ridden post itself, and could therefore adjust its speed to the occasion.

. . . I like to be serious all by myself, and to play when I throw my working-jacket off. Everybody should write on my title-pages, *ridentem dicere verum quid vetat ?* I have had reasons (if any man) for taking life in earnest, but it pleased the Lord to fit me with an " Æolian Attachment," which *will* strike in at the invitation of any breeze that takes it into its head to blow, and I don't think it respectful to balk him.

I had n't forgotten my promise — so far from
it that I had a twinge now and then. But I
found there were some misprints, and was content to wait for a new edition. As I commonly
hate my own books, I don't easily conceive
of anybody else hungering after them. If my
friends only like *me*, forty thousand what's-his-
names may fly away with what I write. Then,
too, I live in Grub Street — so called because
nobody is allowed to turn butterfly there —
and its inhabitants may *call* their time their own
if they will, but it is somebody else's all the
same. But I send a copy by the same post with
the errata corrected in my own neat hand, which
will add to its value whenever it goes to the
book-stall ! . . .

Yes, your scandals are bad enough and sad
enough ; but I saw a good deal of people who
are called of "a certain class" while I was in
England, and they seemed to me as clean as
New-Englanders, and that is saying a good
deal. Take such as the Cowpers, the Greys,
the Stanhopes, the Lytteltons, the Ashleys, to
name no more, and where will you find purer
or better ?

. . . I write to you instead of going to
church — but I sent my oblation to the offer-
tory. I am a conservative (warranted to wash),
and keep on the safe side — with God as
against Evolution — but I do hate going to

church. If Dr. Donne or Jeremy Taylor, or
even Dr. South, were the preacher, perhaps —
but I don't know. . . .

To Walker Fearn

Deerfoot Farm, SOUTHBOROUGH, MASS.,
Christmas Day, 1886.

Dear Mr. Fearn, — I am much obliged by
your very friendly remembrance of me, and
glad to be assured by yourself (I had heard it
from others before) of the interest you take in
the American School of Classical Studies at Athens. In order to hold and manage any funds
that might come to our address, we have had
ourselves incorporated under the Massachusetts
law, and I am president of the Corporation. . . .

Yes, I have been at Athens — *et ego* in Arcadia — and shall never outwear the impression
I brought away. Pardon what looks like a pun
when I say that as I stood gazing up at the
Acropolis, many new sensations were born in
me by a very natural parthenogenesis. Perhaps what comes back to me oftenest when I
think of Greece is the outline of the mountains, inexplicably graceful as if modelled by
Pheidias, and the color of the sea. I am glad
to hear that you are happy there. It is good
to be so anywhere, but in Athens must be best
of all !

I am glad also that you liked my address.

It was first printed in a supplement to the "Atlantic Monthly," and I shall ask my publishers to send you the copies for which you ask through the Department of State. It was a very interesting occasion and went off well. The President, I am glad to say, was received with great warmth and was deeply gratified — as indeed he more than once told me with a great deal of feeling. With all his firmness he has a very tender and sympathetic nature, or I am much mistaken. I think he has made some sad mistakes, but he is gaining ground with general public opinion, and I know how difficult his position is.

You speak of the pleasant people you see. This is one great advantage of Athens, that, being a little harder to get at than Rome, fewer of the wrong kind of people get there. You must find much to interest you also in your other posts, especially of late. You are the very Cerberus of ambassadors — three rolled into one!

I was pleased to hear of your appointment, and should have written to say so had I known just where you were. It is not too late to say so now.

Faithfully yours,

J. R. LOWELL.

To C. E. Norton
Deerfoot Farm, Southborough, Mass.,
January 1, 1887.

. . . I am "awfully" afraid (as my grandchildren *will* say — no d——g will stay this
neophrastic flood) that I have lost my Emerson letters. At any rate, I have mislaid 'em.
They are no longer in the little trunk where I
kept them, and I have no doubt that I took
them out, meaning to give them to you. I
have one hope and only one — that they may
be in a desk I use at my sister's. I am sorry,
for I valued his verses written for a dinner
given me on my fortieth birthday, in 1859. I
read them over when I made away with them
last year. There will hardly be any other copy,
for he gave me the original manuscript, evidently written in haste. I remember he praised
my healthy temperament (I'm glad he didn't
know it so well as I), calling me "well-born
Lowell," and, what interested me more, prophesied that, if the time ever came for it, I
should "lighten" or "thunder," I forget which,
perhaps both, for one is easy after you have
accomplished t' other. I hope I shall find them
yet, for I am sometimes luckier than I deserve
in that way. . . .

Have the clouds been playing the confec-
tioner with you and are your trees all sugar-

candied as ours are? I suppose not, for we are five hundred feet nearer heaven than you — a great start, if I should be put under ground here. I look out of window and see the woods grown grayer than I of a sudden, and find a sort of comfort in it. They have such a knack of renewing their youth in the spring, confound 'em! My sap feels the spur of the young year too, but won't do anything for my hair as it does for theirs. I know a tree or two that I would swap with if I had my life to begin over again. Then one might be made into a violin, perhaps, or into a coffin for somebody one hated, for trees have their likes and dislikes; they 've often told me so. . . .

To Miss Grace Norton
Deerfoot Farm, SOUTHBOROUGH, MASS.,
January 3, 1887.

. . . I don't get on with the world at all since I half promised to write an introduction to the "World's Progress," a megatherium of a book in two volumes quarto. I hear their heavy footfall behind me wherever I go, and am sure they will trample me into the mud at last. . . .

Oh, if you could see *my* moon — for all mine she must be now if, as I have no doubt, I am the last person up in all this village! I am having the luxury of a private view, and has n't she found a new plaything in this plated snow, across which she has drawn a long moon-glade as over the sea ! She is evidently wondering why these multitudinous hill-waves of ours show no emotion, and thinks that either the ocean's heart has ceased to beat or grown as insensible as Endymion's. And every jutting bowlder is a Kohinoor almost big enough for the shirt front of a New York alderman on his way to Sing Sing. How I wish you could see it, with your poor suburban planet vainly trying to get an effect of light and shade out of the enormous flank of Memorial Hall. And all the while the cold is so still that I am sure it means mischief. . . .

To Thomas Hughes

Deerfoot Farm, SOUTHBOROUGH, MASS.,
January 10, 1887.

Dear Tom Brown, — Your friendship is very dear to me, and accordingly I was very glad to get so pleasant a reminder of it, and to be assured that you were happy in your new home, as you, if ever any man, deserve to be. I look forward now to no removal except to the narrow house that contrives to hold us all, and hope to be comfortable there, though it do not command such a prospect as yours. I have seen it, you remember, and thought, as the American young woman of the period (born out

of Boston) would say, that it was " just lovely " !
If I had, or could have, a perch, I think I could
be content there. You are beyond reach of the
noise and smoke of Babylon, but within reach
of its Hanging Gardens, for may I not call so
those of the Temple where you breed your
Judges ! *Felix nimium, tua si bona noris*, as so
few of us do, though you seem to be wiser.

My new book will be coming to you by and
by. It would have come to you sooner, but
that some vile misprints were discovered in the
first edition which held my hand. So don't think
the fifth thousand on the title-page (P. S. It
is n't, I find on undoing the package) implies
neglect, but only the second edition of twenty-
five hundred copies. Rejoice with me that I am
getting popular in my old age, and hope to pay
my this year's trip to the dear old Home without defrauding my grandchildren. I get twenty-
five cents, I think it is, on copies sold during
the first eight months after publication, and
then it goes into my general copyrights, for
which I am paid £400 a year. Not much after
nearly fifty years of authorship, but enough to
keep me from the almshouse.

I am sorry you have no grandchildren, for I
enjoy mine more and more. I have made up my
mind to take them as they are, and not fash my
beard too much when they say *will* for *shall* (the
infection of which is now universal and past cure)

or " I don't know as." They talk as naturally through their noses as friars sing through 'em. 'T is an innovation in our family, and I hope they 'll get over it — but 't will be too late for me. I am thinking of making the eldest (my namesake) take my name in full and receive what heirlooms I have to leave, on condition that a jury of Britons pronounce him not guilty of this offence.

I am to be very busy this winter ; indeed I fear I have undertaken more than I can do well, for I can't always write when I would, though I set myself never so doggedly about it. And Johnson himself, how little he 'd have left us but for Boswell ! However, I am going to talk on politics to the people of Chicago on my next birthday, and to give six lectures before the Lowell Institute in March. The latter will give me three or four hundred pounds, which will be a lift. If ever you have grandchildren you will grow miserly and approve of entails. Depend upon it 't was grandfathers invented 'em. My own died seventeen years before I was invented, or perhaps I should be driving in my coach at this moment. On the whole I think I am better employed in writing to you. . . .

P. S. I have not thanked you for your kindness to young B——. He is carried away just now by the Something Brothers, a kind of Anglican monks (without monasteries) who wear cords round their waists, but resemble St. Francis in no other particular that I can discover. If these hempen girdles were worn in readiness for extemporal application to the gullets of many of our public functionaries, I would join the order myself. We need some strong doses of the herb Pantagruelion.

Pray, who is " F. T." who has been writing about me in so friendly a way in the " Cornhill "? He is a little out now and then, but strikes me as in the main judicious. He is wrong about the second part of the " Biglow Papers." I think had he read these first, he would have seen they had more permanent qualities than their predecessors, less fun and more humor perhaps. And pray what natural scenery would he have me describe but my own? If you know him, tell him I think two European birds beat any of ours, the nightingale and the blackbird. The lark beats any of them also by sentiment and association, though not vocally. I suppose I should have been a more poetical poet if I had not been a professor. A poet should feed on nothing but poetry, as they used to say a drone could be turned into a queen-bee by a diet of bee-bread. However, my poems have mostly written themselves and I cannot account for them. But nothing is so uncomfortable as an analysis of one's own qualities.

Give my love to England in general. I am

as proud of my two doctor's gowns as Dogberry of his two cloaks, or M. Jourdain of his
two lackeys.

To C. E. Norton

. . . What do you suppose I was doing at
between two and three last night? I could n't
sleep and so — I took up Seneca's " Medea."
I had n't read it for forty-eight years, and all I
remembered of it was *Medea superest.* · I had
forgotten that the *venient annis,* etc., was from
there. I suppose his Latin is not very good,
but now and then there is a cadence that sticks
in one's ear, and a kind of Dr. Young sublim-
ity, as where Medea by her incantations draws
down the serpent of Ophiuchus to earth. The
passion is that of a stoic, and leaves one stoical.
He is turgid enough in all conscience, and when
he swells gets turbid too, and brings along with
him whatever he comes across, trees and bridges
and cattle and herdsmen and Orpheus's head
and mud, lots of it. And yet I take a certain
pleasure in watching him go it — only one feels
that it is all let on, as Kauterskill Fall used to
be. Lucan came fairly by his style (a sort of
Roman Cowley he), and I am glad I took up
the book, since I bethought me for the first
time that Lucan was the true protogenist of the
concettisti. . . .

To R. W. Gilder

DEERFOOT FARM, *February* 9, 1887.

. . . I have often wondered if men lying
supine " up back of the meeting-house " (as we
say here) may not sometimes wile away the time
by reading their own epitaphs — no doubt with
some surprise in most cases, and perhaps (if in
Latin) with some difficulty, though probably
with a leaning towards favorable interpretation
where there was any doubt. To a certain ex-
tent I realized my own fancy in reading your
proofs. In a literary life of now almost fifty
years this is the first time I was ever admitted
to the confidence of anything written about myself. I should have refused it now if I had
thought of it in time. But I had forgotten your
promise to send me the proofs. However, as
the Lowell of twenty-four years ago is grown a
comparative stranger and an object of scientific
curiosity to me, I won't send back your proofs
unread through an over-scrupulosity.

I have made a translation such as it is of the
Italian verses. I can't remember now whose
they are. Not Petrarch's I think ; perhaps Leo-
pardi's, whom I used to read in those days.

What you say about Bryant interests me very
much. Never being a great reader of newspapers, and never seeing the " Evening Post "
(which I thought Godwin's mainly), I knew

nothing about the matter. I am all the glad-
der I wrote my poem for Bryant's birthday —
a kind of palinode to what I said of him in the
" Fable for Critics," which has something of
youth's infallibility in it, or at any rate of youth's
irresponsibility. Besides, I wrote it (slapdash,
in less than a week, I think) with no notion of
publication. That was the doing of my friend
C. F. Briggs (with whom I grew acquainted
through Page), and to whom I sent it as fast as
it was written ; if I remember, I gave him the
copyright. It turned out a better gift than I
expected, for it was the first (perhaps the only)
popular thing of mine. Under my own name
I was tainted with Abolitionism, to which I
swore fealty in 1839. The " Fable " (luckily
for Briggs) was anonymous. So were all the first
series of " Biglow Papers " as they originally
appeared, and I had great fun out of it. I have
often wished that I could have had a literary
nom de guerre and kept my own to myself. I
should n't have cared a doit what happened to
him.

But I am writing an autobiography — I must
pull up. . . .

To C. E. Norton
DEERFOOT FARM, *April* 8, 1887.

. . . I am trying to get rested by reading
Dickens, and am over " David Copperfield "

now. I had never read it, I find, though Mr. Micawber has become so proverbial that, finding his name in it, I thought I had. Dickens says in his preface that David Copperfield was his " favorite child," and I don't wonder, for it is amazingly well done so far as I have got.

We have got back the birds again, but in this weather they seem as unseasonable as autumn blossoms on the trees. I hope it is warmer in your parts. The only bird that has my entire sympathy is a woodpecker which has been tapping at an elm opposite my window all the morning, as much as to ask, " Is Spring at home?" He has made up his mind that she is n't even expected, and has flown away. Still, there is a certain cheer in the bluebirds. They bid me not despair every day. . . .

To Thomas Hughes

DEERFOOT FARM, *April* 16, 1887.

My dear Friend, — I have just received your " Life of Fraser," [1] and have read enough of it to see that I shall find it very interesting. He was just the manly kind of fellow to awaken all your sympathy, and accordingly I was not surprised to see (before I got the book) that opinion was unanimous as to how admirably you had written his biography. Notwithstanding his Scottish name, he was a peculiarly English

[1] Bishop of Manchester.

type of man, a type which I trust will long continue to be characteristic of the dear Old Home.

I naturally follow your politics with great interest. You and I don't agree about the Irish question, I think, but we are sure to be of one mind about the Coercion Bill. It amuses me to see the Grand Old Man using the same arguments against this bill that I vainly urged against *his* bill five years ago. You know that I am "principled agin" indulging in prophecy, but I made one at that time which has been curiously verified. I used to ask, "Suppose the Irish nation should strike, what are you going to do about it?" They have struck, and I am still at a loss. I am glad to see that their tone over here is much more moderate than it was. "Studiously moderate," you will say. But I think they begin to see the difficulties more clearly than they did. Meanwhile the coercion policy is crowding the emigrant ships to this country, and we have already as many as we can digest at present. We are really interested in your Irish question in more ways than one. It is really we who have been paying the rents over there, for we have to pay higher wages for domestic service to meet the drain.

But I did not mean to write a letter when I began, still less a political letter, but only to say that I sail by the Pavonia on the 21st, and mean to stop over and smoke a pipe with you before going up to London. So expect me about the 2d May, and get some fine weather and plenty of thrushes and blackbirds ready for me. We have been having a " saltatory " winter, all ups and downs. Old Hiems has behaved like the guest of the Satyr in the fable — blowing hot and cold — till we are glad to turn him out of doors. But the birds are come at last, though our landscape is as sallow as ever. Hardly a blade of green to keep the poor dears in heart. But the wild geese have been flying northward, and of course *they* know. At any rate, the tame ones are supposed to, or else what faith could one have in a government of majorities?

I shall be glad to clasp your honest hand again, which has done so much good work for all good things. Meanwhile, with love to Mrs. Hughes, I am always

Affectionately yours,

J. R. LOWELL.

To Mrs. Edward Burnett
2 RADNOR PLACE, HYDE PARK, W.,
May 22, 1887.

. . . Nothing can be more bewildering than the sudden change in my habits and surroundings. Were it merely from the dumbness of Southborough to the clatter and chatter of London, it would be queer enough; from the rising

and falling murmur of the mill to this roar of
the human torrent. But I can hardly help
laughing sometimes when I think how a single
step from my hermitage takes me into Babylon.
Meanwhile it amuses and interests me. My
own vitality seems to reinforce itself as if by
some unconscious transfusion of the blood from
these ever-throbbing arteries of life into my own.
Upon my word, I think I am beginning in my
old age to find a more impressive and poignant
solitude in the Great City than in the country.
I get all the country I want in the Park, which
is within five minutes of me, and the song of the
thrush is more pathetic there, like a quotation
of poetry in a dreary page of prose.

Last evening as I drove to dinner through
the Edgeware Road I seemed to get a glimpse
of Fairyland in the Saturday-night fair which
stretches along one side of the way and runs
over into the by-streets. A dingy fairyland
truly, and yet so remote from all my ordinary
associations as to become poetic.

At dinner, by the way, I was glad to meet
John Morley for the first time since my return.
He welcomed me most cordially, but looks older
and a little worn with the constant friction of
politics. But the cheerful fanaticism of his face
is always exhilarating to me, though I feel that
it would have the same placidly convinced expression if my head were rolling at his feet

at the exigence of some principle. He knows where he stands on the Home Rule question better than Gladstone, for his opinions are more the result of conviction than of sentiment.

My thrushes are singing under every discouragement, for everybody (with the usual shortness of memory and joy in generalization) agrees that " there never was such weather " ! It has been and is indeed very cold, but the palace of English summer is always built of ice, and I continue to think the London climate the best in the world. At any rate it suits me. . . .

To C. E. Norton
2 Radnor Place, Hyde Park, W.,
May 26, 1887.

. . . I do like London, and it gives a fillip to my blood, now growing more sluggish than it used to be. I love to stand in the middle of the Park and forget myself in that dull roar of ever-circulating life which bears a burden to the song of the thrush I am listening to. It is far more impressive than Niagara, which has nothing else to do and can't help itself. In this vast torrent all the drops are men. There ! I have unconsciously written a pentameter and it is time to stop.

I have seen Gladstone several times, and he is lighthearted as a boy — as lightheaded, too, I might almost say. I am amazed at the slowness of people here in seeing that the ice they have been floating on is about to break up — nay, will at the first rough water. The Irish question is only incidental to the larger question of their whole system of landholding, and the longer they delay settling *that* the more inevitable is it that this should stir itself. It is a misfortune and not a crime to be entangled in an anachronism, but if one won't do what he can to break loose one must share its fate without complaint or hope of compensation. You will be glad to hear that Morley has made himself respected both in Parliament and out of it, though on what is now the unpopular side. I think it will be the winning one in the end, for the stars in their courses are fighting against Sisera, and Sisera refuses to lift his eyes to them. It is a curious touch of nature that there should be such bitterness against Chamberlain — as if a self-made man had no right to opinions of his own, as the sons of dukes have as a matter of course. I met him last night at old Lady Stanley's (of Alderley), and he did n't show any sign of disheartenment. She is one of my favorites. She reminds me of the people I used to see when I was young — so frankly themselves. But this was before our individuality had been trampled out of us by the Irish mob. . . .

To Mrs. Edward Burnett

2 RADNOR PLACE, HYDE PARK, W.,
June 12, 1887.

. . . I was very glad to get your letters day before yesterday, one of them including that of Joe. It was a statistical letter (as those of boys are apt to be), and told me just what I wanted to know — the blossoming of the apple and pear trees and the greenness of the lawn. He forgot to say how my friend the brook was, but as you speak of a three days' rain, I have no doubt he is in good health and spirits, rolling his amber over the dam with a full heart. Many a night have I listened to him crooning his poems to himself and the embowering elm trees. Joe's letter I was glad to find carefully written. I am sorry that he is to lose his European trip, but dare say the Beverly shore will do quite as much for his health. After all, the kind of world one carries about in one's self is the important thing, and the world outside takes all its grace, color, and value from that.

. . . I am glad you have been reading Howell's letters. The book is not so good as Charles Lamb fancied it. His favorites were always a lover's "inexpressive Shes," endowed with every charm out of himself. If it was my copy of the letters you have been reading, you will find some interesting proposals for a reform of spelling (by Howell) on a leaf at the end. . . .

To Sybella Lady Lyttelton
WELLINGTON TERRACE, WHITBY,
August 14, 1887.

I have very pleasant lodgings overlooking the red roofs of the old town, with the Abbey in full view across the river, and every evening see the rays of the setting sun quiver on the cracked panes of the church that stands near it. I mean the Abbey, not the sun. No, not every evening, for yesterday it rained all day, and I was struck more than ever with the warm beauty of the tiles in comparison with the slates which are replacing them. The tiles brighten with the wet. It brings out all their virtue and they make a very good substitute for sunshine. That is better than nothing, is n't it? Don't we spend the greater part of our lives in trying to manufacture the counterfeit? The slates do their duty also as they understand it, and grow more dingily glum with the rain, which touches their sympathies. . . .

As I pause and look out of window, thinking how fruitless consolation is, and how unconsoling submission, I see the long rows of headstones in the churchyard on the hill staring at me with a startled look, as if they had all suddenly sprung up at the sound of the last trump, and were wondering where they should find the bodies of the men they commemorate, so many of whom are buried in the sea. Well, there are worse things than being washed about the stormy Hebrides.

To Mrs. Leslie Stephen

WHITBY, August 16, 1887.

. . . Your letter lost a couple of days by going to seek me at Radnor Place. I have been here for a week, and find Whitby as delightful as ever. The Abbey stares at me with the empty sockets of its eyes, and tries, I think, to get a little friendly expression into them. St. Hilda seems to welcome me back, but I am not sure that Cædmon would be glad to see a brother poet. Goethe, you know, talks of the roaring loom of Time, and I suppose he weaves us all in somehow or other, whether we like it or no. Of you, no doubt, he will make a lovely white rose. I shan't cut much of a figure, I am afraid, but shall be content to be the dull ground on which you are woven.

I do little else than take longish walks by the sea or over the moors, which do me good and make my eyes *feel* a little better at any rate. But I feel that I am come to the period when decay begins to set in, and when I am tired of looking at the ruins of the Abbey I sit among my own and pensively contemplate them. I hope a flower or two will root in a crevice here and there for you to make a nosegay of when you chance that way. . . .

To Miss Sedgwick

2 RADNOR PLACE, HYDE PARK, W.,
August 18, 1887.

Dear Dora,— Many thanks for so kindly remembering me. But how clever women are in
flattering us with their pretended jealousies!
No, there may be another Dora, but the first
will always have that preëminence of priority
that belongs to the first snowdrop and the first
bluebird. You are Dora I., D. G.

In spite of the epigraph of my paper I am
really at Whitby, whither I have been every
summer but '85 for the last six years. This
will tell you how much I like it. A very primitive place it is, and the manners and ways of
its people much like those of New England.
" Sir " and " ma'am " are only half-hardy ex-
otics here. The great difference is that everybody here will take a shilling, failing that, a six-
pence, and, in desperate circumstances, even a
penny, as a kind of *tabula in naufragio*, God
save the mark! The people with whom I
lodge, but for accent, might be of Ashfield.
'T is a wonderfully picturesque place, with the
bleaching bones of its Abbey standing aloof
on the bluff and dominating the country for
leagues. Once, they say, the monks were lords
as far as they could see. The skeleton of the
Abbey still lords it over the landscape, which

III

was certainly one of the richest possessions they had, for there never was finer. Sea and moor, hill and dale ; sea dotted with purple sails and white (fancy mixes a little in the purple, perhaps), moors flushed with heather in blossom, and fields yellow with corn, and the dark heaps of trees in every valley blabbing the secret of the stream that fain would hide to escape being the drudge of man. I know not why, wind has replaced water for grinding, and the huge water-wheels, green with moss and motionless, give one a sense of repose after toil that, to a lazy man, like me, is full of comfort. Not that I am so lazy neither, for I think a good deal — only my thoughts never seem worth writing down till I meet with them afterwards written down by somebody more judiciously frugal than I. Do you know I was thinking this morning that Montaigne was the only original man of modern times, or at any rate the only man with wit enough to see things over again in his own way, and to think it as good a way as any other, never mind how old?

I wish you could see the "yards" — steep flights of stone steps hurrying down from the West Cliff and the East, between which the river (whose name I can never remember) crawls into the sea, and where I meet little girls with trays bearing the family pies to the baker, and groups of rosy children making all manner of playthings of a bone or a rag. And I wish you could see the pier, with its throng of long-booted fishermen, looking the worthy descendants of the Northmen who first rowed their ships into the shelter of the cliffs and named the place. And I wish you could breathe the ample air of the moors — I mean with me.

Your little gift, dear Dora, has been very useful. I carry it in my pocket, not without fear of wearing away the birds and flowers, and so changing its summer to autumn, as my own has changed. I use it almost every day. I dare say you are in Ashfield now. Greet the hills for me, especially Peter's, and the June grass that I still see making them so beautiful in velvet. Give my love to all wherever you are, and tell Sally that I shall write to her soon. I take my letters in order, and yours came before hers; and oh, if I am tardy, remember how many I have to write and that my life is eventless.

Affectionately yours,
J. R. LOWELL.

To C. E. Norton
DEERFOOT, *December 22,* 1887.

. . . I have contrived at last to make a kind of whole of "Endymion," which had been lying in fragments for many years, but fear I have not made a harmonious statue of it after all.

I have finished the "Epistle to Curtis" after

a fashion, well or ill is hard to say. The measure is so facile that one soon loses one's sense of the difference between what sounds like something and what really is something. One needs to brace one's self with a strong dose of Dr. Donne. . . .

To R. W. Gilder
DEERFOOT FARM. *December* 26, 1887.

. . . My dear boy, if ever you *should* attain to entire utterance of yourself you would be the unhappiest man alive. Be happy in having something to strive after. Possession (unless of the Devil) is nine points of the law, but it is *ten* of disillusion. A happy New Year to you both! I am glad you have been seeing the President.[1] To me his personality is very *simpatico*. He is a truly American type of the best kind — a type very dear to me, I confess. . . .

To C. E. Norton
DEERFOOT, *January* 5, 1888.

. . . I brought up one volume of Singer's "Old English Poets," but 't was that containing the "Hero and Leander" of Marlow and Chapman, an old dear of mine. "Thealma and Clearchus" I left behind because I did n't want it — nor do I now. The weight of its dulness

[1] Mr. Cleveland.

left a crease in my memory which will never out any more than that of a dog's-ear in a book. But besides this, a conviction remains from that laborious reading (what a reader I was! I am far fallen from such grace now) that the book could not have been written by a contemporary of Spenser, as Walton said it was. The language was altogether too modern — curiously so even for 1683, when, as I find, Walton published it. And this singularity (of modernness) is very notable in the style of the "Complete Angler" too. I have little doubt that Walton himself wrote "Thealma and Clearchus," though I can well fancy a coroner writing it, or sitting on it and bringing in a verdict of "Found Dead." That Walton should have laid it at the door of his (connubial) great-uncle is, after all, a comparatively innocent *supercherie*. If Walton wrote only the verses in praise of angling printed in the "Complete Angler," how explain Donne's verses to him — unless on the supposition that the opinions of one's friends about one's verses are ninety-nine parts friendship to one of judgment? I, who am just printing mine, am upset by the thought. Or was there another I.W.? I know of none.

I am wondering more and more if my poems are good for anything after all. They are old-fashioned in their simplicity and straightforwardness of style — and everybody writes so plaguily well nowadays. I fear that I left off my diet of bee-bread too long and have written too much prose. A poet should n't be, nay, he can't be, anything else without loss to him as poet, however much he may gain as man.

But this is getting as long as the Epistle to the Corinthians (which had to be cut in two), and is not near as entertaining. But I always write my longest letters when I have something else to do. It seems so like being industrious. 'T is a temptation of the Devil. . . .

To R. W. Gilder
DEERFOOT FARM, *January* 16, 1888.

. . . If the Landor article be not yet printed I should like to make a correction therein. When I wrote it I sought in vain for a note I had made (when my memory was fresh) of what he said to me about "Old Daddy Wordsworth," as Thackeray used irreverently to call him.[1] I have now lighted on it, and this it is : —

"Mr. Wordsworth, a man may mix poetry with prose as much as he pleases, and it will only elevate and enliven ; but the moment he mixes a particle of prose with his poetry it precipitates the whole." If my version in the

[1] "Old Daddy Wordsworth," said Thackeray, "may bless his stars if he ever get high enough in heaven to black Tommy Moore's boots."

"Century" differs materially from this, I should
be glad to have this take its place, for I don't
like a lie even in the milder form of inaccuracy.
If I have got it nearly right in the "Century"
I shall be glad, because it will partly persuade
me that my memory is not so ruinous as I supposed. . . .

To the Misses Lawrence
DEERFOOT FARM, *January* 30, 1888.

. . . I am very busy in my old age, if I may
call my seventieth year so (on which I enter in
twenty-three days), when I feel as young as I
ever did. I have been printing a new collection
of my old poems, some of them already published in magazines (to help boil the pot for
the day), and some out of yellowing portfolios.
I shall send you a copy in due time, and you
must toss up which shall read it first — for I assume a natural eagerness in both of you. Then
I am revising my "Works" for a uniform edition in type so clear that I shall be able to read
them myself should I ever have the wish. I
have already read over one volume of my prose,
and am astonished to find how clever I used to
be. I give you my word for it, I was entertained
by the reading.

We have been having the coldest weather for
many years — cold and clear as a critique of
Matt Arnold's. Night before last our ther-

mometer (a very serious one and not given to exaggerations) marked forty-six degrees of frost on the honor of Fahrenheit. I like it, and if you could see the long stretch of snowy peace (with no track of the interviewer's hoof in it) I look at from my windows, you would think that Winter had his compensations. When you *do* have snow in London, it has lost its innocence and looks as if it had come out of the slums. . . .

To Mrs. Leslie Stephen

DEERFOOT FARM, *February* 20, 1888.

. . . This is the first time you ever said anything to me that made me uncomfortable. But when you tell me that my lovely little goddaughter has been supplied with an autograph-book, an instrument of torture unknown even to the Inquisition, you make me shiver. Albums they used to be called and, after exhausting the patience of mankind, hope to continue their abominable work under an alias.

Stammbücher the Germans call them (who, cunning in the invention of bores, invented this also), and I rather like the name, because *stamm* has an imprecatory sound and rhymes honestly with the d—n that rises to one's lips when one sees a specimen. However, I will write in Virginia's, that she may have the pleasure of wondering one of these days how her mother ever could have loved so dull a fellow. . . .

To Lady Lyttelton

DEERFOOT FARM, *February* 20, 1888.

. . . In one sense it matters very little who our ancestors were, though in another it is of enormous import to us, for they help make us what we are ; but we can't do anything about it. There they were, and here they are, all the while dominant in our lives and fates, whether we will or no. On the whole, the weather is a more substantial topic, and we have had loads of it this winter. It has been so whimsical that one fancies the clerk of the weather gone mad, and asks one's neighbor, "What do you think he is going to do next?" He is like a raw 'pothecary-prentice who, having poured too much out of the wrong bottle, in his agitation pours too much out of the right. He has contrived to mix all four seasons together till neither he nor we can tell which is which. . . . .

I watch your politics from my loophole of retreat and am interested in the Irish question. I admire Balfour's pluck, but am still a heretic, and believe that, when the time comes, Lord L. will borrow Mr. G.'s axe to cut the gordian knot with. In a day of newspapers and of a public opinion enlightened (whether from above or below) to an alarming degree, you cannot govern men by antiquated methods, however good they may once have been. Meanwhile, *plectuntur Achivi*, it is the landlords that are hit, and must make a worse bargain with every day of haggling. All the arguments in such cases are always on one side except one, and that is the strong point with the progress of events. This mysterious because invisible entity — invisible, I mean, at any given moment — has a way of persuading the Court to rule out our evidence on the ground that *la force prime le droit.* " I am stronger than thou " is as incontrovertible now as it was among the cave dwellers. . . .

I look up and see the garden at ——, with its dear group of last summer figures before me, and take heart again. Here are young creatures that can still look forwards confidently, with tow enough on the distaff still to spin long and happy destinies, and Atropos hides the shears behind her back.

To C. E. Norton

DEERFOOT FARM, *February* 21, 1888.

. . . I have n't had much of a week. My wits are sluggish as cold molasses. I have to wait for a thaw like my neighbor the brook here, who is in fine vein this morning, as contemptuous of dams as a Universalist. I never could get any good by Johnson's recipe of " setting doggedly about it." Perhaps I don't take a strong enough dose. . . .

Deerfoot Farm

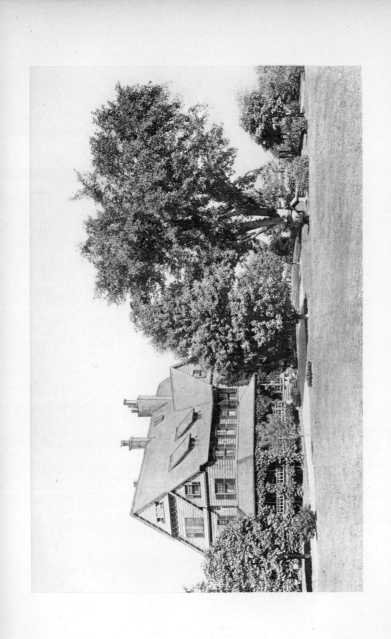

To the Same

DEERFOOT FARM, *March* 11, 1888.

. . . I have been having a very blue week — unable to do anything that I ought to be doing, and of no earthly use (of heavenly there is no question) in the world. . . . But yesterday I received a certain amount of self-satisfaction in a foolish way. I had been reading about Alcott, and was reminded that forty years ago I wrote something about him myself. I read it, and found that, though I could now amend it here and there, I had said gayly pretty much what people are saying seriously now, and this pleased me. Therefore I write to you as my literary executor, to say the second of " Studies for Two Heads " was a sketch from the living Alcott. It must have been written before 1850. Read it and see how you like it. Lord, how easily I used to write ! — too easily, I think now. But I could n't help it. Everything came at a jump and all of a piece. In reading this over again, I doubt if my pencil hesitated once in writing it or made a correction afterwards. Perhaps this is why I never value what I have done till long enough after to have forgotten it (as in this case), and then sometimes, but not often, I am goose enough to be pleased !

. . . Heigh-ho ! everything is beginning to seem long ago to me now and everything grows dreamy — but I shall wake now before long. I think it is partly that I can't realize myself here in Southborough. I don't get wonted. I walk to the post office or over the hills, and though I have every evidence that earth is solid under my feet, yet it crumbles away at every step and leaves me in dreamland. *Is* there anything solid outside the mind ? Or is one a little *cracked* now and then ? Sometimes in my lonely lunes I fancy it, and then Fact gives me a smart rap on the head and it rings clear again. . . .

To T. B. Aldrich

DEERFOOT FARM, *March* 19, 1888.

. . . I liked your little poem about Brownell both for its own sake and for being what Lessing used to call a *Rescue*. But this is not my reason for writing. What I meant to tell you about was one of those coincidences of which so much is made nowadays. Yesterday morning I found myself all of a sudden thinking of Brownell (though I couldn't for my life remember his name) and of those fine Norse-hearted poems of his. I fell into the same line of thought with you in your poem — though mine didn't achieve such gracious curves as yours. Now, I can't recollect that I had thought of Brownell for years, nor could I excogitate any suggestion, by association or otherwise, that should make me think of him then.

I was on my way to take down a volume of
Dyce's " Middleton " from the shelf when he
(anonymously, too, as I have said) dropt in.
So sudden and unforewarned was it that I
thought it very odd at the time and tried in vain
to account for it. The man himself came back
to me vividly as I saw him some twenty years
ago at our Saturday Club. He had a single
touch of vulgarity about him — he dyed his
hair (or beard, I forget which — perhaps both).
But he was so modest that one soon forgot it
as one does a uniform, though a little discon-
certing at first. So I said to him, " I remember
your face perfectly well, but can't recall your
name, and I remember, too, how your great
guns used to *jump* — was n't that the word ? "

Well, in the evening came your poem and
gave me the label for my poet. I really think
it was rather odd. 'T was better to remember
his poems, though, than his name, was n't it ?
But don't you go to rescuing anybody else,
for I might not again verify the proverb that
les beaux esprits se rencontrent, and my story
of how far off your coming shone would be
spoiled. .   .   *

To C. E. Norton

DEERFOOT FARM, *March* 27, 1888.

. . . I have n't had a very blessed week. If
I could manage the gymnastic feat of jumping

off my own shadow, I should do well enough. But it is difficult. And yet I fancy that they who accomplish it are the only ones who have a chance at being happy or reasonably successful. I am such an ill-conditioned mixture of folly and common-sense as makes me despair sometimes. My Folly whispers me, " Now do something really good, as good as you know how," and so I do something, and it is n't so good as I know how. Then comes Common-sense and says, " Why in the dumps? It makes no odds in the end." Very true, but the end may be a good way off, and meanwhile? . . .

Well, I shall hope to see you on Saturday, and I hope the weight will be lifted for a while. But I am to speak in New York, and that depresses me. What can I say that I and everybody else has n't said fifty times before? And then my way of saying things does n't answer for the Philistines, and they are the important people after all. . . .

To the Same

DEERFOOT, *March* 29, 1888.

. . . I was a little consoled yesterday by getting a letter from ——, which she had sagaciously addressed to " Scarborough, Maine," on the cover of which the postmaster of that ilk had written, " No such party known here."

How —— ever found out there was such a place and where it was I can't imagine, but although the P. M. *did* call me a " party," there was a kind of comfort in thinking of a place where I had never been heard of. I am thinking of migrating thither and beginning life anew as an honest burgher whose soul has never ventured into a region above buttons.

But by Jove! there's a bluebird warbling, God bless him! 'T is the best news this many a day. . . .

To the Same

DEERFOOT, *March* 30, 1888.

. . . I was seeing things all night long; they were all beautiful and bright. One night I saw Michael with his scales, and made a poem of it next morning which rescued me from a prose article I was trying to write for a young fellow in Chicago. I sent him the verses (which cost me but half an hour) instead. You will see and like 'em too, I hope.

I am persuaded that the D—l has been abroad in great wrath, but not because his time is short unhappily. I am thankful for the immense ballast of common-sense I carry. It sinks me too deep in the water sometimes for my keel to plough air as a poet's should, but it keeps my top-hamper steady when the wind blows as it has lately.

" Timon " was n't a bad medicine. The text
is one of the worst among all the plays. 'T is
wrapt in smoke, but with awful gushes of flame
now and then as from a world on fire. . . .

To Mrs. Edward Burnett

2 RADNOR PLACE, HYDE PARK, W.,
May 13, 1888.

. . . London has been very pleasant this
week — I mean the weather; not a raindrop
since my last letter. And I find a childish
pleasure in the vision of splendor it offers me.
I like the difficulty I find in crossing the drive-
way in Hyde Park for the throng of equipages.
I like to see so many people capable of lux-
uries that are beyond my reach. I wonder
whether I should like it as well if I could n't
afford to hire a hansom? I half think I should.
It is very odd to be snatched from my cell at
Deerfoot and caught up by this whirl of break-
fasts, luncheons, teas, dinners, and " goings-
on." I am sure I like Deerfoot best, and can't
quite make it clear to myself why I am here.
Yet you would be pleased with the warmth of
my welcome. . . .

It is so fine to-day that I can't help wishing
I were in Kensington Gardens, where the new
leafage brightens into blossoms against the
smoke-blackened trunks, and the thrushes are
singing as if they would never be old. It is

odd to see the battered old trees there come out in their new spring fashions like dowagers who dress young. I shall be walking across presently. . . .

To the Same

2 RADNOR PLACE, HYDE PARK, W.,
June 24, 1888.

. . . You know that my correspondence is apt to have gaps in it, like a saw with which some enterprising boy like Francis has been experimenting, and I felt sure that you would explain this last one by my journey to Bologna.[1] That, indeed, was the immediate cause of it. The heat was of the best quality, and I felt a good part of the time as I suppose a dissolving view must when it is fulfilling its destiny. But the consequence of that and of the fatigues I underwent was in long last a fit of gout from which I am just recovering. Luckily for me it came to a head gradually, and I was able (with the kind aid of my fellow-travellers Professors Ramsay and Ferguson, of Glasgow) to make the journey of thirty-one hours without break from Milan to London. I look back upon it now with amazement when I think that I am on the edge of seventy. Had I stopped on the way I should be there now, for I have been

[1] To be present as a delegate from Harvard, at the celebration of the eight hundredth anniversary of the University.

flat on my back since I arrived here eight days
ago. . . .

. . . The gout hardly tolerates any distrac-
tion on the part of those it visits, and the material for a letter accumulates slowly. I hold
my cup patiently under the faucet, I shake the
cask, and it is odds if a draggling drop fall now
and then. I don't think that one's meditations
on the universe are exactly the material for a
letter or likely to prove so entertaining, not to
say profitable, as Swift's on a broomstick. The
outward world may be an illusion of the senses
— one is often tempted to think it such; but
solitary confinement without even so much as
Bruce's spider, or Silvio Pellico's mouse, soon
teaches one how dependent on it we are for
mental enlivenment. The silk-worm and the
spider are the only creatures which can spin
their own insides to advantage; and the former
is nothing to the purpose, since he spins 'em
only to exclude himself from the world, while
the latter can profit by his gift of nature only
when he finds coigns of vantage on which
to hitch the web that is to catch his flies for
him. This was Montaigne's method, and the
connection of his essays is never logical, but is

dictated by the accidental prominence of corners of his memory to which he can attach the thread of his discourse. But an essay is not a letter, as you have discovered by this time. The meaning of all this is that my life has been wholly without incident for the last three weeks. To-day is marked by an event of grave importance. I have had my boots on and mock at my crutch. . . .

To Miss E. G. Norton
2 RADNOR PLACE, HYDE PARK, W.,
July 12, 1888.

. . . Your letter was even more welcome than you could have expected, for it brought a vision of your gracious presence to me while I was prostrate with gout and specially in need of such consolations. It was very nice of you to think of me and to show me that you did in such a charming way. . . .

I occupied my enforced leisure in reading the comedies of Eugène Labiche, which greatly amused me. Since I have been getting better I have read the lives of Archbishop Trench and of W. E. Forster. I knew them both, and the books interested me accordingly, especially the latter. It is pleasant to read about men whom one can respect so much, however one may dissent from some of their opinions. . . .

To Leslie Stephen
WHITBY, *August 22,* 1888.

. . . I like Whitby as well as ever, weather
or no, but find it harder than ever to be jolly.
I feel that I am going downstairs at last, and
am not even consoled by the *esprit d'escalier*.
But I have found the drawing-room pleasant,
on the whole, and liked the people there. . . .

To Mrs. Leslie Stephen
WHITBY, *August 23,* 1888.

. . . I am rather lame to-day because I
walked too much and over very rough paths
yesterday. But how could I help it? For I
will not give in to Old Age. We started, a
dozen of us, at half past ten, as agreed on the
day before. The clouds were heaping ominously
in the N. W., and soon it began to rain in a
haphazard kind of way, as a musician who
lodges over one lets his fingers idle among the
keys before he settles down to the serious business of torture. So it went on drowsily, but
with telling effects of damp, till we reached Falling Foss, which we saw as a sketch in water-
colors and which was very pretty. We had left
our wagonette at Little Neck, where we were to
lunch, and walked thither to meet it by a footpath along the valley of the stream. This was
a very up-and-down business, and especially

slippery from clayeyness of soil, especially to me who had on tennis shoes for the ease of my feet, the india-rubber soles of which lent themselves gladly to all the sliding passages of the performance. I was unable to maintain that sedateness of gait which Dante commends as essential to dignity, but escaped without a tumble by dint of much impromptu gymnastics.

Thunderstorms loitered about over the valley, like 'Arries on a bank holiday, at a loss what to do with their leisure, but ducking us now and then by way of showing their good humor. However, there were parentheses of sunshine, and, on the whole, it was very beautiful. After lunch, being assured that the footpath (two miles and a half in the Yorkshire dialect) from Little Neck to Sleeghts was much easier, I resolved to attempt it. It turned out harder than we expected, owing to slipperiness, and we had to cross the swollen stream three times, leaping from unsteady stone to stone as we could. Episodes of thunderstorm as before all the way. We got in at last; I with my feet giving me twinges like toothache at every step. The sun came out and the hills were glorious all about us for the last half hour of walking. If you could have seen the golden heaven that deepened in the little mill-pond just before we arrived at Sleeghts! 'T was like the heart of a poet, no bigger than another's, but capable of holding so much! I don't regret my walk.

It is sunny and soft to-day, and I shall crawl out to bask a little, like the other pensioners of nature. It will not be long now ere I head for St. Ives. . . .

P. S. Pardon this letter. As I think back over it, I fear it must be like one of the business passages of the " Excursion." . . .

To the Same

3 Radnor Place, LONDON,
September 29, 1888.

. . . I have not been seriously at work on anything, but only entangled in the briery intricacies of George Meredith, like the poet of the " Romaunt of the Rose," and like him consoling my scratches with the assurance that there was a consummate flower hidden somewhere among them, of which one gets enchanting glimpses now and then. I am now reading Mrs. Green's " Henry II." with great edification.

But I am dissolute also. Last night I went to the Court Theatre, and saw, I am bound to say, one of the stupidest pieces of vulgarity that ever pleased a British public. Ah, if I were only capable of judging English civilization as American is judged, what a sermon might n't I preach! But I forbear. No, I won't give in.

I still insist that Britain produces a saint now
and then as fair as if they had stepped down
from an old painted window.

We have been having snivelling weather, but
to-day is sunshiny, and I am going to the private view of the " Arts and Crafts " Society —
a hopeless attempt, in my opinion, to reproduce
the happy inadvertence of mediæval art by de-
liberate forethought.   But I shall be glad to see
the Burne-Jones windows. . . .

To Miss Sedgwick

2 RADNOR PLACE, *October* 3, 1888.

. . . We are in the beginning of our foggy
season, and to-day are having a yellow fog, and
that always enlivens me, it has such a knack
of transfiguring things.   It flatters one's self-
esteem, too, in a recondite way, promoting one
for the moment to that exclusive class which
can afford to wrap itself in a golden seclusion.
It is very picturesque also.   Even the cabs are
rimmed with a halo, and people across the way
have all that possibility of suggestion which
piques the fancy so in the figures of fading frescos.   Even the gray, even the black fogs make
a new and unexplored world not unpleasing to
one who is getting palled with familiar landscapes. . . .

To F. H. Underwood
LONDON, *November* 3, 1888.

. . . I had recollected that you had asked
me if I would read what you had written about
me, and could not be quite sure whether you
had asked me by word of mouth or by letter.
You know my shyness about such things, so I
shall only say that what you said gave me as
much pleasure as at my age one is able to take
in such things. One's old self becomes with
time a kind of third person, in whom one
takes a certain friendly interest, with no in-
cursion of that partisanship which is apt to
disturb any discussion of one's actual self—
though less, I would fain think, in my own case
than in most. I fancy I might have accomplished more if I could have contrived to take
a greater interest in myself and my doings.
Perhaps not, for I should have been more conscious. . . .

To Lady Lyttelton
RADNOR PLACE, HYDE PARK,
November 11, 1888.

Dear Lady Lyttelton, — The last motive I
should ever attribute to you would be a selfish
one, and whenever you write to please yourself
you may be sure of pleasing me. Indeed, how
can one write naturally (which is the secret of

writing well) unless one contrive at the same time to please one's self. . . .

It is foggy to-day. You know that I don't mind that, but it is raining too, which is pushing a good thing too far, and shows a want of tact on the part of the weather. I can hardly see what I am writing, which prevents me from discovering whether I am dull or no. So you must not read me in too strong a light.

I sent you back the Life of Principal Shairp on Friday. You must have been surprised at my swift punctuality, but the truth is I am learning in my old age to skim over books at a pace like that of the swift Camilla. I get a very good notion of the general landscape and leave statistics to the gazetteers. . . .

I ventured to abuse the margin with a few comments in pencil as I went along, and hope you will forgive me. If you don't like it india-rubber will set all right again, or I will give you a clean copy. 'T is only stains on the mind that are ineffaceable. Meanwhile, I have a little poem in my head about some goldfish in a vase, which I think will be pretty, if ever I get it out. Oddly enough the picture part was impressed on my memory more than sixty years ago, when there was such a vase at Elmwood — I forget whether my mother's or my sister Mary's. With what unfailing delight I used to watch them, — the faint pulse of their fins as they rested, the heave of the gills, the sudden whirl into flashing motion, the unwinking eye with its vein of yellow ominously magnified by the liquid lens till it seemed the very eye of conscience herself! This is a sign of senescence, perhaps, that I recall early memories so vividly.

I hope it is n't raining at Perystone, but the English climate is such a dab at water-colors! Nevertheless I wish I was not going to leave it so soon.

To C. E. Norton
2 RADNOR PLACE, HYDE PARK, W.,
November 11, 1888.

. . . It is noon, and I am writing by candle-light. If I look over the way I can just see the houses vague as the architecture of Piranesi. But I like fogs; they leave the imagination so wholly to herself, or just giving her a jog now and then. I shall go out into the Park by and by, to lose myself in this natural poesy of London which makes the familiar strange. It is as good as travelling in the interior of Africa, without the odious duty of discovery, which makes the strange familiar. There is an ominous feel about it to which I never get wonted, as of the last day, and I listen with a shudder sometimes for the *tuba mirum spargens sonum*. I am still so much of a Puritan that the English words would shock me a little, as they did the other day at ———'s table, when I blurted them out to a parson's wife in my impulsive way, and made her jump as if she had heard the authentic instrument with her accounts but half made up.

There is nothing new here — there seldom is, and this is what makes it so comfortable. The Parnell Commission, like a wounded snake, drags its slow length along with an effect of bore silently and sootily pervasive as the fog of which I was just speaking. Unless some sudden Chinese cracker of *révélation intime* should go off, the world in general will have forgotten it ere it be over. I think Gladstone has at least effected so much — that he has brought Irish and English together on a common ground. Surely this is good so far as it goes, but how long the Irish will allow any ground on which they get a footing to remain common is to me at least problematical. I for one am getting tired of seeing *our* politics playing bob to *their* kite.

The Sackville squall has amused me a good deal, bringing out so strangely as it did the English genius for thinking all the rest of mankind unreasonable. One is reminded of the old story of the madman who thought himself alone in his sanity. I seldom care to discuss anything — most things seem so obvious — least of all with the average Briton, who never is willing to take anything for granted and whose eyes are blind to all side-lights. Yes, there is one thing they always take for granted, namely, that an American *must* see the superiority of England. They have as little tact as their *totem* the bull. I have come to the edge of my temper several times over the Sackville business — always introduced by them. " All Europe is laughing at you, you know," said Sir—— —— to me genially the other day. " That is a matter of supreme indifference to us," I replied blandly, though with a keen temptation to pull a pair of ears so obtrusively long. But with all that there is a manliness about them I heartily like. Tact, after all, is only a sensitiveness of nerve, and there is but a hair's-breadth between this and irritability. . . .

P. S. Fancy! I shall have reached David's limit in three months.

To Mrs. Edward Burnett
2 RADNOR PLACE, HYDE PARK, W.,
November 12, 1888.

. . . Alas! in this world we do not cast off our hair shirts. At best we turn them or put on clean ones that have n't lost their bite by wear. . . . If one is good for anything, the world is not a place to be happy in — though, thank God, there are better things than being happy. . . .

To Mrs. James T. Fields

68 BEACON STREET, *January* 21, 1889.

. . . It is very kind of you to offer me books, and I thank you heartily. But alas! it is not books — it is I that am wanting. I read as a swallow peruses the pool, with briefest dips at the surface. I suppose I shall feel the wind in my sails before long. At present I am be-calmed. In some corner of the sky there must be a breeze waiting. Or am I (as some teach) a machine? and has a grain of sand blown in somewhere? Never mind, I am much obliged to *you*. . . .

To Mrs. Edward Burnett

1608 K Street, WASHINGTON,
February 13, 1889.

. . . Philadelphia was very dinnery, of course, with lunches and Wister parties thrown in. No-thing could have been more agreeable than my host and hostess the Weir Mitchells, and every-body was kind. . . .

Here I am busy dining and receptioning again, but not now for the first time do I find that I am not the stuff of which lions are made. I feel as if I had on a false mane which might blow off at the first gust. Like Bottom "I no lion am, nor yet no lion's dam." But the shak-ing up I get does me good.

Yesterday afternoon Ned [1] and his chum gave me a tea which was very pleasant, and which Mrs. Cleveland honored with her presence. She is very pretty and gracious and bears herself very well.

I met the President and her at dinner with the Endicotts. He was very cordial, and there is a look of sentiment in his eyes in odd contrast with the burliness of his person. It is odd to be in a capital again and to renew the familiar round of official receptions with unfamiliar faces and ways. I have been struck with the fine figures and heads of the senators. They are really imposing, and seem to have been sifted out by a kind of natural selection. This morning, after a call on Mr. Bayard at the State Department, I called on Mrs. Cleveland at the White House. She was again very pleasing in a very pretty morning-gown. . . .

To C. E. Norton
1608 K Street, Washington,
February 15, 1889.

. . . I fear I never had that lively interest in folks that becomes a wise man — I mean *folks* in general. I somehow get to the end of them so soon that they begin to bore me sooner than they should.

I have seen some interesting people, never-

[1] Mr. Burnett, who was at this time a Member of Congress.

theless, and have been lucky in my hosts (the Mitchells and S. G. W.), who are always good company and hold out, having native springs in them, and not being merely taps of the general system of milk-and-water works. Ward is wonderfully young and like his former self. Hanging before me as I write are two landscapes of his in pastel, as good in their way as anything of the kind I ever saw, and his interest in good things is as lively as ever. Mrs. Ward, too, is little changed since I last saw her, and together they give me a queer feeling that I have come back to a place where we called a halt twenty years ago, and that in retracing my steps I have abolished the years between.

I have seen Bancroft twice and found him as vivid as ever. In answer to a question of mine he told me the odd fact that he learned German of Sidney Willard, who knew the language well, but must have been his own teacher, for he knew nothing of the pronunciation, so that Bancroft, when he arrived in Germany, had only to learn that in order to speak easily.

I have made also a very pleasant acquaintance in Mr. McCulloch, who called on me, a dear old man of eighty-five, rosy and fresh and gentle, looking more like an emeritus professor of philosophy than like a financier. . . .

To Mrs. James T. Fields
68 BEACON STREET, *February* 23, 1889.

. . . A rain of flowers came down on me yesterday as on a virgin-martyr, and the hard seventieth step of my climb was velveted with them. They were very sweet, but such gracious words from you two (to me, too) were even sweeter. That two such charming women[1] — since there are two of you I can say what I like without impertinence — should think of me so kindly makes all *man*kind a matter of indifference.

I shall hope to see you this afternoon, but may be circumvented. If I should be so lucky as to come, and you should observe a pinch of condescension in my manner, you will bear with it when I tell you that I was listening to my own praises for two hours last night[2] — and have hardly yet got used to the discovery of how great a man I am. A poison, you know, may be distilled from laurel leaves, and I think the very smell of them goes to the head. But, after all, *every*body is n't seventy, and there is a certain promotion from the mob in that! . . .

[1] Mrs. Fields and Miss Jewett.
[2] At a dinner in his honor at the Tavern Club.

To Mrs. Leslie Stephen
68 BEACON STREET, *February* 27, 1889.

. . . I have been forging over the reef of
my seventieth birthday into the smooth water
beyond without much damage to my keel, so
far as I can discover. Even had I been wrecked
I should have saved your box, as Camoëns did
his Lusiads. 'T is a beauty, and I shall fill my
pipe from it with a sense of virtue as if I were
doing something handsome. How adroitly in-
dulgent you women are. If you can't cleanse
us of our vices, you contrive to make them so
far as possible becoming.

I was dined on my birthday, and praised to
a degree that would have satisfied you, most
partial even of your sex. But somehow I liked
it, and indeed none but a pig could have helped
liking the affectionate way it was done. I suppose it is a sign of weakness in me somewhere,
but I can't help it. I *do* like to be liked. It
gives me a far better excuse for being about
(and in everybody's way) than having written
a fine poem does. *That'll* be all very well when
one is under the mould. But I am not sure
whether one will care for it much. So keep on
liking me, won't you?

It is very droll to be seventy. Don't scold
me for it — I 'll never do it again; but I don't
feel any older, I think, and I am sure I don't

III

feel any wiser, than I did before. 'T is a little depressing to be reminded that one has lived so long and done so little. When I measure the length with the achievement there is a horrible overlapping, but I shall expect a certain deference. Whatever condescension I show will be multiplied by seven instead of six, remember, and precious in proportion. . . .

To Mrs. S. Weir Mitchell

68 Beacon Street, BOSTON,
March 9, 1889.

Dear Mrs. Mitchell, — I am not so clever as you show yourself to be in the size of your sheets of paper, which reminds me of that prudence one learns in Italy of ordering one ration (*una porzione*) for two persons. Nor, though I have so many letters to write, and using as I do a more generous sheet, can I divest myself of the feeling that there is a kind of inhospitality in leaving my fourth page blank. Am I flattering myself, as we generally do when there is a choice of motives, by assuming that we act from the better? and is this feeling but a superstition derived from those heathen times (before yours) when a single postage was $18\frac{3}{4}$ cents (written in red ink, as if in the very life-blood of the correspondent), and one felt that one did n't get an honest pennyworth unless one filled every scribable corner of his foolscap?

Now, you think I mean by this that I should have answered your note sooner had I as tiny quarto as your own to write upon. But nothing of the kind. It was because I remembered that I had promised you something. . . .

I have been doing my best to be seventy, and have had a dinner, and all kinds of nice things were said about me, and it was very pleasant to think that people were so kind. But I feel that they were trying to make it up to me for having been guilty of some sort of gaucherie, as when one knocks over a stand with some frail thing on it that can't be replaced, and is condoled with " It 's not of the least consequence." Well, I have made up my mind never to do it again. But really I am quite ashamed to find how well people think of me, and yet I can't help liking it too. I feel as if it somehow justified my friends.

I often think of my pleasant week with you in Walnut Street. I have now two memories of Philadelphia, antithetic one to the other — the Quaker one of forty-five years ago, and that of yesterday so very unlike it, and both so good. How far away seems and is the first, for it is extinct as the dodo. It was very sweet in its provincial valley of self-sufficientness and contentment. It had a flavor beyond terrapin. But the telegraph has cosmopolitanized us in spite of ourselves; the whole world has but one set

of nerves, and we all have the headache together. And, after all, Europe has the advantage of us still, for it has been endowed with
the gift of prescience and hears what happens
here before it has happened. Do what we will,
they get the elder brother's portion. But I am
droning.

And I had taken my passage for the 27th
April, and now they insist on my being in New
York on the 30th to speak for Literature. I
had twice refused, for I think I am fairly entitled to my share of silence now; but they set
Holmes at me, they set Eliot at me, and I am
almost afraid I shall give in. I console myself
by stating and thinking that length also has in
it an element of majesty.

Well, I must leave you a small mercy of
blank paper yet, for I fly to the Cunard office
to see if I can make some arrangement that will
comport with my martyrization. Would I had
the proper spirit that Borachio showed when
they told him to come out and be hanged.

With kindest regards to Dr. Mitchell and
your daughter and the MacVeaghs (of whom I
had too short a glimpse here) and Marguerite,
and with remembrances to whoever remembers
me,

        Affectionately yours,

                    J. R. LOWELL.

To Lady Lyttelton

68 BEACON STREET, *March* 13, 1889.

Dear Lady Lyttelton, — This time I should score a point against you by writing while you are still in my debt, were it not for my consciousness that between us two the debt must always be on my side. I saw you in fancy at the Parnell Commission the other day. The letters (as I always supposed they would) have turned out to be forgeries, and my old proposition to make Parnell Irish Secretary does not look so whimsical as it did then. I suppose the Liberals will be as foolish in their exultation as the Tories were in their confidence, as if the real matter of dispute were of persons and parties and not the old Irish question, which survives as unpleasantly pertinacious as ever. I confess that I feel a profound sympathy for Parnell, in whose sincerity I have always believed, and who is the only hope of a conservatory policy in Ireland.

After several months of a very draggly and dowdy condition I have managed to be seventy without any particular personal exertion and have felt better and younger ever since. . . .

Yesterday Mabel and I went up to Southborough together to hunt for some papers. . . . I found what I sought, which will surprise you who are painfully familiar with the confusion (as you think it) of my papers. It was odd to find Southborough already grown so strange to me, though it is not yet a year since I saw it last. I felt like a ghost revisiting its old haunts, and was astonished when anybody saluted me. But I am used to this ghostly feeling now. I can hardly believe that anything outside me is real. . . .

To S. Weir Mitchell

68 BEACON STREET, *April 2*, 1889.

Dear Mitchell, — Your letter of St. Valentine's day would not have waited so long for an answer had the address on the cover been in your own handwriting. As it was, I too hastily concluded the missive to be from an autograph hunter, one of those perverse persons who seek for a sign and to whom no sign shall be given. I tossed it among a heap of others on the top of a revolving bookstand at my elbow, and there it lay all these weeks without any sign of ill humor. But yesterday, as I reached for a book, one letter disengaged itself from the rest and fell on the floor at my feet. I picked it up, observed that it had never been opened, again took it for an autograph beggar, and was about to toss it back among its fellows, when it struck me that it was too thin to contain a stamped envelope. So I opened it, and there was your valentine. The thing struck me as odd. There was a heap of letters, this one was not on top,

and yet was the only one that struggled forth
and fell. How explain these mysteries? Chance
is a mighty clever fellow.

I was deeply interested in your pamphlet. I
think it lays most of the ghosts, perhaps not
all. I believe them all (so far as they seem to
be objectively visible) figments of the brain.
But my doubt is whether there must not have
been some preceding impression of the near-
ness of that person whose eidolon seems to be
seen in order to produce the image. Given that
impression, the imagination sees that person
(with all the accidents of gait, gesture, dress
even) as the eye had been accustomed to see
him when in the body. (I am thinking of a
German ghost which paraded in a bottle-green
coat with brass buttons.) To be sure this perhaps is only proposing an alternative explanation of phenomena better, at least more simply,
accounted for by your cases. I have long believed my own visions to be *all my eye*, though
I cannot remember that they were ever followed
by headache. Those could be shut out by clos-
ing the lids; but what of those I see with my
eyes shut, that come and go and change without my will, or even in spite of it? Is everything one has ever seen laid away in the eye as
a photographer stores his negatives? And is
there something analogous in the mind's eye,
the memory?

I was particularly struck with the case of the lady who observed that the movements of her sister's image were governed by that of her own eye. What a happy example of the difference between lookers and seers, between the ordinary and the scientific habit of mind.

By the way, have you sent your pamphlets to the psychical-research men? To William James, for example. To me a physical marvel is as interesting as a spiritual one, though in a different way. Pardon my garrulity, busy man that you are, and, with kindest regards to Mrs. Mitchell, be sure that I am

Faithfully yours,

J. R. LOWELL.[1]

To the Same

BOSTON, *May* 16, 1889.

My dear Mitchell, — I am vainly trying to work my correspondence up to date before I

---

[1] Note by Dr. Mitchell : —

"My sending the essay alluded to arose out of a long talk about ghosts, which took us deep into the night twice during the fortnight spent with us in 1889. Mr. Lowell told me that since boyhood he had been subject to visions, which appeared usually in the evening. Commonly he saw a figure in mediæval costume which kept on one side of him. The last vision he had was while staying at an English country-house. After dinner, in the drawing-room, he saw a figure in the dress of a mediæval scholar. The form was very distinct. It beckoned to him, and, determined to see where it would go,

sail day after to-morrow. I have been thoroughly fagged with an introduction to the "Complete Angler," which I had pledged myself to finish ere I went. But I must write a line of thanks for the book which came this morning. I have stolen time to read so much as would enable me to tell you how much I like it (the "Dream Song" is exquisite) — almost more than the other, and that is saying a great deal. It is rather hard on us old fellows to wait so long and then push us from our stools. I am half minded to study medicine if that's what does it.

With kindest regards to Mrs. Mitchell,
Cordially yours,
J. R. LOWELL.

To R. W. Gilder
68 BEACON STREET, *May* 16, 1889.

. . . When I saw you last I told you I had disappointed you, and so I had, and quite rightly too, though you denied it as you were bound to do. I don't mean that the speech[1] was bad as speeches go, to judge by the latest quotations, but I delivered it as if I thought it

he followed it out on to the terrace, where of a sudden it disappeared."

[1] In response to the toast, "Our Literature," at the banquet in New York, given in commemoration of the hundredth anniversary of Washington's Inauguration.

was. The truth was that they made me write it out before I was ready, and that tempted me to try committing it to memory and I could n't, and I had no entire copy and that bothered me. Then I was disheartened by the size of the house. The sort of things I am apt to say are not exactly to be bawled, and without bawling I might as well have expected to fill the Cave of Kentucky. I felt as Jack Ketch must after the Star Chamber was abolished and the fine crops of the plentiful Prynne and Bastwick years were gone, when he looked about on the harvest of ears ripening for his sickle, but denied to its hungry edge. There were the ears (long or otherwise), but I knew they were beyond my reach. I slumped into my temperament.

However, I did not cry over it. I was too busy. I have been writing an introduction to the " Complete Angler," and a poem which I have had in my head for a good while, and which buzzed so the moment my brain went a-Maying that I had to let it out. I wonder whether you will like it. I rather hope you may.

You will be glad to hear that I hope to have a home of my own again when I come back in the fall. I think it probable that I can arrange to live at Elmwood with my daughter. I could n't without her. 'T is worth trying. . . .

To Mrs. W. K. Clifford
2 RADNOR PLACE, HYDE PARK, W.,
June 11, 1889.

Dear Mrs. Clifford, — You ask me as many questions as if you were a Royal Commission, and two of them — " Do I know you ? " and " Do you know me ? " — are simply unanswerable, though I think I might answer one of them after a fashion by saying that I never knew a single woman in my life — each of them being so various (I won't add the poet's other epithet) and so apt, like Darwin's insects, but more quickly, to put on whatever self-protective color of sympathy suits their immediate purpose or need.

Somewhere in Scripture (in Proverbs, I think, attributed to Solomon, who had an unrivalled experience in this branch of natural history) a great many disagreeable things are said about women, but I do not remember that " putting their foot in it " is to be found in the indictment. But you have managed to do so — just the smallest foot in the world, of course. You say you had " forgotten " me last winter. Precisely what I supposed. *Habeo confitentem deam!* Why could n't you have said " neglected " and saved my pride ?

As for the weather, you put your case very prettily, but so far as I am concerned I always make my own. My weather is purely subjective. When I say I make my own I mean that it is made for me, but in my own workshop and in my own little theatre.

Typewriters quotha! They are as bad as postal-cards. Both of them are unclean things I have never touched. Typewriting is hard to read also, harder even than you. I am sure I could never say what I would if I had to pick out my letters like a learned pig, and on a wooden keyboard too. But what is all this to the purpose? What I mean to say is, that I will come Wednesday afternoon. . . .

Faithfully yours,
J. R. Lowell.

To Mrs. Edward Burnett

Whitby, August 4, 1889.

. . . I came hither two days ago and was received with enthusiasm by the Misses Galilee, my landladies. 'T is my third year with them, and they vow they will never let my rooms (the best in the house) so long as there is any chance of my coming. I like it as much as ever. You know the view from my window by Chadwick's little sketch. I never weary of it. The Abbey says to me, " The best of us get a little shaky at last, and there get to be gaps in our walls," and then the churchyard adds, " But you 've no notion what good beds there are at my inn."

We made a tea-party yesterday afternoon to
Rigg Mill, where dwell a dear old couple named
Harrison. He talks a pure Yorkshire that delights my soul. The mill runs no longer, but
the stream does, down through a leafy gorge
in little cascades and swirls and quiet pools with
skyscapes in them, and seems happy in its holiday. It is a very pretty spot and belonged to
the monks once. . . .

To Mrs. Leslie Stephen
WHITBY, *August* 11, 1889.

. . . The Abbey looks across over the red
roofs into my window and seems to say, "Why
are you not at church to-day?" and I answer
fallaciously, "Because like yourself I have gone
out of the business, and, moreover, I am writing to a certain saint of my own canonization
who looks amazingly as your St. Hilda must
have looked (as I fancy her), and the thought
of whom has both prayers and praise in it."
The Abbey does n't look satisfied, but I am —
so the Abbey may go hang! Besides, am I not
honoring the day with a white shirt and well-
blackened boots? and when I presently go out
shall I not crown my head with a chimney-pot
hat? which, rather than the cross, is the sym-
bol of the Englishman's faith — being stiff,
hollow, pervious to the rain, and divided in
service between Babylon and Sion.

This is my ninth year at Whitby, and the place loses none of its charm for me. It is better than Cornwall, except inasmuch as Cornwall has St. Erth's in it, where sometimes one has beatific visions. I find a strange pleasure in that name too, so homely and motherly, as if some pope had suddenly bethought himself to canonize this dear old Earth of ours so good to us all, and give the body as well as the soul a share in those blessed things. My happiness is so much at the mercy of obscure sympathies and antipathies that perhaps I am less at ease among a Celtic population (though I fancy them more refined) than among these men of Danish stock with whom I own kinship of blood. But you are enough to leaven the biggest batch of Celts that ever was baked, so I am coming to you as soon as I leave Whitby, or shall it be later? . . .

Whitby is coming more and more into the great currents of civilization. We have a spasmodic theatre and an American circus that seems a fixture. Last year there was a delightful clown who really looked as if he could n't help it, and was a wonderful tumbler too. How the children would have liked it! One other amusement is the Spa, where there is a band of music bad enough to please the Shah. It is brilliantly lighted, and at night it is entertaining to sit above and watch the fashionable world laboriously diverting themselves by promenading to and fro in groups, like a village festival at the opera. The sea, of course, is as fine and as irreconcilable as ever. Thank God, they can't landscape-garden *him*. I think I have confessed to you before that our colors are not so southern as yours. On the land they are as good as they can be in range, variety, and fickleness. . . .

To C. E. Norton

WHITBY, *August* 18, 1889.

. . . You are a little severe in your judgment of English society. Buffalo Bill has been taken up by a certain layer of society, but not, I should say, by society in its better sense. The —— has debased a considerable circle, the circumference of which is spreading, as in stagnant pools a circle once started will. There is a partial truth in what you say about society here losing its fastidiousness, but this is mainly true of the ——'s set, and those who are infected by it or wish to be of it. I have not met B. B., but Colonel Colville told me (you know him, I think ?) that B. B. was one of the finest men he ever saw and of princely manners. Moreover, he is really a Somebody and the best of his kind. But I think the true key to this eagerness for lions — even of the poodle sort — is the dulness of the average English mind. I never come back here without being struck with it.

Henry James said it always stupefied him at
first when he came back from the Continent.
What it craves beyond everything is a sensation,
anything that will serve as a Worcestershire
sauce to its sluggish palate. We of finer and
more touchy fibre get our sensations cheaper,
and do not find Wordsworth's emotion over a
common flower so very wonderful. People are
dull enough on our side of the ocean-stream
also, God wot; but here, unless I know my
people, I never dare to let my mind gambol.
Most of them, if I ever do, look on like the
famous deaf man at the dancers, wondering to
what music I am capering. They call us super-
ficial. Let us thank God, dear Charles, that our
nerves are nearer the surface, not so deeply em-
bedded in fat or muscle that wit must take a
pitchfork to us.

I am fairly contented here, almost happy
sometimes, nay, should be often, could I jump
off my own shadow. I know no expedient to
get rid of it but Peter Schlemihl's, and alas,
nobody, not even the D—l, thinks mine worth
buying. 'T is a beautiful place, with associations
that touch me deeply when I am conscious of
them, and qualify my mood insensibly when I
am not. I have done some reading in Lope de
Vega, but am not drawn to him or by him as
to and by Calderon. Yet he is wonderful, too,
in his way. . . .

Whitby

To Mrs. Edward Burnett

WHITBY, *August* 20, 1889.

. . . To-day it is raining (as it rains here) with a gentle persistence, as if to convince one by degrees that it is the proper thing to do. I think of the burthen of the old ballad,

> " The rain rins doun through Merryland toun,
> Sae does it along the Po."

I fancy the old fellow who made it was trying to console himself for a rainy day like this by making believe it was raining even in Italy, too, all the time. But we have had good weather on the whole, and the moors are born again in the purple. I went to Aislaby Moor yesterday and lay on my back on the springy heather, making the bees very wroth. They querulously insisted that the heather I covered was the very heather they had been saving for that morning. But they did not push things to extremities with me. I couldn't help wishing the children had been there, they would have been so happy in that wilderness of bloom. They would have thought, as everybody does, that the blossoms a little farther on were finer than those about their feet. . . .

III

To Mrs. James T. Fields

WHITBY, *August 27,* 1889.

Dear Mrs. Fields, — . . . I must write now while it rains, for Whitby is a place that won't let you have a moment to yourself if it can be prevented. The Abbey wants you, the beach wants you, Robin Hood's Bay, Sands-end, Rigg Mill, Falling Foss (is n't that a name to seduce from virtue?), the Moors, all want you. And while one is here, everybody expects letters from one because one has nothing to do — as if that did n't make it all the harder to do anything else. Oh, could you only see my Abbey, as gray as a ghost there on the cliff across the river! Could you only see my moors! I walked over the highest and broadest of them yesterday with the cairn of some nameless old British chief at the top, where he could see the northern ocean as he lay. All about were other hills and other moors in all the glory of their heather, flushing with pleasure as the sun fondled them with a careless ray now and then from between the downy clouds and swept on to nestle among the wheat-sheafs in the field below. But is not all this written in the guidebooks which may be had for twopence halfpenny? . . . And so you liked my poem even without the succor of the voice? I am glad to think so. And the "Herald" liked it too? All very well, but the thing is to like it oneself. I wish I could learn that trick. 'T is the prettiest in all authorship. And I never could hit it off. While the metal is molten and running, it is as it should be, or seems so. But afterwards one finds so many flaws in the moulds one runs it into ! I never could be pleased with anything I had done when it was three days old. I take comfort in liking what other people do. It does n't matter. I dare say the old chief up in the cairn there wrote verses when he was young. What does he care about 'em now? We shall all be behind the impregnable rampart of a headstone ere long. And yet I like to write things too. I have just been writing another of a totally different kind which perhaps you will see some day and must try to like. Poets are the only miners who don't discover when their vein runs out. They keep picking away as if nothing had happened. I always try honestly to put some meaning into what I write and to pack it in as small compass as I can. Perhaps I have not allowed Music so much place as she deserves, but, after all, Music is but Thought's trainbearer and should n't try to walk in front at the manifest risk of tripping up her mistress. . . . How it will be with me, when I get back to Elmwood, I cannot say. There will be much food for moodiness there, and the edges of a broken life will never quite match, even were there any cement that would knit them together, and who has ever invented that? However, I think I shall be compelled to work, if only to keep the blue devils away, and that is a good in itself. This is a queer life of ours, and could we have it as we would, it would perhaps disappoint us oftener. One is apt to moralize a good deal at a watering-place, you see.

I am coming home towards the end of October, by which time you will be in Charles Street again, looking out at the prettiest view in the world. It has but one fault, — there is no ruined Abbey in it to set one an example of dignity in dilapidation. The tower of Memorial Hall makes but a poor fist of it as a substitute. But you have water and sunset, and they go a good way towards happiness.

Now I am called for to go down Flowergate (what do you say to that for a name?) to do some shopping. Give my kindest regards to Miss Jewett if she be with you, as I hope she is for both your sakes.

The bells in the Abbey Church are chiming for a wedding.

          Faithfully yours,

               J. R. LOWELL.

To Thomas Hughes

WHITBY, *August* 28, 1889.

. . . Whitby is as good as ever, and has now another pleasant association in recalling you and Mrs. Hughes. We go to the old moors and the old mills as usual, though our weather has been a little wrong side out a good deal of the time. Yesterday we had a thrilling experience in being taken (as we suppose) by the hostile fleet. At any rate, three men-o'-war first came in — very unlike the noble creatures that landed royal Charlie — and fired three heavy guns at us, and as we have no visible means of support, I take it we surrendered and that I am now a prisoner of war. I am glad I saw those guns fired, for the smoke behaved in a very strange and beautiful way, first rising a little in a dense cloud and in a semicircle of lingering Staubbachs, completely veiling the villanous-looking monsters that belched them forth.

As they did n't put us on parole, Mrs. —— and I went to Scarborough — an expedition I had promised her these nine years, which I thought it hardly safe to put off any longer at my age. We had a fine day, and enjoyed ourselves highly. I had always wished to see the place since I read " A Trip to Scarborough," of which I remember now nothing more than the name. We went up to the Castle (which had a superbly impregnable aerie before the invention of gunpowder), where we saw the volunteer artillery encamped, resolved to save Scarborough from the fate of Whitby or die. But the fleet never came, and the band did its best to keep up the spirits of the men under this disappointment. We saw them drilling with the stretchers, which had a grewsome look, and heard the far-off grumble of a sea-fight which was going on somewhere behind the haze. We had the satisfaction of communicating to one of the officers the fall of Whitby, which hardly seemed to sadden him so much as it ought — so little do rival watering-places feel each other's misfortunes. Then we went to the Spa, lunched at an eating-house as good as it was cheap, and then sat watching the crowd. They all had the air of second-hand gentility trying very hard to make itself believe it was first-hand. It wasn't shabby gentility, but the profusely new thing which is far worse. It takes several generations to make clothes unconscious. But the place was gay and as many-colored as Joseph's coat, and I liked it for an hour or two. Particularly I liked the little open traps with one horse ridden by a postilion with silken jerkins and caps of the brightest hues. I sat with immense satisfaction behind one whose jacket (stripes red and white) recalled the flag of my country. On the whole we had a successful day, and on the way home one of the most surprisingly original and beautiful sunsets I ever saw. . . .

Affectionately yours,

J. R. LOWELL.

To Mrs. Leslie Stephen

WHITBY, *September 11, 1889.*

. . . For the last few days we have been having American weather, except for the haze which softens and civilizes (perhaps I should say, artistically generalizes) all it touches, like the slower hand of time. It does in a moment what the other is too long about for the brevity of our lives. How I do love this unemphatic landscape, which suggests but never defines, in which so much license is left to conjecture and divination, as when one looks into the mysterious beyond. And how the robins and some other little minstrels whose names I don't know keep on pretending it is the very fresh of the year. I think few people are made as happy by the singing of birds as I, and this autumnal music (unknown at home), every bush a song, is one of the things that especially endear England to me. Even without song, birds are a perpetual delight, and the rooks alone are enough to make this country worth living in. I wish you could see a rook who every morning busies himself among the chimney-pots opposite my chamber window. For a good while I used to hear his chuckle, but thought he was only flying over. But one day I got out of bed and looked out. There he was on the top of a chimney opposite, perambulating gravely, and now and then cocking his head and looking down a flue. Then he would chuckle and go to another. Then to the next chimney and *da capo*. He found out what they were going to have for breakfast in every house, and whether he enjoyed an imaginary feast or reckoned on a chance at some of the leavings I know not, but he was evidently enjoying himself, and that is always a consoling thing to see. Even in the stingy back-yards of these houses too, wherever there is a disconsolate shrub a robin comes every morning to cheer it up a bit and help it along through the day.

Since I wrote what I did about the weather (one should always let the Eumenides alone) it has begun to rain, but gently, like a rain that was trying to discriminate between the just and the unjust, and sympathized with those confiding enough to leave their umbrellas behind them (I hate to expose *mine* any more than I can help, for reasons of my own). So the rain let me get back dry from the beach, whither I had gone for a whiff of salt air and a few earfuls of that muffled crash of the surf which is so soothing — perpetual ruin with perpetual renewal.

I wonder if your moors have been as gracious as ours this year. I never know how deeply they impress me till long after I have left them, and then I wonder at the store of images wherewith they have peopled my memory. But what is the use of my asking you any questions when you tell me you could not read my last letter? Was it the blue paper with its ribs that made a corduroy road for my pen to jolt over, I wonder, or my failing eyesight, or — and this is saddest to think of — the dulness of the letter itself? Is this better? I am trying to write as well as I can for my dear and admirable friend, but what would you have? How should one write letters worth reading who has so many to write as I? But never mind. The true use of a letter is to let one know that one is remembered and valued, and as you are sure of that, perhaps I need not write at all! No, the true use of writing is that it brings your friend to you as you write, and so I have your sweet society for a while, and you need have only just as much of mine as you choose to give yourself. . . .

To Mrs. W. E. Darwin

WHITBY, *September 13, 1889.*

. . . The charm of this place and the kindheartedness of the weather have Capuaed me here longer than I meant.

There is no use in trying to tell you how beautiful our moors have been — pensively gorgeous like the purple mourning that used to

be worn for kings — as if they were still com-
memorating the lonely funerals of the chieftains
whose barrows crown their summits. And our
Abbey — did n't I see it a few nights ago with
the moon shining through its windows till one
fancied it lighted up for service with corpse-
lights for candles, and heard the ghostly mise-
rere of the monks over their ruin? And then
its fantastic transformation by the sea-mists!
Do you wonder that I linger?

I hear the robins singing in your shrubbery
and wish you joy of them. They gladden me
every morning from the mangy back-yards of
the houses opposite. What is it Donne calls
them? "The household bird with the red
stomacher," or something prettier. I am doubtful about "household."[1] But what would you
have of a memory as tumble-down as the
Abbey yonder? . . .

To Mrs. Edward Burnett

ST. IVES, *September 23, 1889.*

. . . I am very well — really so absurd a
septuagenarian is seldom met with — and my
stay at Whitby, where the weather grew to be
almost weakly good natured at last, did me

---

[1] Lowell's recollection of the verse was correct. It oc-
curs in Donne's "Epithalamion on Frederick, Count Pala-
tine of the Rhine, and Lady Elizabeth being married on
St. Valentine's Day."

good. A poem even got itself written there (which seems to me not altogether bad), and this intense activity of the brain has the same effect as exercise on my body, and somehow braces up the whole machine. My writing this was a lucky thing, for when I got back to London I found a letter from the New York "Ledger" enclosing a draft for £200 for whatever I should choose to send. So I sent them what I had just written, pacifying my scruples with the thought that after all it was only my *name* they were paying for, and that they knew best what it was worth to them. The letter, by great good luck, had been overlooked and not forwarded to Whitby as it should have been. Had I got it before my poem got itself out of me, I should have been quite disabled and should have sent back the draft. . . .

To C. E. Norton

St. Ives, *September* 24, 1889.

. . . *Amor che nella mente mi ragiona* has often bid me write to you, and I should certainly have done so, even without the added prompting of your letter, which came to me just as I was starting for my visit here. I am at best a poor correspondent, and at worst no correspondent at all. I make a feint of excusing myself (since one could never get on with one's faults so complacently if one could not palliate them) by reminding myself that I grew up in the ampler days of quarto, nay, folio letter-paper, and of postage that inspired reflection. I can't get over the feeling that less than four pages is niggardly in point of friendship and spendthrift in point of postage. Moreover, I am far past the period when I was a constant novelty to myself and eager to communicate it to all and sundry. I envy the careless profusion with which a younger generation scatters its hasty notes as fish their spawn, while I, a serious barn-door fowl, am inclined to cackle when I succeed in laying my single eggs at decorous (increasingly decorous) intervals. Things don't happen in one so often as they once did.

I also read Fitzgerald's " Letters " with great interest and satisfaction. I quite agree with you that they are among the best we have. I fancy he took enough pains with them to make them as easy as they are. They were his only means of communication with the outward world, of *translating* himself as it were into the vulgar tongue. He was a scholar and a gentleman — I change the order of the words because I fancy a distinction and a pleasing one. I agree with you as to the general sanity of his literary judgments — though he would not have been so agreeable as he is without a few honest prejudices too. We are so hustled about by fortune that I found solace as I read in thinking that here was a man who insisted on having his life to himself, and largely had it accordingly. A hermit, by the bye, as he was, has a great advantage in forming secure conclusions. Another charm of the book to me was that it so often reminded me of J. H.

I spent my usual month at Whitby and indeed stretched it to six weeks, the weather grew so obliging. I did very little, but felt remarkably well, which at my age is perhaps as wise an employment as another. I read a little of Lope, a little of Dante, and a good deal of Milton, convincing myself of what I had long taken for granted, that his versification was mainly modelled on the Italian and especially on the " Divina Commedia." Many if not most of his odd constructions are to be sought there, I think, rather than in the ancients. I read something of Byron, too, with an odd feeling of surprise that the framework of the fireworks (*feux d'artifice* says more) which so dazzled my youth should look so bare. I read some Old French, having received about a dozen volumes of the " Anciens Textes " that were due me. Mainly dull — nothing like the " Galerant " of last year. I dread falling under its spell again when I go back to Elmwood and the old associations, for I can't see exactly what good it has done me or anybody else.

The average result of my Whitby seems to be that the moors and shy footpaths round about it are dearer to me than ever.

After getting back at last to London, where I halted a day to copy and correct a poem which I forgot to say was one of my Whitby results, I went down for a visit of two or three days in Hampshire. On my way up again I stopped a few hours at Winchester, where I had the advantage of going over the Cathedral with the dean. The Norman transept seemed to me the best of it — so massive that it gives one the impression of being a work of nature, like a cliff in which the fancy pleases itself with tracing marks of architectural design. . . .

To the Misses Lawrence
2 RADNOR PLACE, HYDE PARK, W.,
October 2, 1889.

. . . I am looking (they tell me) younger than ever, which is almost indecent at my time of life when I consider the Psalmist. However, I don't much mind being young. 'T is the other thing I dread, and I hope I shan't have much of it. Thus far the earth seems to me as beautiful as ever, and the new song of the birds in spring renews me with the renewing year. The grasshopper is not yet a burthen, and as for the ceasing of desire, I think the fewer we have the more likely they are to be gratified. . . .

To Mrs. W. K. Clifford
2 RADNOR PLACE, HYDE PARK, W.,
October 18, 1889.

. . . Old poets need encouragement far more than young ones, for with youth and inexperience they sometimes lose their better muse. Art may be won, but inexperience once lost can never be recovered. . . .

Well, good-by till next spring, if next spring shall come to me. . . .

XI

1889–1891

To Lady Lyttelton

ELMWOOD, *November* 7, 1889.

HERE I am in my own library again,
after so many years' alienage. My own
clocks measure my time for me. They
have just sounded noon, the cuckoo with hilar-
ity (as if it were a new discovery), and all at suf-
ficient intervals to show their independence of
mind. The veteran in the hall, which has been
running nigh two hundred years, came in later,
with breath enough left to declare with emphasis, " You youngsters are always in such a hurry !
It is now authentically twelve o'clock." . . .

I found the country looking green, and our grass has a bluer tint than yours, borrowed of the sky, perhaps, but all the trees are bare except the great English elms in front of the house, which still have tatters of gold about them. I watch the moon rise behind the same trees through which I first saw it seventy years ago, and have a strange feeling of permanence, as if I should watch it seventy years longer. It is very odd that I cannot feel old, though I know that the children whose voices I hear are by two generations my junior, and I am a great-great-uncle. I shan't be sorry if this feeling lasts till I fall suddenly, as old trees do in our forests, in the windless noon of a summer sky! . . .

To Mrs. Leslie Stephen
ELMWOOD, *November 9,* 1889.

. . . It is a very strange feeling this of renewing my life here. I feel somehow as if Charon had ferried me the wrong way, and yet it is into a world of ghosts that he has brought me, and I am slowly making myself at home among them. It is raining faintly to-day, with a soft southerly wind which will prevail with the few leaves left on my trees to let go their hold and join their fellows on the ground. I have forbidden them to be raked away, for the rustle of them stirs my earliest memories, and when the wind blows they pirouette so gayly as to give me cheerful

III

thoughts of death. But oh, the changes! I
hardly know the old road (a street now) that I
have paced so many years, for the new houses.
My old homestead seems to have a puzzled
look in its eyes as it looks down (a trifle super-
ciliously methinks) on these upstarts. "He
who lives longest has the most old clothes,"
says the Zulu proverb, and I shall wear mine
till I die.

It is odd to think that the little feet which
make the old staircases and passages querulous
at their broken slumbers are the second generation since my own. I try to believe it, but
find it hard. I feel so anomalously young I
can't persuade myself that *I* ever made such a
rumpus, though perhaps the boots are thicker
now.

The two old English elms in front of the
house have n't changed. The sturdy islanders!
A trifle thicker in the waist, perhaps, as is the
wont of prosperous elders, but looking just as
I first saw them seventy years ago, and it is a
balm to my eyes. I am by no means sure that
it is wise to love the accustomed and familiar
so much as I do, but it is pleasant and gives a
unity to life which trying can't accomplish.

I began this yesterday and now it is Sunday.
You will have *not* gone to church five hours
ago. I have just performed the chief function of
a householder by winding up all the clocks and

adjusting them to a *striking* unanimity. I doubt if this be judicious, for when I am lying awake at night their little differences of opinion amuse me. They persuade me how artificial a contrivance Time is. We have Eternity given us in the lump, can't believe in such luck, and cut it up into mouthfuls as if it would n't go round among so many. Are we to be seduced by the superstitious observances of the earth and sun into a belief in days and years? . . .

To Josiah Quincy

ELMWOOD, *December* 10, 1889.

Dear Mr. Quincy, — I regret very much that I cannot have the pleasure of joining with you in paying respect to a man so worthy of it as Mr. Cleveland.[1]

> Let who has felt compute the strain
> Of struggle with abuses strong,
> The doubtful course, the helpless pain
> Of seeing best intents go wrong.

> We, who look on with critic eyes,
> Exempt from action's crucial test,
> Human ourselves, at least are wise
> In honoring one who did his best.

Faithfully yours,
J. R. LOWELL.

[1] At the banquet of the Boston Merchants' Association, where ex-President Cleveland was the chief guest, on December 12.

To R. W. Gilder
ELMWOOD, *December* 22, 1889.

. . . I should have been glad to preside at the breakfast of the Copyright League, but I really could n't. Such things worry me nowadays more than you could easily conceive. They take more life out of me than I can afford to give. Kept in this shelter, my candle seems to have some stuff left and shortens at a hopefully moderate rate; but set it in a flurry of air and the deuce is in it, it so swales and runs to waste. . . .

To the Misses Lawrence
ELMWOOD, *January* 2, 1890.

. . . Here I am again in the house where I was born longer ago than you can remember, though I wish you more New Year's days than I have had. 'T is a pleasant old house just about twice as old as I am, four miles from Boston, in what was once the country and is now a populous suburb. But it still has some ten acres of open about it, and some fine old trees. When the worst comes to the worst (if I live so long) I shall still have four and a half acres left with the house, the rest belonging to my brothers and sisters or their heirs. It is a square house with four rooms on a floor, like some houses of the Georgian era I have seen in English pro-

vincial towns, only they are of brick and this is
of wood. But it is solid with its heavy oaken
beams, the spaces between which in the four
outer walls are filled in with brick, though you
must n't fancy a brick-and-timber house, for
outwardly it is sheathed with wood. Inside
there is much wainscot (of deal) painted white
in the fashion of the time when it was built. It
is very sunny, the sun rising so as to shine (at
an acute angle, to be sure) through the northern windows, and going round the other three
sides in the course of the day. There is a pretty
staircase with the quaint old twisted banisters
— which they call balusters now, but mine are
banisters. My library occupies two rooms opening into each other by arches at the sides of the
ample chimneys. The trees I look out on are
the earliest things I remember. There you have
me in my new-old quarters. But you must not
fancy a large house — rooms sixteen feet square
and, on the ground floor, nine high. It was
large, as things went here, when it was built,
and has a certain air of amplitude about it as
from some inward sense of dignity.

Now for out of doors. What do you suppose
the thermometer is about on this second day of
January? I was going to say he was standing
on his head — at any rate he has forgotten what
he 's about, and is marking sixty-three degrees
Fahrenheit on the north side of the house and

in the shade ! Where is that sense of propriety
that once belonged to the seasons ? This is flat
communism, January insisting on going halves
with May. News I have none, nor other re-
sources, as you see, save those of the special
correspondent, who takes to description when
events fail. Yes, I have one event. I dine to-
night with Mr. R. C. Winthrop, who remembers your father very well nearly sixty years
ago.

I have all my grandchildren with me, five of
them, and the eldest boy is already conspiring
with a beard ! It is awful, this stealthy advance
of Time's insupportable foot. There are two
ponies for the children and two dogs, bull-ter-
riers, and most amiable creatures. This is my
establishment, and four of the weans have had
the *grippe*. I remember it here in '31, I think
it was. You see I make all I can of age's one
privilege — that of having a drearier memory
than other folks.

I forgot one thing. There are plenty of mice
in the walls, and, now that I can't go to the
play with you, I assist at their little tragedies
and comedies behind the wainscot in the night
hours and build up plots in my fancy. 'T is a
French company, for I hear them distinctly say
wee, *wee*, sometimes. My life, you see, is not
without its excitements, and what are your
London mice doing that is more important ?

I see you are to have a Parnell scandal at last, but I overheard an elopement the other night behind the wainscot, and the solicitors talking it over with the desolated husband afterwards. It was very exciting. Ten thousand grains of corn damages !

Good-by, and take care of yourselves till I come with the daffodils. I wish you both many a happy New Year and a share for me in some of them. Poets seem to live long nowadays, and I, too, live in Arcadia after my own fashion.

Affectionately yours,

J. R. L.

To Lady Lyttelton

ELMWOOD, *January* 7, 1890.

. . . We have lost Browning. . . . His later work shows that we had had the best of him. He had singular force and intensity, — passion, in short, of an *oriental* kind, new in English litera-ture, and which therefore gave a fillip to Anglo-Saxon sensibilities, — but I think his main charm for many people was an obscurity that made them think they were thinking. A man who fur-nished an endless series of conundrums, capable every one of a dozen different solutions, was a public benefactor. But when he is fine, he is so in a very fine way, and he never lets us forget that we have blood in our veins.

And so you are to have a Parnell scandal.

Cherchez la femme never had an odder illustration than in the name of the Lady in *O'Shea* as if she summed up in herself all the feminine elements of catastrophe. But nothing will come of it, I fancy, I mean politically, for the Irish cat always comes down on its feet, no matter from how high a roof it falls. . . .

To W. D. Howells

ELMWOOD, *January* 10, 1890.

. . . And now let me say something I have been wishing to say this great while. I have seen some of the unworthy flings at you in the papers of late. I know you will not feel them more than an honest man should. But I have indignantly felt them. You are one of the chief honors of our literature, and your praises are dear to us all. You know I don't share some of your opinions or sympathize with some of your judgments, but I am not such an ass as not to like a man better for saying what *he* thinks and not what *I* think. Though I thought those Chicago ruffians well hanged, I specially honored your courage in saying what you did about them. You can't make me fonder of you, but I am sure you will make me prouder of you.

And so I am

Always affectionately yours,

J. R. LOWELL.

To S. Weir Mitchell
ELMWOOD, CAMBRIDGE, MASS.,,
April 4, 1890.

Dear Doctor Mitchell, — Just after getting your note I was put to bed (where I ought to have been sooner, only I would n't), and found myself, almost before I knew where I was, under the charge of a nurse and with two doctors in consultation over me. I have had a hard time of it, and was much pulled down. But I had a very present help in the constant encouragement and kindness of my old friend, Dr. Wyman, who even went so far as to watch three nights running at my bedside, and he in his seventy-ninth year. For a fortnight now I have been mending, and have had no return of acute symptoms. Yesterday I was able to dress and get downstairs for the first time, and one of the first things I had on my mind to be done soonest was to thank you for your kind note, and to say that the printing of the poems will begin soon — as soon, I believe, as I shall be in condition to read proofs without too much fatigue.

With affectionate regards to Mrs. Mitchell,
Faithfully yours,
J. R. LOWELL.

To Mrs. W. K. Clifford
LMWOOD, CAMBRIDGE, MASS.,
April 9, 1890.

Dear Mrs. Clifford, — It was very good of
you to be anxious about me, and I wish I could
drop in to ask you for a cup of coffee and thank
you in person. That *would* be delightful, but
my gratitude must find vent in ink, which
sometimes runs cold in spite of us. Pen in
hand, one has n't always the courage of one's
feelings. Spoken words may be as warm as one
likes — there is always air enough about to
temper them to the right point. . . .

I have been really ill — six weeks on my back
in bed, whither I refused to go till I could sit
up no longer. I could n't conceive of anything
but Death strong enough to throw me. And
he did look in at the door once, they tell me,
when I was worst, but changed his mind and
took his ugly mug elsewhere.

I have now been mending for nearly three
weeks and begin once more to have legs and
things. But I had grown very weak and am
still very easily tired. I have been out of doors
thrice, once to bask for an hour in the sun on
the veranda, twice to crawl about a little — the
last time for nearly a hundred yards, one of the
triumphs of pedestrianism. I am bidden to re-
cline as much as possible and am on my back

now in a *chaise-longue*. The doctors say I must on no account venture across the water this summer, and I myself have n't the courage, for I have had rather a sharp warning that I am over forty — which I never believed before. When you see me again I shall be an old man — that was a slip, I meant to say "elderly," but it is out now and I must make the best of it. I shall be little better than a tame cat. You will stroke me in a pause of your talk with some more suitable person, and I shall purr.

I could n't endure my deprivation did I not think my renunciation this year would insure my coming the next. Only by that time, I fear, you will have forgotten me and wonder who I am when I call. Please don't if you can help it. And yet, if you have to make an effort, I should n't quite like that either. But I must n't write any more, for my head begins to grumble, and already has the stitch in its side. Write when you happen to think of it.

Faithfully yours,
J. R. LOWELL.

To Thomas Hughes
ELMWOOD, CAMBRIDGE, MASS.,
April 20, 1890.

Dear Friend, — What a good old-fashioned Scripture-measure letter was that of yours! It annihilated penny-posts and telegraphs, and grew to a quarto sheet as I read with all the complicated creases of its folding. Pleasant indeed was it to hear such good news from your Deeside hive, which through the boys bids fair to be a true *officina gentium*, peopling our Western emptinesses with the right kind of stock.

And so our bright and busy-minded —— is married, and happily too. After mature deliberation with the help of a pipe, I don't think her husband's not smoking is a fatal objection. A—— would tell you that Napoleon did n't, and Goethe and several other more or less successful men. I consent, therefore, on condition that he stuff his pockets with baccy for his poor parishioners when he goes his rounds; they know how good it is and how they "puff the prostitute (Fortune) away," or snuff up oblivion with its powdered particles. I remember an old crone whom I used to meet every Sunday in Kensington Gardens when she had her outings from the almshouse and whom I kept supplied with Maccaboy. I think I made her perfectly happy for a week and on such cheap terms as make me blush. She was a dear old thing, and used to make me prettier curtsies than I saw at court. Good heavens, of what uncostly material is our earthly happiness composed — if we only knew it! What incomes have we not had from a flower, and how unfailing are the dividends of the seasons!

I can't help having a sneaking sympathy with
————, as I think I once wrote to Mrs. Hughes.
Philosophy and liberty are excellent things, but
I made the discovery early in life that they had
one fault — you can't eat 'em, and I found it
necessary to eat something, however little. For
the celibate (if his father have a balance at his
banker's) they will serve, but on no other condition and at best not for long. ———— tried it, and
do you know what Mrs. ———— once said when
somebody asked "if her husband did n't live
with his head always in the clouds?" "Yes, and
I'm sometimes tempted to wish he'd draw his
feet up after it!" But his were the dreams of
middle-age and senescence. Those of youth are
sometimes the best possession of our old age. . . .

Association with so generous a nature as Auberon Herbert's would do any man good —
unless, to be sure, they give up for the moment
making themselves good to quarrel about the
best way of making other people so. I have
known that to happen. But never mind; the
desire to sit in the *siege perilleus* is a good thing
in itself, if it do not end in sitting there to watch
the procession of life go by, papa meanwhile
paying a smart fee for young Hopeful's excellent seat.

Speaking of these things reminds me of
Howells's last story, "A Hazard of New For-
tunes"; have you read it? If not, do, for I

am sure you would like it. A noble sentiment
pervades it, and it made my inherited comforts
here at Elmwood discomforting to me in a very
salutary way. I felt in reading some parts of it
as I used when the slave would not let me sleep.
I don't see my way out of the labyrinth except
with the clue of coöperation, and I am not sure
even of that with over-population looming in
the near distance. I would n't live in any of the
Socialist or Communist worlds into the plans
of which I have looked, for I should be bored
to death by the everlasting Dutch landscape.
Nothing but the guillotine will ever make men
equal on compulsion, and even then they will
leap up again in some other world to begin
again on the old terms.

You will be glad to hear that Carl Schurz (a
good judge), who had several talks with the new
emperor both as crown prince and after, thinks
that he is intelligent, means business, and knows
what he is about. As emperor he has done away
with some of the old fusses and feathers. Once
he sent for Schurz, who was ushered at once into
the cabinet of the emperor, with whom he was
left alone, and who pushed an easy-chair towards
the fire for him, seating himself on a hard stool.
Bismarck, by the way, said a good thing to
Schurz with which I am growing into sympathy
— "I am beginning to think that the best half
of life is before seventy."

I am glad to be remembered by your fair neighbors, and wish my image in their minds could, in the nature of things, be as charming as theirs in mine. Tell them that my power of seeing faces with my eyes shut is a great blessing to me, since it enables me to see two such (let their glasses fill up the blank) ones whenever I like. I have just taken a look at them. Love to Mrs. Hughes. Thanks for her kind note.

Affectionately yours,

J. R. LOWELL.

I am still doing well, but have to be very careful. The doctor won't hear of my going abroad this year. Alas!

To Leslie Stephen

ELMWOOD, April 21, 1890.

Dear Leslie, — I have just got your letter and write to say that your coming would be a great joy to many, and above all to me. But what I wish to urge is that, if you can come, I hope you will come as early as you can, because everybody here, except me, runs away in summer, and there are a few whom I should like you to see and who would like to see you. Norton's going would make no odds, because you would seek him at Ashfield, though I shall keep you as long as I can.

I remember well our parting at the corner of

my lane, and how strangely moved I was. It has mingled with and distinguished my affection for you, and I shall forget it only when I forget everything.

I shan't be able to walk with you, but, by the time you get here, I suppose I shall be allowed to drive, and we can see Beaver Brook and the oaks again together. Wellington Hill (where you started a fox) I could not attempt.

You *must* come. It will do you good and me too. By the way, what do you think was the first [book] I chose to entertain me after I got downstairs? Your " History of Thought in the Eighteenth Century." I read it over again with unqualified satisfaction. More love to Julia and to the weans. I am tired.

Affectionately yours,

J. R. LOWELL.

To Mrs. W. K. Clifford

ELMWOOD, CAMBRIDGE, MASS.,
April 27, 1890.

Dear Mrs. Clifford, — It is the evening of a drizzly Sunday. I have just been helping my second grandson in his Greek exercise (with an uneasy apprehension that he would find out he was a better Grecian than I), and now lay down " Redgauntlet," in which I am deeply interested, in order, so far as a letter may, to maintain your interest in me. . . .

Yes, I have read Kipling's stories, and with real pleasure. I read them while I was still in bed and under the spell of opium, and so was adopted into their Orientalism. Some of his verses, too, I liked, especially the Omar Khayamish at the head of the last chapter. I find something startlingly vernacular in Oriental poetry (which I know only through translations, mainly German), as if I had lived some former and forgotten life in the East. How potent is this Oriental blood — in Napoleon, in Goethe, in Heine, Victor Hugo, in Browning, to go no further back ! In Montaigne probably ; in Dante possibly. I am not so sure that I like the West-Oestliche as Goethe exemplified it. But I have hopes of the volume Mr. Kipling seems to promise us in that last chapter, but I hope he will drop his Hindostanee pedantry. 'T is as bad as Mrs. Gore's French used to be. Be truer to your sex, my dear. He is not Burne-Jones's nephew, but Mrs. Burne-Jones's, and his book constantly reminded me of Phil. Burne-Jones, by whom I set great store. How good he was to the children when I stayed with him at Talland House ! I adore that kind of goodness afar off, for I have n't it myself. They tell me I had it once, and perhaps I shall get it again before long in my second childhood.

I am doing well, thank you. When I get up in the morning I feel about thirty, but when I

go upstairs to bed I seem to carry a Nestorian
weight of years. This I shall get over when
I am allowed to take exercise. What I can't
get over yet is apprehension. My malady came
upon me so without warning that I live in
hourly dread of ambushes. Still, I should like
to drop in at 26 Colville Road and fence with
you a little. I don't think you would find *much*
difference. Good-by ; write when you remember me. No, not that exactly, but oftener. Is
that a bull ? I don't mind if it bring me Europa.
Our Spring is just beginning, and the buds are
peeping to see if it be really she at last. I am
encouraged by finding that my sap still stirs
with the rest. There must be some life in my
roots yet. Give my love to the two girls.

Faithfully yours,

J. R. LOWELL.

To the Misses Lawrence

ELMWOOD, CAMBRIDGE, MASS.,
May 3, 1890.

. . . Septuagenarians are allowed to talk about
themselves, a license, I am inclined to think,
which they are beginning to abuse, if one may
judge by the number of autobiographies, reminiscences and things we have had of late. It
must have been through a well-founded dread
of such garrulities that the ancient Scythians
put an end to their old people before these had

a chance to become public nuisances. It is whispered that they feasted on them afterwards, but this is doubtful. What is certain is, that no toughness of digestion would have been competent to what their memoirs would probably have turned out to be.

As I say, I have no news because I am not yet permitted to go about and gather the stale stuff we call so. My "Court Journal" is a record of the comings and goings of birds and blossoms. My births, deaths, and marriages are new moons, sunsets, and the pairing of innocent winged creatures. Two days ago I was much excited by the first appearance of a summer-yellowbird, one of the most graceful of our songsters. Yesterday a sparrow-hawk perched in one of my trees, and a bird with a gleaming white waistcoat, that made him twice as big as he really was, and a purple necktie. Have you never seen people whose costume lent them a fictitious greatness? I will not go higher than a lord mayor for an example. You see that morals flit about among my boughs as thick as sparrows. And, by the way, the English sparrows which we carefully imported are grown as great a nuisance as rabbits in Australia. They are beyond measure impudent. If you take off your hat to wipe your brow, they have built a nest in it before you are ready to put it on again, and then dispute possession with you. They seize all unoccupied territory, as I won't say who sets them the example of doing. They build in a twinkling half a dozen nests over one's front door, and if one evict them and tear down their homesteads as thoroughly as if they were Irish tenants, the nests are there again next day with young in them, which the birds borrow as beggars do to excite compassion. If they let fall nothing worse than oysters (or whatever it was that the osprey dropt on the bald pate of Æschylus), one would n't mind. They bully our native birds out of their lives, as British officials used to bully us poor provincials in the good old times. What is there in your island — but no, I won't generalize on so narrow a foundation, as if I were an English traveller in America. To tell the truth, I rather like them, and they amuse me immensely, the cock-birds are such insufferable coxcombs. In our sunny and clear air they are by no means the chimney-sweep-looking creatures you are familiar with in London, but have almost a brilliant plumage.

So you have been at Avignon (Babylon) and Arles (did you observe how pretty the women are?) and Orange (did you think of Guillaume au Court Nez?) and the Pont du Gard. But you say nothing of Vaucluse and its living waters, one of the most beautiful things I ever saw, though a little brackish with Petrarch's tears — not very, for they had more sugar than salt in them. I first saw the Pont du Gard in '52, and next in '78. The same man was in charge and we made a laughing bargain that I should come again after another score of years: And I am already within two years of my tryst. You never saw in the south of France a day more lovely than this. One must make a cloud in one's own mind (as modern poets do) if one would have a cloud, and the breeze is like the waft of one's mistress's fan, cooling and fragrant at once. Time leans on his scythe and rests. . . .

To Mrs. Leslie Stephen

ELMWOOD, *May 4*, 1890.

. . . We are beginning to look very pretty here in our new spring dresses, and all my pear trees with fresh flowers in their bonnets. But, alas, how my trees and shrubs have pined for me in my absence. And they have been shamefully broken, too. For my part, I feel the pain in the limb of a tree as in one of my own. But I am sure they all know me, and will take heart again now that I am come back. They are not quite reconciled with me yet, and I wish I could show you to them as one of the arguments for my absence. That would bring them all round.

The birds are here again in reasonable numbers, but my orioles not yet. They build a

pendulous nest, and so flash in the sun that
our literal rustics call them fire hang-birds. . . .

To Miss Kate Field

CAMBRIDGE, *May* 15, 1890.

Dear Miss Field, — I have had too long an
experience of the providential thickness of the
human skull, as well as of the eventual success
of all reasonable reforms, to be discouraged by
the temporary defeat of any measure which I
believe to be sound. I say "providential" because the world is thereby saved many a rash
experiment in specious legislation. Were it
otherwise, the Huon's horn of inconsiderate
enthusiasm would lead us a pretty dance among
the briers. Unfortunately there is, as usual, an
exception to this general rule, for the sutures
of the political cranium are so loosely knit as
to leave a crevice through which considerations
of ephemeral expediency find a too easy en-
trance. Such considerations, it should always
be remembered, are most liable to disastrous
recoil.

I grant that our hope has been long-drawn-
out, but since material for it (as for every hope
that has a moral base) has been constantly supplied, it has never become too attenuated to
bear the strain put upon it. It is seventy-one
years since Irving wrote: "You observe that
the public complain of the price of my work;

this is the disadvantage of coming in competition with republished English works for which the publishers have not to pay anything to the authors. If the American public wish to have a literature of their own, they must consent to pay for the support of authors."

(And why not, I may add, if we consent to pay Senator Jones for the support of a silver mine?)

It is fifty years since Irving wrote: " How much this growing literature may be retarded by the present state of our copyright law I had recently an instance in the cavalier treatment of a work of merit, written by an American who had not yet established a commanding name in the literary market. I undertook as a friend to dispose of it for him, but found it impossible to get an offer from any of our principal publishers. They even declined to publish it at the author's cost, alleging that it was not worth their while to trouble themselves about native works of doubtful success, while they could pick and choose among the successful works daily poured out by the British press, *for which they had nothing to pay for copyright*."

This was in 1840, and in the same year Mr. Clay's bill was defeated. We have been fighting for the same cause with the same weapons ever since, and apparently with the same result.

But for all that we have made progress. We

have secured public discussion, and a righteous cause which has done that has got the weather gauge of its adversary. I am too old to be persuaded by any appearances, however specious, that Truth has lost or can lose a whit of that divine quality which gives her immortal advantage over Error. The adversary has cunningly intrenched himself in the argument that there can be no such thing as property in an idea, and I grant that this is a fallacy of which it is hard to disabuse the minds of otherwise intelligent men. But it is in the form given to an idea by a man of genius, and in this only, that we assert a right of property to have been created. The founders of our republic tacitly admitted this right when they classed the law of copyright with that of patents. I have known very honest men who denied the public expediency of such a right in both cases, but I cannot understand either the logic or the probity of those who admit the one and deny the other. This right is visible and palpable in a machine, invisible and impalpable in a book, and for this very reason the law should be more assiduous to protect it in the latter case, as being the weaker.

But, after all, every species of property is the artificial creature of law, and the true question is whether, if such property in books did not exist, it would be wise in our own interest to create it. The inventions of Whitney, of Ful-

ton, and of Morse added enormously to the
wealth of the nation. Have not those of Ed-
wards and Irving and Cooper and Emerson
and Hawthorne and Longfellow (to speak only
of the dead) added also to that wealth and in
a nobler kind? Or is not moral credit, then,
worth something too? Is it not, indeed, the
foundation on which financial credit is built and
most securely rests?

The foreign right to property of this description stands on precisely the same footing
with the domestic right, and the moral wrong
of stealing either is equally great. But literary
property is at a disadvantage because it is not
open, gross, and palpable, and therefore the
wrongful appropriation of it touches the public conscience more faintly. In ordinary cases
it is the thief, but in this case the thing stolen,
that is invisible. To steal is no doubt more
immediately profitable than acquisition by the
more tedious methods of honesty, but is apt to
prove more costly in the long run. How costly
our own experiment in larceny has been those
only know who have studied the rise and progress of our literature, which has been forced
to grow as virtue is said to do — in spite of the
weight laid upon it.

But even though this particular form of dis-
honesty against which we are contending were
to be always and everywhere commercially pro-

fitable, I think that the American people is so
honest that it may be made to see that a profit
allowed to be legitimate by us alone among civ-
ilized nations — a profit, too, which goes wholly
into the pockets of a few unscrupulous men —
must have something queer about it, something
which even a country so rich as ours cannot
afford.

I have lived to see more than one successful
appeal from the unreason of the people's repre-
sentatives to the reason of the people themselves.
I am, therefore, not to be tired with waiting.
It is wearisome to ourselves and to others also
to go on repeating the arguments we have been
using for these forty years and which to us seem
so self-evident, but I think it is true that no
reformer has ever gained his end who had not
first made himself an intolerable bore to the
vast majority of his kind. I have done my share
in my time to help forward such triumphs of
tediousness, but you will not thank me for es-
saying it again in the sprightly columns of your
paper.[1]   Faithfully yours,

J. R. LOWELL.

To Lady Lyttelton
ELMWOOD, *May 25,* 1890.

. . . As for myself I am getting on very well,
though I find that at seventy odd it is far easier

[1] This letter was published in *Kate Field's Washington.*

to go down hill than to get back again. I get
tired sooner and on less provocation than I was
wont. But I shall come round with patience —
a commodity, I find, which is always scarce when
one particularly wants it.

The spring is lovely here as everywhere, but
with a special grace from lifelong association
and because I take a special interest in the for-
tunes of trees I have known and loved from
childhood. My lilac hedges have been superb
with their waving plumes for the last week.
Having assisted at the coronation of Queen
May, they are now becoming sober citizens
again. We have had one event of real importance — the rose-breasted grosbeak has come to
us and is evidently building his shanty somewhere about the grounds. He is a finch, cousin
to the linnet, and a rapturous singer, whose
wings quiver with the ecstasy of his song all day
long. In great moonlights he sings all night
too. He is not a common bird here, though
he has been known for years a few miles away
from us. So I rejoice in his coming. My place
is very small, but there are many trees and
thickets, so that the birds love it, and this year
we are populous with them.

I have just been out for a few moments to
soak in the sunshine and listen to the birds. It
is a perfect day, such as makes one in love with
earth. Not a speck in the sky except the pale

ghost of the new moon in the east on her way
back to life like Alcestis. She will be beautiful
over my pine crests this evening.

Since I can't go to England this summer, I
have been reading over again Hawthorne's
" Our Old Home." Have you ever read it? It
is full of sensitive observation and of description really vivid without effort — of genius out
of harness, as it were. I read it in the way of
business, for I hope to write my little book
about him before the summer is over.

To the Misses Lawrence

ELMWOOD, CAMBRIDGE, MASS.,
July 6, 1890.

Dear Dual-mood, — It is Sunday morning
and as fair as George Herbert's, a happy bridal
of Earth and Sky presaging a long felicity of
married days — all honeymoon that is n't sunshine. Yet I can't help hoping that some spite-
ful fairy has hidden a seed of storm somewhere in
the *trousseau*, for we have had no rain these three
weeks, and our turf is beginning to show symptoms of jaundice. The partiality of the solar
system (due, no doubt, to the insular prejudices
of Sir Isaac Newton) gives you a five hours'
start of us; so I suppose you have both been
to church by this time, and have put away your
prayer-books with a comfortable feeling that
you have played your parts in maintaining the

equilibrium of the British Constitution and have done with religion for a week. With us there has been a divorce of Church and State, and the children are given over to their own guidance.

Why must you be so cruel as to flout me with the nightingale when you knew (or was it *because* you knew?) we had n't him? I am not sure we would have him if we could, for, in spite of the poets, who naturally try to make the best of him, he has a bad character among you as a *somnifuge*, and I have heard no music so ill-spoken of as his save only that of the barrel-organ. Even his flatterers seem savagely happy in thinking that he sings with his breast against a thorn and suffers some proportion, inadequate though it be, of the misery he inflicts. In any case you need not give yourself airs, for our nights will never want for music while we have the mosquito. What is your nightingale to him, whether for assiduous song or as a prophylactic against inordinate and untimely slumber? He would have prevented the catastrophe of the Foolish Virgins — not that I liken you to those — God forbid! On second thoughts I am not sure that I don't, after all, for I have been some-times tempted to think that I liked them better than the wise. 'T is a question of gold spectacles.

I have no news except that my smoke-trees have vapored into rosy clouds that carry on the

tradition of sunrise all through the day to the
sunset. Sweet-peas, too, are in blossom, and
honeysuckle, but, alas, I have n't seen a hum-
ming-bird this summer. I never before knew a
summer without them.

Your London world seems a great way off,
for I am gone back to my old books, and live
chiefly two or three centuries ago, sometimes
much farther back. I find no nicer creatures
than you there.

My grandchildren grow apace and my eldest
grandson goes to college this year. My con-
temporaries drop faster and faster about me,
but one gets used to it as the leaves to the falling of their fellows and playmates in autumn.
I am not conscious yet of any loosening of my
stem. But who ever is?

Affectionately yours,

J. R. LOWELL.

To Lady Lyttelton

ELMWOOD, *August* 10, 1890.

. . . Your reproaches have always a lining of
caress in them which makes them very nice to
take. But I had not the least notion that I
deserved anything of the kind. One who spends
so much of his time in reverie, as I in my *chaise
longue* naturally do, is unconscious of the passage of time. Add to this the heat with the
thermometer at 90°, and an uncompromising

sun by which all the energy I had left, not much at best, has been distilled out of me, and you will have some faint notion of my disabilities. I was asked for an autograph the other day by some-body I could n't refuse, and I had only strength enough for something like this : —

> The hot hours come, the hot hours go,
> So listlessly, so more than slow,   •
> That I believe old Time, like me,
> Has dropt asleep beneath some tree,
> While, slipping from the loosened hand,
> His hourglass lies, nor stirs its sand.

To C. E. Norton

ELMWOOD, *August 23*, 1890.

. . . Tied by the leg as I am, I should envy the spryness with which you are skipping over the hills and seeing them golden with the June grass — as good as heather in its way. But I am by nature so stolidly content with seeing the things I have seen all my life, and find such a comforting sympathy in them, that I am on the whole satisfied to sit on the veranda and enjoy a vegetative life with my trees, with Panks and Gobble for company. Gobble is getting to be as interesting a little soul — for I am sure he has one — as I ever saw, and the patience of his father with him, letting him bite his ears, tail, legs, or what not, just as he has composed him-self for a nap, is worth many a sermon to me.

The newspapers have n't told you our most important event. The crickets have come, and are trilling away, each on his own hook and without unison, like an orchestra tuning their fiddles. This means that the curtain is going to rise for the entry of autumn. I find no sadness in it — cheer rather. It is *my* season of the year now, and I heard my crickets long ago, only they creak in the joints instead of the grass.

I have finished my " Areopagitica " [1] business after a fashion, that is, I sent it off yesterday, and am now beginning to think of what I might have said and meant to say. This is an old phenomenon, but I suppose it only means that the Muse is a woman and saves all she wishes to say for a postscript.

Anyhow, I was well tired of the thing (it has two clever things in it), and so after posting it I gave myself a good bath in Calderon. He always entertains and absorbs me after everybody else has given it up. I am quite conscious how much sameness there is in him, and yet there is endless variety too, and if his horizon be not of the widest, heat-lightnings of fancy are forever winking round the edges of it. Partly, perhaps, the charm is in the language and the verse,

---

[1] An Introduction to an edition of the "Areopagitica," printed by the Grolier Club, of New York, in facsimile of the first edition.

which slips along thoughtless as a brook. There are greater poets, but none so constantly delightful. His mind is a kaleidoscope, at every turn making a new image of the same bits of colored glass — cheap material enough, but who cares? Not so cheap either when one comes to think of it, for these are fragments from painted windows, deepened in hue with incense fumes and thrilled through and through with organ and choir. Well, it is a comfort that there *used* to be poets, at any rate, only it is despair to see how easily they did it!

Pongame el ruego á los pies de Peter's Hill, and tell the park-like trees there that I shall never cease to love them. And take off your hat for me to Monadnock, the most high-bred of our mountains. There must be something rarely fine in the Ashfield landscape, it has stamped itself so on my memory. I see it more clearly than many more familiar.

Dr. Wyman has just been in, and still forbids my walking. I grin and bear it. . . .

To Miss E. G. Norton

ELMWOOD, *7tember* 7, 1890.

Dear Lily, — Do you observe my date? You would infer wonders from it as from a seventh son's seventh son. But I pray you in advance to do nothing of the kind, for my letter is predestined to dulness. And it is this conscious-

III

ness, not infidelity, that has kept me silent so long with your dear letter on my table and on my conscience too. I have been dronish all summer. I don't mean lazy, but derive my adjective rather from the drone of a bagpipe, which is as oppressive to everybody else as it seems inexhaustibly delightful to the manipulator of it. I am struck, on after-thought, with the infelicity of my comparison, for I am not eager to bestow myself on the rest of mankind. Much rather am I incommunicable as a jelly-fish on the sands — did you ever essay conversation with one? Southampton Water would give you a chance. I fancy you making the experiment and whisking away with a pretty flutter of scorn in your skirts and a "Good-by, Uncle James; I give you up as a bad job!"

What would you have? The birds have ceased to sing, and I drag out my long days on the veranda with no company but that of Panks (my dog), who generously shares his dumbness with me and looks up at me as who should say, "You are become unspeakable as one of us, poor old fellow; I pity you!"

I said the birds had ceased, but I was wrong. The screech-owl is in season, and every night yodels mournfully about the house like a banshee. How they used to scare me when I was a boy! And even now I don't feel quite secure in the silenter watches of the night. But the crickets have come, too, and are cheerful enough in their monotonous way. I venture to think they have told me the same thing before. But that makes them all the more like human society.

I have n't the least notion where you are, and have to invent epicycles for you, as old astronomers for the moon, to account for your aberrations and fix you for a moment in the right spot for my fancy. So I shall suppose you at Basset, which must be delightful at this season, if Aquarius have set his watering-pot in the corner at last. Are the robins and finches cheery in the garden? Our ancestors brought hither with them laws, language, and other engines of oppression; why did they leave those behind? Yet we are not wholly comfortless. A robin forgot himself yesterday and sang once, but stopped short with a twinge of conscience, like a child that catches itself feeling happy in church. Meanwhile we are having pears.

Your latest sensation is Newman's death. A beautiful old man, as I remember him, but surely a futile life if ever there was one, trying to make a past unreality supply the place of a present one that was becoming past, and forgetting that God is always "I am," never "I was." He will be remembered chiefly by his "Lead, kindly light," which is as far from

poetry as I hope most hymns are from the ear
to which they were addressed. Else would it be
shut to all our petitions. . . .

Your affectionate
UNCLE JAMES.

To S. Weir Mitchell

ELMWOOD, *September* 24, 1890.

Dear Mitchell, — The other day I wrote to
my publishers asking them to send you a copy
of my new edition " Hommage de l'Auteur."
They replied that you were already a subscriber
for a large-paper copy, an *Edition de looks*. This
is a cross too heavy for my strength, and accordingly I beg that you will permit your subscription to be transferred to me and accept the copy,
not as a requital for many obligations, but as a
record of my affection and respect.

I am elated by the chance to step into your
shoes, which, under any other circumstances,
would be a world too wide for me, but under
these will not wobble unpleasantly. You must
not deny me this; indeed, I shall so far pre-
sume upon your friendship as to direct Messrs.
Houghton & Mifflin accordingly.

I cannot do much, for I get more easily tired
than before my illness. I had a slight relapse
in the latter part of June, and this was in one
sense an encouragement, for it was soon over
and without any of the anguish I had before.

But it has left me with an irksome feeling that my malady may be lying in wait for me around the next corner, and floor me again at any moment. This is not a frame of mind auspicious for any continuous or fruitful work.

I beg you to make my affectionate regards acceptable to Mrs. Mitchell, and remain

Always faithfully yours,

J. R. LOWELL.

To Thomas Hughes

ELMWOOD, CAMBRIDGE, MASS.,
October 1, 1890.

My dear old Friend, — With the cooler weather of autumn (and it is the most fountain-of-youthy I know of) I am beginning to feel like my old, or rather my young, self again. When you write next it must be in words of one syllable, and with everything adapted to the apprehension of a boy. Since my illness I have been under the weather, but a week ago this meteorological incubus was suddenly lifted away and life was lightsome again.

I wish you could share my day with me. It is simply what a day should be that has a good conscience — nothing left in it but a well-manner'd sunshine and the mere pleasure of being. I can't bear to think that our politicians should have any share in it. It was meant for better men. However, it may make them think there is a God in heaven, and that he visits earth sometimes in his mercy.

This morning I read that the Tariff Bill is passed — the first experiment a really intelligent people have ever tried to make one blade of grass grow where two grew before, by means of legislation. A reaction is sure to follow, and what I fear is, that their excesses may make it so sudden as to be calamitous. It is a comfort to think that nations, if they have any stuff in them, survive even folly.

I have felt so sluggish and unwieldy this summer that I have found it hard to write even a letter, and all that I have done is a short preface to an exact reprint of the first edition of Milton's " Areopagitica." It will be a pretty book, and I shall send you a copy. If the preface do not attract you, there is good pasture in the text. It is published by a club of book-and-binding lovers — the Grolier.

My eldest grandson enters college this year, a shocking anachronism, for I could swear I was n't forty this very morning — not a day older for love or money — and the sun shining in on me as I write seems to say, " Strike off another [decade] and done with it." The only thing that makes me doubt is helping Joe with his Greek. I seem to have got farther away from it than my years would warrant. And the absurd quiddities with which the grammarians

have made the language indigestible nowadays !
If the Greeks had had to think of all these
things when they were writing, they could n't
have managed it at all. . . .

Why did Balfour make martyrs of all those
fellows who were making fools of themselves
to his advantage ? But, as I have always said,
" the stars in their courses fight against you in
the Irish question." . . .

To W. W. Story
ELMWOOD, *October* 2, 1890.

My dear William, — It was very pleasant to
see your well-remembered handwriting again,
and to see it without any hint of that quaver
in it into which the hand as well as the voice
is betrayed by the accumulating years. I say
this not in malicious sympathy but as a respectful tribute to your seniority. It is n't
great, to be sure, but at our time of life even
ten days have a value of which youth could
not conceive.

But why do I talk of old age, I, in whom
autumn (of all seasons of the year) has renewed
my youth ? I was seriously ill last winter and
spring, even dangerously so, I believe, for a
day or two, and all summer have been help-
lessly languid and inert. Not that I did n't
feel well enough in body, but my mind had no
grip — " could n't seem to catch hold," as our

vivid American phrase puts it. And my memory fumbled in vain when it tried to pick up
anything smaller than a meeting-house. But
all of a sudden ten days ago I got up in the
morning a new man. My memory still boggles
a little about dates, but, as well as I can make
out, I am about fifty. Pray Heaven it may last !

I am here in my birthplace, and find it very
gracious to me. I look upon the trees and fields
I first saw and find them good as then. Your
letter naturally recalled the old days. In my
house and the ten acres in which it stands there
is no change, but the Old Road (now Brattle
Street) as far as the corner of my lane is now
crowded with houses, and the cross streets between it and the New Road thickly dotted with
them. Mr. Wells's grandchildren (*my* eldest,
by the way, has just entered college) still live
in the old house, but a new one usurps the
playground and two the garden. I still have
elbow-room, but I am more and more persuaded that the new generation should n't be
allowed to start till the old be off the stage. It
would save much unseemly hustling and many
heart-burnings.

It is very good of you to tempt me with
Rome and the Barberini, but, setting aside any
scruples I might have as an American about
living in a palace, I am anchored here for the
winter. . . .

I shall send you one of these days a little book to which I have written a preface and which will have the value of being at once pretty and scarce — two hundred and fifty copies printed for a club. It is n't much of a preface, but a good deal of a book, being Milton's " Areopagitica."

Though I cannot come now, I am not without hope of seeing you in Italy again before I vanish. A longing has been growing in me for several years now, chiefly, I confess, for Venice, but with subsidiary hankerings after Rome and Florence. Neither of them is the old one, of course, but they are better than anything else. But it grows harder and harder for me to get away. For reasons into which I need not enter, but which are imperative, I am not my own man so much as I should like to be and as I expected to be in my old age. For better or for worse one is married to duty and must n't dally with the other baggages.

Give my love to Emelyn and thanks for her note. I suppose the Alpine air has driven you away by this time, and so shall address this to Rome. Good-by.

                    Affectionately yours always,
                              J. R. LOWELL.

. . . A cold northeaster is blowing and drizzling and whatever else the D——l prompts it to do. I have just touched off the heap of wood that has been waiting in the chimney all summer, and it is blazing and crackling merrily. I put under a modest veil of French the fact that *aussi j'ai allumé ma pipe*, and there you have me. . . .

I entirely sympathize with you in your tenderness about Thoby, for I have a grandson who goes off to a boarding-school to-morrow. He does n't look as if he were a bit sentimental, but his heart is so full that it spills over in tears at the least jar. And *such* tears! as big as those of Jacques's stag! I never saw any with so much water in them. Whether the salt be in proportion is another matter. They drop silently upon his expansive waistcoat to rebound in spray. They are of the Roman fashion — they could not have filled their lachrymatories else. And Gobble, my puppy, whom Leslie will remember, was he not carried away howling to a boarding-school where he is to be taught dogmatics! Yes, dear friend, I weep with you, tear for tear. They are grandfather's tears, to be sure, and not worth so much as a mother's, but they will serve at a pinch. I

continue as well as when I wrote. After growing younger every day for a fortnight, I have
resolved to draw the line at forty and intrench
me there for the rest of my days. 'T is an
age that does not carry me beyond the circle
of a woman's interest, and so will do very
well. You won't be putting cushions behind
me or tame-catting me, if you please. A man
of sense ought never (ought he?) to get a hair's-
breadth beyond fawty. Shall I send you my
photograph?

Joe has just come in with his Greek lesson
for to-morrow, so if I get a little higgledy-
piggledy you must n't mind. When he finds a
difficulty he consults the oracle, who is no longer
so glib in that tongue as in that of Dodona,
and cannot like that save his credit by an am-
phibolous answer. (The oracle uses that adjective with design, to make you think him not
quite so shady in his Greek as he pretends.)
'T is an excellent exercise for me, and my li-
chens are getting a little rubbed off, revealing
unsuspected Attic inscriptions underneath. My
embarrassments are increased by the new-fan-
gled pronunciation, so unlike that of the ancient
Grecians of my time. Fancy their calling εἰμί
(I 'm I) *amee!* The world certainly *is* going to
the bad heels over head. I had long supposed
it, but this convinces me.

I was wrong about the hydrangea. It does n't

turn blue, but pale-green, like the sky sometimes after sunset, or like a bit of green cheese
from the new moon. It is I that turns blue
sometimes, but I shan't any more, now that
I'm fairly forty. It was looking forward to
that which depressed me. One really does n't
feel any older after one gets there, as you will
find out one of these days. . . .

To R. W. Gilder

ELMWOOD, *October 9, 1890.*

My dear Gilder, — You recall very happy
days with your " Conversations " and things.
Dio mio, how full of hope and confidence I was,
how young, in short! I was twenty-three when
I wrote the prose, and many of the verses are
even younger. Mabel's mother designed the
illuminated covers before we were married.

But, thank God, I am as young as ever.
There is an exhaustless fund of inexperience
somewhere about me, a Fortunatus-purse that
keeps me so. I have had my share of bitter
experiences like the rest, but they have left no
black drop behind them in my blood — *pour
me faire envisager la vie en noir.*

You must know, then, that after a summer
of helpless inertia, I got up one morning about
a fortnight ago as if nothing had ever happened
— not even a birthday later than my fortieth.
I have n't the smallest notion how it was done,

what Fountain of Youth I drank in dream, but so it was. May it only last!

I don't know De Quincey well enough to write anything about him. I have not read a line of him these thirty years. I never write about anybody without reading him through so as to get a total impression, and I have not time enough to do that in his case now. The only feeling I find in my memory concerning him is, that he was a kind of inspired *cad*, and an amplification of that with critical rose-water would n't answer your purpose.

But I begin on "Parkman" to-morrow. My bugbear in respect of him has been that I wrote two or three short things about him from twenty-five to thirty years ago, and can't say them so well again. Do you think I might quote a sentence or two from my former self? I may be driven to it. . . .

I am almost afraid to say how well I am lest the Liers in Wait should be listening, but meanwhile it is delightful.

Affectionately yours (both),

J. R. LOWELL.

From the *Universal Eavesdropper*:

"ANECDOTE OF JAMES RUSSELL LOWELL.

" Passing along the Edgeware Road with a friend two years ago, their eyes were attracted by a sign with this inscription, 'Hospital for

Incurable Children.' Turning to his companion, with that genial smile for which he is remarkable, Lowell said quietly, 'There's where they'll send *me* one of these days.'"

To the Misses Lawrence

Elmwood, CAMBRIDGE, MASS.,
October 12, 1890.

. . . Φίλτατα ἀμφότερα — which, being interpreted, means, I believe, My dears both — I was on the point of writing to ask how you did, or what I had done that you should be silent so long, when your welcome letter came to relieve me of my doubts. It was as full of the warm South as the beaker Keats wished for, and of names that set one's fancy dancing. I hope, now you are so near, that you will go to Venice — 'tis the only city that deserves to be called *she*. Perhaps this feminine charm of hers works less strongly on those of your sex, but you will be foolish virgins if you don't call upon her when you have so good a chance. Except London, Venice is the one place I care to see again, and I still hope it if I live. She always receives me like an old lover, put upon a footing of friendship, of course, yet with a secret between us that sets me apart from ordinary friends. And yet would she ever forgive me if I accepted the position as if there were no risk in it?

And so you have seen and heard avalanches? I am not sure that I don't like best the silent white flash so far away that one does n't hear the thunder. Snow has no business to make a noise any more than a young maiden has. When it falls, it seems as if the great silence Up There were filtering down upon us flake by flake. When it joins in the mob of an avalanche it belies its own nature, and ought to be ashamed of itself. Besides, I need n't go to the Alps in search of this wonder, for I am familiar with the tame, domestic species, the cat of this tiger, here when the deep snow loosens and slides from the roof at night in a thaw, and wakes me just soon enough to hear the last throb of its muffled thunder.

And the Lago Maggiore, too, how has it been vulgarized by the rows of hotels that prink themselves along its shores and stare into its mirror with eyes as dull as those of tourists! Not that I don't think fondly of *two* tourists, and should be glad to have been with them there. And did you climb up into the empty noddle of San Carlo Borromeo and put more cleverness into it than was ever there before?

Well, well, *we* are looking rather pretty here, and think ourselves well worth seeing in our new autumnal fashions. Our autumn beats the porphyrogeneti, for he is born not only in the purple, but in every other color that is brilliant, and in gold too, if you come to that. *Per Bacco!* I think Nature grows more and more beautiful and companionable as one grows older, and the Earth more motherly-tender to one who will ask to sleep in her lap so soon. But, in the nature of things, I am happy to think you won't reach this point of view for a long while yet.

I do little else than read of late, and have been re-reading Rousseau. I went to him to look up something, grew interested, and went on for weeks. He is (or seems) many ways a very complex character, and one feels as if the two poles of the magnet were somehow mixed in him, so that hardly has he attracted you powerfully, when you are benumbed with as strong a shock of repulsion. He is always the victim of a fine phrase — a monstrous liar, but always the first dupe of his own lie. I don't know why I am telling you this, and I can't tell you any more, you will be glad to hear, for one of my grandsons is studying his Cicero at my side, and asks me so many questions that I am puzzled as to whether Catiline or Jean Jacques were the greater rascal, or Cicero a greater liar than J. J. However, you will acknowledge that I seldom put such stuff into my letters, but good wholesome nonsense rather, keeping my seriousness to bore myself with.

You will be glad to hear that I am suddenly begun to be much better — Heaven only knows why, unless it be that I was fairly tired of being good for nothing. If ever you see me again within any reasonable time, you will be shyer of me, I am grown so young. You won't be able to treat me as if I were shelved among the seventies any more. But I will try to be as old as I can. . . .

Good-by.

Affectionately yours,
GIACOPO IL RINGIOVENUTO.

To R. W. Gilder
ELMWOOD, CAMBRIDGE, MASS.,
November 10, 1890.

My dear Gilder, — You probably have been expecting to receive ere now my little piece about Parkman. I have been trying at it, but my wits nowadays are like a cow trying to bite a pumpkin (did you ever see that illustration of *magnis excidit ausis?*) and can't seem to git no kind o' purchase on anything. My illness has wrought some subtle change in me which I feel, but can't explain. I live in a state of nervous apprehension, like timid folk when burglars are about, or an Irish landlord when there is a hedge within gunshot. I was getting over it when I last wrote to you, but since then I have had two attacks — the last yesterday — which both, to be

sure, passed away without any serious consequence, but left me depressed and disheartened
again. I know it is foolish, but I can't help it
as yet. By and by, when I have made up my
mind that my malady is something I must reckon
with for the rest of my life, I shall take it more
easily.

I am rather languid to-day after the enemy's
raid, but I shall always have energy enough to
send my love to Mrs. Gilder and you.

Faithfully yours,

J. R. LOWELL.

To Edward Everett Hale

Elmwood, CAMBRIDGE,
November 11, 1890.

Dear Edward, — M. Guizot asked me, "How
long do you think the American Republic will
endure?" My answer was, "So long as the ideas
of its founders continue to be dominant." I
quoted this in an address before the New York
Reform Club in 1888. Of course I condensed
it. In my conversation with Guizot, I naturally explained that by "ideas" I meant also
the traditions of their race in government and
morals.

Faithfully yours,

J. R. LOWELL.

To Mrs. Leslie Stephen
ELMWOOD, *December* 4, 1890.

. . . I am not half what I was this time last year. For the first time in my life I am on ill terms with the weather, which indeed has been of late as unaccountable as Sarah Bernhardt, without her motive of advertising itself. Yesterday morning the mercury stood at 1° below zero of Fahrenheit. At two o'clock it had risen only to 10°, blowing hard from the northwest. At five the wind went round to the east and it was raining. In the night it took a miff at something, whisked back to the northwest, and is now a gale, with the glass sinking as rapidly as a disappointed child's heart. . . . To-day, however, I have the sun, which is always a consoler, but if you could hear the wind. The surges break thunderously in my chimneys, and the house whines and whistles like the cordage of a ship in heavy weather. —— Here I was suddenly called away by hearing a blind slam in the third story, threatening my window glass. I found three swinging loose. Such are the cares of a housekeeper with sixty windows on his conscience. How often I recall the saying of Montaigne that a loose tile on his roof gave him far deeper concern than matters of real import.

I am sitting in the sun as I write, and letting

him bake me like a pot in the furnace. I hope
he may give me (poor earthen vessel) a firmness of consistency to resist the brazen fellows
against whom I am jostled by the current of
life. I spend most of my time in my chair, for
I am denied any exercise that would count. I
don't miss it as much as I thought I should, but
miss it, nevertheless. Were it not for Mabel's
sharp eye over me, I should break through all
rules and take my chance. Still, I cling to what
hope of life I have left, and tighten my clutch
as I feel the end of the rope slipping through
my fingers. I don't bother about Death, but
shan't be sorry if he delays as long as he honestly can. This is all stuff, by the way. I am
feeling uncommonly well. . . .

To the Misses Lawrence

ELMWOOD, CAMBRIDGE, MASS.,
December 18, 1890.

. . . You live in the world's capital city, and
the only advantage I can see in such centres
of over-population is that they supply endless
topics for correspondence. Something is always
happening there. But what topic has a hermit
like me save himself? — supremely interesting
at one end of a correspondence; liable to lose
flavor at the other, three thousand miles away.
Unless, to be sure, the hermit be important
enough, like St. Anthony, to attract the special

attention of the Evil One. And even then the spectacles provided by the Arch Tempter were hardly of a kind wherewith to entertain two demure young women, though dwelling in Babylon.

Shall I tell you of the weather? You have enough and to spare of your own. No doubt we had a great storm last night, and my chimneys bellowed like bulls of Bashan — or rather like those of the Pope, for nothing came of it, and this morning the winds have bated their breath. Or shall I tell you what I have been reading? I read old books mostly, and am apt to think that they tell me a secret or two which they have saved for me. Of course I should n't think of blabbing, and, besides, how do I know that they don't say the same thing to everybody? They may be like women in such matters. And what do you care about Terence, for example, whom I have just read through again, when you can go to the French play? I found him rather amusing for a poor devil who had to do his writing before America was discovered. And I have been re-reading South's sermons, and like the handsome way he has of taking everything for granted while he seems to be arguing its probability. But you can hear as good at St. Paul's — I was going to say. I had forgotten Dean Church's death, a great loss to friendship and to literature, one of the few men

worthy to sit in Donne's stall. I am grateful to
him for more than one kindness.

To come back to lighter matters. I have also
been reading Charles de Bernard for the I know
not what[th] time. I wonder if you know him and
like him as much as I do. He is one of the
Balzacidæ, no doubt, but he knew the Great
World far better than Balzac knew it, and has
a far lighter touch. He was waited on, too, by
a guardian angel of gentlemanly humor that generally saved him from yielding to the temptation of melodrama as Balzac so often did. I
like his shorter stories best, though the devil-
may-care artist in "Gerfaut" is a masterpiece.

22d. Here I found myself such a bore that
I put by my letter for a luckier day. To-day
is one of triumphant sunshine, which is always
medicinal, and then, too, the days have begun
to lengthen, which always comforts me, I don't
know why, for I do nothing with 'em, and my
own are shortening all the while. Moreover,
my malady has let me alone for five weeks, and
I have every reason to be jolly. The children
are all busy and mysterious about Christmas —
an anniversary which I am beginning to look
on as sourly as my Puritan ancestors did, it has
become such a *corvée* of unmeaning presents.
It was much merrier when I was young, and
got a gift or two that were worth something for
their rarity and because they came from nearest

and dearest. Nor do people eat so manfully as
they used before stomachs were invented. My
grandson Frank, to be sure, is a doughty and
scrious trencher-man who, after eating straight
through a *menu*, could turn round and eat back-
wards to the soup again with entire self-possession. He is a stay to me in the general back-
sliding and my only mitigation of the approaching
festival.

You see what a cross old thing I am become !
It all comes of living too much out of the world.
I fancy hermits are mostly dull. I am sure
Parnell's is — I don't mean C. S., but the doctor. As for C. S., I pity him. I don't like to
see anybody tumble, and he had qualities as a
captain that are not too plenty. McCarthy occupies his throne as the two kings of Brentford
might. The Irish half of him will be always
consulting the English half, and there will be
no single sharp-edged will as before.

Good-by ; forgive, but don't forget

Your affectionate and tiresome

J. R. Lowell.

To E. L. Godkin

Elmwood, *January* 5, 1891.

. . . As for my poor self, I have had no sharp
attack since the 16th November, though an unwonted languor and ease in getting tired remind
me feelingly that I got a severer wrench last

winter than I have been willing to think. At seventy-one, I was far short of my age. At seventy-two, I have overtaken and passed it. But patience, and shuffle the cards!

I am beginning to think that Ireland " is almost damned in a fair wife," but I fancy Parnell will come to the top again, for none of the others have his quality of captaincy. McCarthy is too mushy. But the Devil seems to have a finger in every Irish pie. . . .

To Mrs. R. W. Gilder

ELMWOOD, *January* 12, 1891.

. . . Yes, thank you, I am fairly well — but not what I was. I need no Gil Blas to tell me that — and I would dismiss him if he did, though, all the same. I am no longer an invalid exactly, but a val-e-tu-di-na-rian. 'T is a noble long word and seems to imply promotion. In short, I am as well as need be, but I can't *do* anything. My spurs, somehow, seem to have been lost overboard in the rough weather of last spring, as Dr. Johnson's were on his tour to the Hebrides. My Pegasus only shakes his ears and won't budge. That 's the way I am.

Tell Gilder how much I liked his poem in the " Atlantic " the other week. The " New Day " is still authentically shining on him. 'T is a good sign and makes you both younger than ever. . . .

To the Same

ELMWOOD, CAMBRIDGE,
January 26, 1891.

P. S.

I had hardly posted my answer to your last letter when I recollected with a twinge that I had left a question you asked me hanging like a hook without its eye. (There is a sex in images, you will observe, which can be judiciously fitted to one's correspondent.) You asked me what I thought of Adams's " Dana." Well, I like it. He has been immitigably, but not, I think, obtrusively frank. . . . But the Adamses have a genius for saying even a gracious thing in an ungracious way. The Adams flavor is as unmistakable as that of the Catawba grape. It won't out of the wine, do what you will. I rather like it. It reminds me of New England woods. 'T is the conscience we have inherited from our Puritan fore *bears* (*ursa novanglica*). There are occasions where it should appear in evening dress, with the reticences and connivances which that implies, and perhaps biography is one of them — but I am not sure. I fancy an honest man easier in his grave with the bare truth told about him on his headstone. Perhaps we pardon superiority more readily if we can comfort ourselves with a knowledge of its weaknesses. Dana had great powers, but he lacked that touch of genius which communizes, which puts a man on a level with the highest and lowest of his kind. He had a talent for locking himself in, with "no admission except on business" on the door. But he had a courage of perfect proof. I knew him well from boyhood up. . . . His highest quality was forensic. He could state a case with a force and lucidity that belong only to minds of the first rate. He could convince, but somehow without persuading. Do you find the real inside of him in his letters? I think not — and this is a pretty sure test. . . .

To Mrs. Leslie Stephen
February 11, 1891.

. . . I wish you could see my dogs lying before my fire, each making a pillow of the other and looking round to me from time to time lest I should forget they loved me. Human eyes have generally precious little soul in them, but with theirs there comes sometimes the longing for a soul and almost overtaking it that is desperately touching. It makes me believe in the story of those poor transmogrified sisters in the "Arabian Nights." I do a good deal of loose reading, too, after a fashion. I lately read Boswell's "Johnson" through again, for the fourth time, and have just finished "Scott's Diary," a refreshingly manly book. I read novels also, a new habit with me — and have to thank your friend, Mr. Norris, for much pleasant disposal of time which I knew not what to do with. I shall begin another story of his the moment I have posted this.

A cold snap is just beginning with us, and the northwest wind is crowing lustily in my chimney. But the sun is shining, and the mere consciousness of that always keeps me warm. It is by imagination that we mostly live, after all. I more and more doubt whether I shall get across this spring. Perhaps I may later, and drop in on you at St. Ives. . . . What could possess Leslie to go to Switzerland, where it is as cold as science, and they have given up Tell? But it is well for him to get away from the Dixery. I hate to think of his giving his life for the lives of fellows of whom we were blessedly ignorant; they were most of them dead and damned, and we hoped we were rid of 'em. . . .

To Mrs. Francis G. Shaw

ELMWOOD, *February* 18, 1891.

. . . Your letter was a cordial to me. You are quite right in thinking that I don't like my own things so well as I wish I did. But that does n't hinder my liking very much that you should like them better than I do. There is no valid reason why you should n't, for you don't know how much poorer they are than I hoped they were going to be. . . . I have been a very miserable creature for a month or more, but things are beginning to go better with me, and I hope to be young again with the year — never so young as you, to be sure, but fairly so for a veteran. . . .

To Thomas Hughes
ELMWOOD, *March* 7, 1891.

Dear Friend, — I was just going to write to you when I was knocked flat by the sharpest attack of gout (save one) I have ever had. . . .

I am glad you got the books and like them. I did n't mean by this collected and uniform edition to write " Finis," though I am not sure my health won't write it for me. But I have enough uncollected essays of one kind and another to make a volume which I shall publish in the spring or autumn. I have also poems enough to fill a small other volume. If the summer does as much for me as I hope, I suppose that I shall wet my pen again. . . .

You make my mouth water by what you say of your fair neighbors, whom I venture to count among my friends, but neither you nor they must think the Irish Question settled, or near it. You know how highly I value Balfour, and I think he has done much and well, but the Irish trouble is something too deep for railways or transplantation to cure. It is a case of suppressed gout. *Experto crede* — don't I live in the midst of a population chiefly Irish? It is proof against everything — even against the exquisite comicality of its own proceedings. Boulogne must be in the Grand Duchy of Gerolstein.

You are having daffodils and things ere this. We are still in the depth of winter, if that is to be measured in snow. The view from my windows would gladden the heart of a polar bear. But this will make our spring less unendurable when it comes.

Our politics are going well. The Congress just ended has spent all our surplus and more. This brings us down to hard-pan at last, which will be good for us. . . .

To A. K. McIlhaney [1]

ELMWOOD, CAMBRIDGE,
April 5, 1891.

Dear Sir, — I sympathize warmly with the gracious object for the furtherance of which Arbor Day was instituted. I have planted many

---

[1] I owe this letter to the kindness of Mr. McIlhaney, to whom it is addressed. He writes to me concerning it (January 27, 1894): "In 1891 the pupils of the public schools of Bath, Pennsylvania, celebrated Arbor Day by planting a tree in their school grounds, and naming it in honor of James Russell Lowell. I was then principal of schools here. Mr. Lowell, being informed of the fact that the tree was to bear his name, wrote the letter which I send to you."

trees, and every summer they repay me with an abundant gratitude.   There is not a leaf on them but whispers benediction. I often think of the Scottish farmer's words quoted by Scott, " Be aye stickin' in a tree, Jock, 't will be growin' while ye 're sleepin'." In my childhood I put a nut into the earth from which sprang a horse-chestnut tree whose trunk has now a girth of eight feet and sustains a vast dome of verdure, the haunt of birds and bees and of thoughts as cheery as they. In planting a tree we lay the foundation of a structure of which the seasons (without care of ours) shall be the builders, and which shall be a joy to others when we are gone.

I need not say how great a pleasure it is to me that my young friends should decorate my memory with a tree of their planting. I wish I could be with them to throw the first shovelful of earth upon its roots.

Faithfully yours,
J. R. Lowell.

To W. D. Howells

Elmwood, April 15, 1891.

My dear Howells, — How could you doubt that I should like anything you wrote — even about myself? [1] I am, perhaps, less able to judge what you have sent me, because I am less

---

[1] In the Editor's Study, *Harper's Magazine*.

intimate with my own works than with those of
other people, but I was altogether pleased that
you should have found in them the motive for
saying so many pleasant things about me.

Always affectionately yours,

EL VIEJO.

To E. R. Hoar

ELMWOOD, *June* 1, 1891.

Dear Judge, — I missed you and marvelled,
and am grieved to hear that you had so painful
a reason for not coming. I trust you are more
than convalescent by this time, and there is nothing pleasanter to look back upon [than] the
gout — unless it be a prison. Even in the very
frenzy of its attack I have found topics of con-
solatory reflection. Is it podagra ? I think how
much better off I am than the poor centipedes
must be. Is it chiragra ? I imagine Briareus
roaring.

I call *my* gout the unearned increment from
my good grandfather's Madeira, and think how
excellent it must have been, and sip it cool from
the bin of fancy, and wish he had left me the
cause instead of the effect. I dare say he would,
had he known I was coming and was to be so
unreasonable.

My neighbor, Mr. Warner, came in last
evening and tells me the doctors pronounce it
[your attack] to be inflammatory rheumatism.

But from his account of it I am sure it was acute gout. *Experto crede Roberto*, as our old friend Democritus Júnior used to say. Three more than intolerable days, and then a gradual relaxation of the vise, one turn at a time, but each a foretaste of Elysium — *that 's* gout and nothing else. Our doctors don't know gout. . . .

Don't think because I have had a consultation over me that I am worse. I *have*, to be sure, been very weak lately and scant o' breath, but for a day or two I have felt lighter in the spirit and in the flesh too. Sleeplessness has been my bother, owing to a nervous cough which lies in ambush till I go to bed and then harries me without ceasing. The mere bodily weariness of it is such that I get up more tired than I went to bed. I am now fighting it with opium, and if I can once break up its automatic action (for such it has become) I shall begin to gain at once, I think. Then, perhaps, I shall be able to get up to Concord, which would do me good in more ways than one.

Day before yesterday I should not have had vital energy enough to write all this, nor resolution enough to write even a notelet, for which *I* thank God, though perhaps you may n't.

Convalescence is an admirable time for brooding over mares'-nests, and I hope you may hatch an egg or two. Several handsome chicks of whimsey have clipped the shell under me.

Good-by and God bless you. Make the first use of your feet in coming to see me.

Affectionately yours,

J. R. LOWELL.

To Mrs. Edward Burnett

ELMWOOD, *June* 14, 1891.

. . . Thermometer 76°, north veranda a paradise, the pale green of the catalpa so beautiful against the darker of the English elms that I can hardly keep my eyes on my paper to write ; Joe sitting near me doing his algebra, which he is using, I fear, as a prophylactic against the piety of church-going, and I weakly submitting, in the absence of the domestic despot — such is the *mise-en-scène*. My handwriting *will* run downhill. I suppose because *I* am — in spite of continued watchfulness on my part.

The house goes on quietly enough so far as I can see. . . . Shall I send you " The Moonstone " ? I found it very interesting — not such a breakneck interest as Reade's, where one follows the scent of the plot headlong as that of a fox in the hunting-field, but still with an interest keen enough for the armchair. I am now in the midst of " Armadale."

I have said all that I know, except that George continues to worry the lawn with his two machines, one of which perfects the roughness left by the other. His air when mounted

III

on the horse-machine puts me in mind of Neptune in the Iliad. . . .

To Leslie Stephen
ELMWOOD, *June* 21, 1891.

Dear Leslie, — If I have not written it has been because I had nothing good to say of myself. I have been very wretched with one thing and another. And now a painful sensation is taking its turn. I could crawl about a little till this came, and now my chief exercise is on the nightmare. I can't sleep without opium.

Your affectionate letter was refreshing to me, and there was not a word in it to which I did not heartily respond. I thank God for that far-away visit of yours, which began for me one of the dearest friendships of my life. How vividly I remember our parting under the lamp-post when you went away ! I beguile the time now chiefly in the reading of novels, and am looking forward eagerly to a new one by your friend Norris which I see announced. I never read so many before, I think, in my life, and they come to me as fresh as the fairy tales of my boyhood. . . .

All your friends here are well, and each doing good in his several way. . . .

Always affectionately yours,
J. R. LOWELL.

Mr. Lowell died on the twelfth of August.

APPENDIX

APPENDIX

Letter of Leslie Stephen

LONDON, *February* 11, 1892.

My dear Norton, — I send you, as I promised, a few notes relating to our friend Lowell.
You are, of course, at liberty to make any use
of them you please. I will only say that I do
not even attempt to draw a complete likeness
of the man. At the most, I hope to suggest a
few characteristics which I happened to have
opportunities of observing.

I first saw Lowell in 1863. The date is
sufficiently fixed by the fact that I had just
landed at Boston and there received the news
of the battle of Gettysburg and the taking
of Vicksburg — events which had taken place
during my voyage. Lowell's name was already
familiar to me. By some accident, I had come
across the " Biglow Papers " before I went to
college. I knew absolutely nothing of American
politics ; but, in spite of the consequent obscurity of many of the allusions, I had been
fascinated by the humors of John P. Robinson
and Birdofredum Sawin. In 1863, I had become a young Cambridge " don " of the radical

persuasion, and was profoundly interested in the American Civil War. I began to appreciate a little more clearly the spirit and purpose of Lowell's poems ; and when, in that year, I re- solved to see something of America for myself, I was unusually eager to make his acquaintance. A letter of introduction opened the doors of Elmwood, and in a very short time I felt my- self surprisingly at home in a new atmosphere. I know that I am boasting by implication ; but I am not ashamed in this case to boast ex- plicitly. I feel a greater respect for myself when I remember that I was able to win Lowell's friendship so rapidly. I will not attempt to decide what it was that he found in me. What I found in him is more to the purpose.

At first sight I found a singularly complete specimen of the literary recluse. I remember, with a curious vividness, the chairs in which we sat by the fireplace in the study. I look at the dedication of " Under the Willows," and feel that I, too, have heard his " Elmwood chim- neys' deep-throated roar," and, indeed, can al- most hear it still. I need hardly add that we worshipped

> " Nicotia, dearer to the Muse
>   Than all the grape's bewildering juice."

All round us were the crowded book-shelves, whose appearance showed them to be the com- panions of the true literary workman, not of the

mere dilettante or fancy bibliographer. Their
ragged bindings, and thumbed pages scored with
frequent pencil-marks, implied that they were a
student's tools, not mere ornamental playthings.
He would sit among his books, pipe in mouth,
a book in hand, hour after hour ; and I was soon
intimate enough to sit by him and enjoy intervals of silence as well as periods of discussion
and always delightful talk. I feel as though I
could still walk up to the shelves and put my
hand upon any of the books which served as
texts or perhaps as mere accidental starting-
places for innumerable discussions. One book
which I always associate with Elmwood is the
" State Trials," into which I first dipped under
his guidance. Sometimes it gave him the delight of discovering a so-called Americanism
already familiar in the vernacular of undoubted
seventeenth-century Britons ; or it suggested
quaint and graphic vignettes from the old English country life, or restored to momentary
vitality some forgotten humorist whose plea-
santries lie buried in evidence given before Coke
or Jeffries. The great lights of literature were
there too, of course, and would suggest occasional flashes of the playful or penetrative criticism which is so charming in his writings, and
which was yet more charming as it came quick
from the brain. Or he would look from his
" study windows " and dwell lovingly upon the

beauties of the American elm or the gambols of the gray squirrels on his lawn. When I was last at Elmwood, in 1890, the sight of these squirrels (or their descendants) took me back twenty-seven years at a bound, and I was pleased to find how clear was the vision of the old days.

To see Lowell in his home and the home of his father, was to realize more distinctly what is indeed plain enough in all his books, how deeply he had struck his roots into his native earth. Cosmopolitan as he was in knowledge, with the literature not only of England but of France and Italy at his fingers' ends, the genuine Yankee, the Hosea Biglow, was never far below the surface. No stay-at-home Englishman of an older generation, buried in some country corner, in an ancestral mansion, and steeped to the lips in old-world creeds, could have been more thoroughly racy of the soil. And, at this period, his patriotism was of course at a white heat. The language of the most widely known English newspapers at the time could hardly have been more skilfully framed for the purpose of irritating Lowell if it had been consciously designed with that end. A man proud of belonging to a genuine national stock, sprung from the best blood of old England, was virtually told that the Americans had no right to be a nation at all, but were a mere mob accidentally aggregated by a loose bond of contiguity, moved by no nobler motive than dollar-worship, and governed, on the whole, by blackguards. Lowell has expressed his feelings in some well-known writings far better than I could do. I remember, however, one illustration of them which impressed me at the time.

He showed me the photograph of a young man in the uniform of the United States army, and asked me whether I thought that that lad looked like a " blackguard." On my giving the obvious reply, he told me that the portrait represented one of the nephews whom he had lost in the war. Not long afterwards I read his verses in the second series of " Biglow Papers," the most pathetic, I think, that he ever wrote, in which he speaks of the " three likely lads,"

> " Whose comin' step ther' 's ears thet won't
> No, not lifelong, leave off awaitin'."

Any sympathetic reader of them will understand better than I can describe what was the mood in which I first found Lowell and what was the secret of his attraction. His thorough scholarship and his wide reading, the brilliancy of his wit and the shrewdness of his observation, would in any case have been interesting, but they might have been very far from agreeable. His patriotism was then in a highly aggressive state; and though I do not own to especial sensitiveness in that direction, I am not sure that he did not tell me some home-truths, not

altogether agreeable, about John Bull. But
then I must have been dull indeed not to see
what his patriotism really meant. It was not the
belief that the country which had produced him
must be the first in the world; or that the opinions which he happened to have imbibed in
his childhood must be obviously true to every
one but fools; or a simple disposition to brag,
engendered out of sheer personal vanity by a
thirst for popularity. It was clearly the passion
which is developed in a pure and noble nature
with strong domestic affections; which loves all
that is best in the little circle of home and early
surroundings; which recognizes spontaneously
in later years the higher elements of the national
life; and which, if it lead to some erroneous
beliefs, never learns to overlook or to estimate
too lightly the weaker and baser tendencies of
a people. Most faiths, I fear, are favorable to
some illusions, and I will not suggest that
Lowell had none about his countrymen. But
such illusions are at worst the infirmity of a
noble mind, and Lowell's ardent belief in
his nation was, to an outsider, a revelation of
greatness both in the object of his affections
and in the man who could feel them. I could
realize more clearly after knowing Lowell the
great national qualities which could call forth
such a devotion, and could value him for ap-
preciating them so profoundly. The "Com-

memoration Ode," with the fine passage upon the necessity of the poet "keeping measure with his people," explains all this far better than any clumsy analysis of mine.

At that time, when the passions roused by the war were at their height, and every day brought news to make patriots' nerves quiver, I had naturally opportunities to see Lowell's true feeling and to admire his profound faith in the success of the good cause. Anyhow, I made a friend for life. I have always remembered how, when I was taking my final leave, he walked with me to the corner where his avenue joins the highroad, and how we parted with a cordial shake of the hands. It seemed to me to be a kind of seal put upon a bond which, as it turned out, was to last as long as he lived. I was greatly pleased to find more than one reference to that little incident in letters written to me long afterwards, and we spoke of it when I last saw him in Cambridge, in 1890. We were to meet again oftener than I had hoped. As years went on my affection strengthened, and during our whole intercourse I never had to regret a word that passed between us, or to feel that there was a temporary abatement of his kindness.

I was again in America in 1868, and stayed at Elmwood under circumstances which gave me additional reasons for gratitude.

Our later meetings (except the last) were upon this side of the water. After he had become Minister in England we met as frequently as was possible in London ; and for several successive summers he paid me a visit at St. Ives, in Cornwall, and, I need not say, was the most welcome of visitors. It often amused me to contrast the Lowell of Elmwood with the Lowell of London society. The contrast, indeed, was in the purely outward circumstances. In his quiet New England home day after day passed with no interruption to study, so far as I could see, except the occasional intercourse with his cherished friends. In London his remarkable popularity left him very little time for anything. I need not speak of his singular success in social functions of all kinds, and especially in after-dinner oratory. If he had been studying all his life to hit off the taste of an English audience, he could not have done it better. But I speak rather from concurrent testimony and newspaper reports than from my own knowledge. My own occupations scarcely ever led me to the places where he won his social triumphs, and I only once heard him speak. It was my great pleasure to fill up some of his interstices of leisure by dropping in for a pipe and a chat at his house or welcoming him at my own. Even in the height of his occupation as Minister, there were always a few of his literary favorites resting in pleasant disorder upon tables and chairs, and waiting for a brief audience. An interview with Cervantes or Montaigne afforded, I imagine, a very pleasant contrast to some of the conversations with which he was favored.

Our pleasantest meetings, perhaps, were in the quiet little country retirement where there was no danger of interruption from the outside world. No man, I need hardly say, had in a higher degree the capacity, not altogether a common one according to my experience, of thoroughly and heartily enjoying country scenery. In Cornwall we had the advantage of being in a granite country, which so far has a certain affinity to his native State. Every year we paid a visit to the Land's End. He confirmed my rooted belief that it is one of the most beautiful headlands in the world. He admitted that our Cornish Sea can be as blue as the Mediterranean, to which in other respects it has an obvious superiority. I argued, indeed, that one main charm of the Land's End to him was that nothing intervened between it and Massachusetts. Be that as it may, he showed the most commendable appreciation of its charms. Hereditary instincts, he declared, enabled him to appreciate our English scenery; he always had a good word for our climate, for the soft mists and haze which impress your real foreigner unfavorably, and he could see the good side even of a London fog. Then he loved the British blackbirds and robins for their own sakes as for their connection with the old English poets. There is a rocky perch or two, from which we look over the Atlantic, which will always be associated in my mind with strolls in Lowell's company. But to give any impression of the charm of his talk on such occasions, I must again refer to his own works. They are himself, except, indeed, that no author whom I have known can quite put all his charm into his books.

No friend of Lowell's could, I fancy, stoop to vindicate him from the charge of having allowed his patriotic feelings to be in any degree blunted by the cajolery of the British aristocracy or other evil-disposed persons. But some such random bit of party dirt-throwing incidentally suggested one remark to me. He was one of those men of whom it might be safely said, not that they were unspoiled by popularity or flattery, but that it was inconceivable that they should be spoiled. He offered no assailable point to temptations of that kind. For it was singularly true of him, as I take it to be generally true of men of the really poetical temperament, that the child in him was never suppressed. He retained the most transparent simplicity to the end. If he had any vanity, it was of the inoffensive kind, which goes with an

utter absence of affectation. He knew, I pre-
sume, that he could make a good speech and
be pleasant in conversation. The fact was a
great deal too obvious to be ignored. But his
good things came up as spontaneously as bub-
bles in a spring. He was never acting a part or
claiming any more attention than came to him
naturally. He was quite as good at listening
as at talking. Any little vanity that came up
seemed to be the delight of a genuine humorist in some pet fancy of his own. There were
little matters on which he could not help sup-
posing that nature must have endowed him with
abnormal penetration. There was, for example,
his astonishing faculty for the detection of Jews.
He was so delighted with his ingenuity in discovering that everybody was in some way de-
scended from the Jews because he had some
Jewish feature, or a Jewish name, or a Gentile
name such as the Jews were in the habit of assuming, or because he was connected with one
of the departments of business or the geogra-
phical regions in which Jews are generally to be
found, that it was scarcely possible to mention
any distinguished man who could not be con-
clusively proved to be connected with the chosen
race. The logic sometimes seemed to his hearers to have trifling defects; but that was all the
greater proof of a sagacity which could dispense
with strict methods of proof. To say the truth,

this was the only subject upon which I could conceive Lowell approaching within measurable distance of boring. I remember once showing some traces, very obscure, I flatter myself, of some slight sense that I had heard enough of the subject, and becoming immediately aware of his awkward power of penetrating one's obscurer feelings. His perceptions of his companion's feelings were indeed so acute that he was naturally secure of never becoming tiresome. Of the qualities that make an agreeable companion, certainly one of the chief is an intuitive perception of the impression you are making. Lowell was so quick at knowing what were the dangerous topics, that I do not think he could ever have given pain unless he felt it to be a duty. Probably an offence to his patriotic sensibilities would have led to a retort, and he had powers of sarcasm which one could not have roused with impunity. I only remember one friend who complained to me of rough usage. That friend was not only one of the most good-tempered, but one of the most cosmopolitan of men, and especially free from any excess of British sensibility. But somehow or other the British lion and the American eagle had been waked to life in the encounter and must have used their claws pretty freely. No such personal experience ever occurred to me.

Lowell's presence in the too short periods

when he was an inmate of my family was inva-
riably unmixed sunshine. Though he did not
set up like some excellent people as a child-
fancier, he was as delightful with children as with
adults, and entered into their simple pleasures
with all his ineradicable boyishness.

As I try to call back the old days, I feel the
inadequacy of attempted description, and the
difficulty of remembering the trifling incidents
which might speak more forcibly than general
phrases. But I have one strong impression
which I can try to put into words. It is not of
his humor or his keen literary sense, but of his
unvarying sweetness and simplicity. I have
seen him in great sorrow, and in the most unre-
served domestic intimacy. The dominant impression was always the same, of unmixed kind-
liness and thorough wholesomeness of nature.
There did not seem to be a drop of bitterness
in his composition There was plenty of virtuous indignation on occasion, but he could not
help being tolerant even towards antagonists.
He seemed to be always full of cordial good-
will, and his intellectual power was used not to
wound nor to flatter, but just to let you know
directly on occasion, or generally through some
ingenious veil of subtle reserve, how quick and
tender were his sympathies, and how true his
sense of all that was best and noblest in his
surroundings. That was the Lowell whom I

III

and mine knew and loved; and I think I may say that those to whom he is only known by his books need not look far to discover that the same Lowell is everywhere present in them.

Yours affectionately,
LESLIE STEPHEN.

INDEX

INDEX

Titles of Mr. Lowell's poems and other writings referred to in his Letters are entered in *italics* in the following index.

Good resolutions, i. 21.

Gordon, General, sends regards to Lowell from Khartoum, iii. 121.

Gore, Governor, ii. 195.

Goschen defeated at Edinburgh, iii. 160.

Gothic architecture, iii. 44.

Gout, ii. 23, 335, 338; iii. 210, 320.

Gower, John, ii. 115.

Gower, Leveson, visit to, iii. 79, 159.

Grahamism, i. 127.

Graham's Magazine, i. 79, 83, 87, 145, 254, 281.

Grail, Holy, ii. 252.

Grandfathers, ii. 369.

Grant, U. S., ii. 90, 203, 255; as a presidential candidate, 179; at Madrid, iii. 58; and Sumner, 59.

Gratitude, ii. 45.

Gray, Thomas, ii. 239, 290; odes of, iii. 9.

Greece, its history, ii. 349; visit to, in 1878, iii. 42.

Greek art as seen in the Naples Museum, ii. 328.

Greek grammar, iii. 294.

Greek pronunciation, iii. 299.

Green, Mrs., her "Henry II.," iii. 214.

Greenough's Franklin, ii. 9.

Greenwood Cemetery, i. 129.

Grolier Club, iii. 294.

Grosbeak, rose-breasted, iii. 283.

Grote, George, his "History of Greece," ii. 349.

Grub Street, iii. 172.

Guizot, M., iii. 306.

Gurney, E. W., ii. 151.

Gymnastic exercise, i. 198.

Hale, Edward E., ii. 86.

——, Letter to, 1890, iii. 306.

Hale, Nathan, Jr., i. 76 n., 81, 82; ii. 351.

Hamon, French painter, i. 311.

Hanging, puns on, i. 245.

Happiness, expression of, in poetry, i. 54; other expressions of, ii. 394; better things than, iii. 220; *also*, ii. 105; iii. 268.

Harper's Weekly, ii. 28.

Hartzenbusch, his notes on "Don Quixote," iii. 34, 37.

Harvard Advocate, ii. 402.

Harvard College, Freshmen and Seniors, i. 27; Lowell on his college life, 33; the pursuit of truth in, 36; the library, 115; Lowell appointed professor, 296; the Harvard-Oxford race in 1869, ii. 231; the Commencement dinner, 359; the triennial catalogue, iii. 15; the library, 34, 38; the quinquennial catalogue, 106; confers LL.D. on Lowell, 111; Lowell's 250th-anniversary address, 167; the 250th anniversary, 174; Lowell delegate of, at Bologna University, 209.

"Harvard Graduates," Sibley's, ii. 344.

Harvardiana, i. 26; ii. 351.

Hats, beaver, ii. 71.

Hawkins, Sir Richard, ii. 96

Hawthorne, Nathaniel, i. 105, 106; the "Marble Faun," ii. 48; the "Scarlet Letter," 48; his death, 93; proposed life of, 127; his genius, 171; iii. 147; Fields on, ii. 272; his "Our Old Home," iii. 284; proposed biography of, 284.

——, Letter to, 1860, ii. 51.

Hayes, R. B., nomination in 1876, ii. 395; and the South, iii. 4; his appearance, 14.

Hayes, Mrs. R. B., iii. 14.

Haying, i. 217.

Hayne, Paul H., ii. 190.

Haze, iii. 247. *See also* Fog.

Hazlitt, ii. 386.

Heath, John Francis, i. 80 n., 222.

——, Letters to, 1842, i. 80, 81, 91, 99; — 1850, 247.

Mitchell, S. Weir, iii. 221, 223, 232; his "Dream Song," 233.
——, Letters to, 1889, iii. 230–232; —1890, 265, 292.
Mitchell, Mrs. S. Weir, Letter to, 1889, ii. 226.
Modesty, ii. 85.
Monadnock, iii. 289.
Money, i. 38, 250; its use, ii. 306.
Montaigne, ii. 249, 303; iii. 194; his essays, 210; petty cares, 307.
Montgomery quoted, i. 27.
Montpensier, Duke of, entertains Lowell, iii. 22.
Mood, A, ii. 185.
Moon, the, in winter, iii. 176.
Moon-clarities, ii. 136.
Moon, G. W., ii. 132.
Moore, Mr., landlord in Trenton, i. 298.
Moore, Thomas, and Wordsworth, iii. 198.
Moosehead Journal, i. 270.
Moral nature, ii. 188.
Moralizing, ii. 105.
Morley, John, iii. 120, 187, 189; on Macaulay, ii. 391.
Moroni, ii. 285.
Mosquitoes, iii. 285.
Mothers and babies, ii. 114.
Motley, J. L., ii. 185; his contributions wanted for the "North American Review," 88.
——, Letter to, 1864, ii. 88.
Mount Auburn Cemetery, ii. 383.
Mount Vernon, visit to, iii. 137.
Mountain-climbing by spy-glass, ii. 319.
Mountains, i. 320.
Musset, A. de, ii. 287.
Mutual admiration, ii. 226.
My Appledore Gallery, i. 289.
My Study Windows, ii. 275.
Mysticism, in Lowell's character, i. 164.

Naples, i. 339; in 1874, ii. 326; changes in, 330; museum, 328.

Napoleon III., ii. 46, 258, 259, 262, 295.
Narni, bridge of Augustus at, i. 328.
Nation, The, ii. 107, 111, 128, 144, 175, 186, 189, 190, 209, 210, 223, 349.
Nationality, Civil War fought for, ii. 396.
Naturalized citizens, iii. 128.
Nature, familiarity with, i. 219; the beauties and delights of, ii. 11; its quiet indifference, 121; the satisfaction of sympathies with, 125; human life and, 266; companionship of, iii. 304; savage instinct in, 141.
New England, i. 27; ii. 105; its provincialism, 344; Journal of a Virginian travelling in, 354; quality of its literature, iii. 126.
Newman, Cardinal, iii. 114, 291.
Newport, contrasted with Beverly, i. 286; the people of, ii. 258.
Newspapers, ii. 63, 329.
Newton, Sir Isaac, iii. 284.
New Year's day, ii. 77.
New York, i. 116; ii. 15.
New York Ledger, iii. 251.
Niagara Falls in winter, i. 302.
Night, sounds of, ii. 155.
Nightcaps, ii. 122.
Nightingale, iii. 285. *See also* Birds.
Nightingale in the Study, ii. 149, 154, 365.
Nippers, ii. 382.
"Njal's Saga," ii. 60.
Nocedal, Señor, iii. 57.
Noise as an expression of happiness, ii. 393.
Nom de guerre, literary, iii. 183.
Nooning, The, i. 226, 230, 232, 268; ii. 133, 184.
Nordhoff, Charles, Letters to, 1860, ii. 54; —1869, 251.
Norris, W. E., iii. 315, 322.
North American Review, i. 170, 172, 233; ii. 4, 88, 97, 108, 115, 129, 145, 185, 351, 353.

INDEX

Weimar, Goethe's house at, iii. 89 ; character of the place, 146.

Wells, Judge, i. 265.

Wesselhoeft, Dr., i. 137.

West, the message of the East to, ii. 75.

West Roxbury Station, i. 263.

Westerners, ii. 390 ; iii. 76.

What Rabbi Jehosha said, ii. 111.

Wheeler, C. S., i. 94.

Whigs, i. 253.

Whist club, ii. 345.

Whistler, iii. 166.

Whitby, iii. 192, 242.

White, Maria, i. 93 ; knowledge of poetry, 62 ; character, 64 ; praise of, 71 ; fills his ideal, 74 ; presents a banner to a temperance society, 89 ; Joe Bird's praise of, 90. *See also* Lowell, Mrs. M. W.

White, Miss L. L., Letter to, 1845, i. 127.

White, Mr., of Watertown, i. 61.

White, Richard Grant, ii. 30.

White, W. A., Letters to, 1841, i. 76 ; —1843, 112.

Whitechokerism, ii. 119.

Whitman, Walt, i. 319.

Whittier, i. 26 ; ii. 170 ; his poem, "Skipper Ireson's Ride," ii. 18.

——, Letter to, ii. 18.

Whittling, ii. 289.

Wickliffe, Bob, ii. 235.

Wilbur, Parson, ii. 40.

Wild, Hamilton, ii. 185.

Willard, Sidney, taught Bancroft German, iii. 223.

William II., of Germany, iii. 270.

William, factotum at Elmwood, ii. 305.

Willis, N. P., i. 116 ; in *Fable for Critics*, 180.

Willows, to be cut down and sold for firewood, ii. 163.

Wilson, Henry, ii. 208.

Wilton House, i. 312.

Winchester Cathedral, iii. 254.

Wind, i. 57.

Windharp, The, i. 291.

Winter, Cambridge scenes in, ii. 21, 250, 254.

Winter evening described, i. 200.

Winter weather, ii. 270, 280, 350 ; iii. 5, 177, 199.

Winthrop, R. C., iii. 262.

Wit and humor distinguished, i. 164.

Without and Within, iii. 62.

Women, social stimulus needed by, ii. 320 ; letters from, 355 ; happiness as expressed by, 393 ; all aristocrats, iii. 123 ; *also* iii. 75, 81, 146, 147, 225, 235, 309.

Woodberry, George E., ii. 402.

Wood-cutting, Lowell's early attempts at, i. 14.

Wood-fires, ii. 331.

Woodpeckers, iii. 184.

Woods, silence of, i. 286.

Words — decuman, ii. 253 ; downshod, 266 ; extend, 244 ; in and into, iii. 151 ; misgave, ii. 266 ; rote, 265 267 ; transpire, 244 ; *virtus*, and *virtu*, 298 ; weariless, 181 ; whitt, 266, 267.

Wordsworth, i. 119 ; ii. 126, 242 ; iii. 9, 94, 147, 240 ; lines from a poem compared by Poe with lines of Lowell's, i. 143 ; imagined meeting with Pope in the Fortunate Isles, 322 ; his "Laodamia," ii. 161 ; his early unpopularity and later fame, 290 ; Thackeray's estimate of, iii. 198 ; the "Excursion," 214.

Wordsworth, Essay on, ii. 362, 365.

Work, the faculty of, i. 221.

Workingmen's college, address at, iii. 81.

World, the, iii. 220.

World's Fair, 1876, ii. 373.

Worthy Ditty, A, ii. 113.

Wright, Henry C., i. 211.

Writing, i. 181.

Wyman, Dr. Morrill, iii. 265, 289.

Wyman, Rufus, ii. 132.

THE END